LOCATING EUROPE

STUDIES IN CONTINENTAL THOUGHT

John Sallis, *editor*

Consulting Editors

Robert Bernasconi
John D. Caputo
David Carr
Edward S. Casey
David Farrell Krell
Lenore Langsdorf

James Risser
Dennis J. Schmidt
Calvin O. Schrag
Charles E. Scott
Daniela Vallega-Neu
David Wood

LOCATING EUROPE

A Figure, a Concept, an Idea?

Rodolphe Gasché

INDIANA UNIVERSITY PRESS

This book is a publication of

Indiana University Press
Office of Scholarly Publishing
Herman B Wells Library 350
1320 East 10th Street
Bloomington, Indiana 47405 USA

iupress.org

© 2021 by Rodolphe Gasché
All rights reserved
No part of this book may be reproduced or utilized in any form or by any means, electronic or mechanical, including photocopying and recording, or by any information storage and retrieval system, without permission in writing from the publisher. The paper used in this publication meets the minimum requirements of the American National Standard for Information Sciences—Permanence of Paper for Printed Library Materials, ANSI Z39.48-1992.

Manufactured in the United States of America
First edition 2021

Library of Congress Cataloging-in-Publication Data

Names: Gasché, Rodolphe, author.
Title: Locating Europe : a figure, a concept, an idea? / Rodolphe Gasché.
Description: First edition. | Bloomington, Indiana : Indiana University Press, 2021. | Series: Studies in continental thought | Includes bibliographical references and index.
Identifiers: LCCN 2020044839 (print) | LCCN 2020044840 (ebook) | ISBN 9780253054838 (hardback) | ISBN 9780253054852 (paperback) | ISBN 9780253054845 (ebook)
Subjects: LCSH: Europe—Philosophy.
Classification: LCC B105.E68 G385 2021 (print) | LCC B105.E68 (ebook) | DDC 940.01—dc23
LC record available at https://lccn.loc.gov/2020044839
LC ebook record available at https://lccn.loc.gov/2020044840

CONTENTS

Preface vii

Acknowledgments xvii

1 Archipelago *1*
2 Without a Horizon *12*
3 In Light of Light *29*
4 The Form of the Concept *49*
5 Axial Time *65*
6 Eastward Trajectories *87*
7 Feeling Anew for the Idea of Europe *110*
8 An Idea in the Kantian Sense? *133*
9 Responsibility, a Strange Concept *150*
10 An Immemorial Remainder: The Legacy of Europe *168*
11 Beyond the Idea of Europe *193*

Bibliography 225

Index 233

PREFACE

Even though this book is primarily devoted to phenomenologist and postphenomenologist thinkers in the second half of the twentieth century who have made significant philosophical contributions to "Europe" as a philosophical issue, I wish to begin these prefatory remarks with a bold statement by a philosopher who not only comes from a different philosophical tradition but, in her own words, also from a part of Europe whose "extremism at times brings to light certain deep European roots, which Europe deliberately conceals."[1] I am referring to the Spanish modernist philosopher Maria Zambrano.[2] *La Agonia de Europa*, published in 1945 in Buenos Aires, where she sought refuge after the rise to power of the fascists in Spain, is, in light of the death that Europe underwent at that time, an inquiry into what Europe had been. However much she is committed to the Greek heritage, she is also a deeply, though in many ways, heretical, Christian philosopher. One of the distinctly original points of Zambrano's work is, indeed, her claim that Saint Augustine is "the father of Europe, the main protagonist of European life."[3] But he, significantly enough, is not a European. He came, as Zambrano offers, from abroad "in order to nurture Europe by familiarizing it with the wisdom of forgotten and far away Africa."[4] In other words, the Christian origin of Europe, rather than something native to Europe, comes from abroad. However, the figure of Saint Augustine is not just a stand-in for the Christianity of Europe. On the contrary, he is the main actor of Europe in that with him a specific conception of Europe takes form. Indeed, after the death of the ancient world, it is a Christian Europe in which Greek philosophy and Roman law undergo a resurrection through Christian faith that, at the same time, transforms this faith itself. What comes into being with Saint Augustine is something that cannot die, and will always resurrect through the amalgamation of the Christian conception of hope with the Greco-Roman heritage concerning a *polis* for all human beings here on Earth. Within the frame of the history of salvation that characterizes Saint Augustine's thought, a new way of discovering the subject's innermost self is discovered. Indeed, as Zambrano points out, at the transition of antiquity to modernity, Saint Augustine creates a new genre—the "confessions"—aimed at acquiring "knowledge about oneself," a knowledge that "becomes important at that moment at which one wants to be reborn, in which one wishes to resurrect, not only once, but as often as is necessary in order to become whole."[5] This new genre is also the form that the subject "Europe" takes, beginning with Saint Augustine. Its heart is constituted by this unrelenting self-reflection and self-critique at the moments of its many deaths, and which seeks to accomplish a self-transparency so as to be resurrected. In short, if Saint Augustine is the father of Europe it is because with him a Europe comes to life that is constituted by rebirth from its many deaths. According to Zambrano, it is precisely this hope of resurrection at the heart of Europe, grafted on its Greek and Roman origins, that gives it its Christian character. To reflect not only on the wealth of its diverse forms and the multiple styles of European life but also on the decay of these forms and styles in order to discover what about Europe is "indispensable," this is, the Spanish philosopher holds, the way of keeping Europe alive; of bringing it to life again. She avers, "Europe will live when it gets our mental powers going."[6] This is the context in which she makes the following statement: "Europe is not dead, Europe cannot die completely; it decays. For Europe is perhaps the only thing—in history—that cannot die; it is the only thing capable of resurrection."[7]

In a political and cultural climate such as today's, when unified Europe is not only threatened from within by right-wing and populist authoritarianisms but from outside as well, by Russia's aggressive attempt to divide the European Union and by the current protectionist US administration that wants if not to dismantle, then at least to weaken it as an integrated and multilateralist institution, a statement like the above sounds like a deluded and chimerical dream. Is it just a coincidence if in North American academia a similar attempt to get rid of Europe is underway in several respects? It is under attack, first, as far as the shape of the institution of the humanist university itself is concerned; second, regarding the context of the present study, in its form of being a mode of thinking that seeks an intelligibility in which everyone can participate. In academia, this attack is waged by tribal culturalism. Here, Zambrano's statement will be judged not only to be deluded but to be the expression of European arrogance.

In no way do I wish to question the fact that new efforts to include domains and topics hitherto excluded or underrepresented in academic work have led to signal contributions in scholarship. But the nativist mentality that more than occasionally is part and parcel of these studies is as disquieting as the concerted political efforts of the illiberal and nationalistic forces that seek to undermine Europe's transnational project. Indeed, there is a call in a considerable part of North American academia to wall itself off and to police its boundaries in order to be able to "feel safe" from concepts and ideas that—*because* initially they originated in Europe or came with a demand of universal rational accountability and of responsibility to the other—are judged imperial and to override differences and particularities. In extreme cases, this is a call to "feel safe" from any other who might be seen as a threat to one's identity. Needless to say, in the context of such a culture of particularism, Zambrano's statement sounds completely out of tune.

So why continue to be concerned with Europe, which Hegel, distinguishing it from the New World, already characterized as "Old Europe"?[8] Why not drop the issue once and for all? Yet, before even beginning to ponder such a question it might be appropriate to remind oneself of what the name *Europe* stands for. As the title of this book already suggests, rather than as a geographical, geopolitical, or economic entity, Europe is here being considered philosophically, as a figure, a concept, or an idea. It is the name for a cluster of interrelated, at times aporetic, exigencies or injunctions such as the following: rationality, self-accounting, self-criticism, responsibility toward the other, freedom, equality (including for the different sexes), justice, human rights, democracy, and the list goes on. To hold that Europe is a topic that no longer deserves reflection is to demonstrate a lack of historical judgment and, ultimately, to dismiss all these ideas and values that make up the core of the European heritage. By contrast, to reflect on these concepts, values, and ideas that historically have their origin in Europe, is to reflect on Europe and to measure it against them; in turn, to consider that the idea of Europe is still important today is to hold that these concepts, values, and ideas still matter, not only in relation to Old Europe but also to all parts of the world without distinction, in fact, more than ever, in a now transnational and multicultural world. But in the context of this philosophical approach to the question of Europe, it must be recalled that the name *Europe* also stands for a distinct mode of thinking, namely philosophical thinking. In phenomenological thought in particular, to which almost all the analyses in this book are consecrated, Europe as a concept or idea is synonymous with rational, scientific, and philosophical thought. But this mode of thinking is also one that, because of its inherent self-questioning and self-criticism, never comes to an end. European thinking is not only characterized by a methodology that leads to universally verifiable results but also by an unremittingly critical vigilance that questions all results in which thinking could congeal, such as systems of thought in which this thinking would then take the form of a definite representation of what Europe is. It is not a form of representation that would usher in the formation of a cultural identity; on the contrary, it is a kind of thinking that is critical of itself and that, therefore, is suspicious of any self-sufficient outcomes. For such a thinking, however fragile and vulnerable it may be, there is no end. It remains open. It is not a nostalgic thinking of some lost identity but, because of its self-critical nature and for structural reasons, a thinking that always again pulls itself together anew, resurrecting its critical potential from its failures and deaths.[9] In short, because of the very structural nature of this thought associated with Europe, it cannot simply die or reveal itself to be superfluous or obsolete. Although I do not share Zambrano's optimism—on the contrary, I hold that the kind of critical thinking characteristic of Europe experiences within itself and from outside itself resistances today on many fronts—I believe that European thought requires incessant attention, because only on this condition is there any chance that its critical impetus, its ideas and values, will survive. But there is a further reason why this kind of thinking demands its renewal without end. As its very name—*philosophy*—intimates, it is a mode of thinking that has come to Europe from the outside, from classical Greece. In all of the many European languages, this foreign word designates a mode of thinking that has not grown on European soil, that is not native to it, but that has come to Europe as something alien. According to Zambrano, European thought originates in North Africa, to others in Greece, and, if one takes the Greek myth about Europa into account, even farther East. Precisely because it is a mode of thinking that is not native, it remains a challenge that never loses its provocation and urgency. Indebted to the Other, Europe's responsibility to the latter is infinite and thus demands that this thought be unremittingly renewed, given new vigor, and always again a new life. Only at the price of a disavowal of the responsibility toward this gift from the other could European thought—the thought *of* Europe—be done away with. This would, then, also be the moment when Europe would close in on itself in an identity blind to what is dissimilar from itself.

It is against the background of Zambrano's statement that Europe cannot die: that after each death it inevitably springs forth again into life, not only because the concepts, values, or ideas that are associated with it are "indispensable" but also because the very nature of the thinking that is involved with Europe—its self-critical attitude and force—cannot come to, or rather cannot be allowed to, come to a close. Like all genuine thought, its life is that of a restlessness (*Unruhe*) without end.

The essays reunited in this book are not only testimony to the enormous wealth of thought regarding the "essence" of Europe in the phenomenological tradition alone but also of its restlessness, that is, the aliveness of this thought. They also map out the geography of thinking Europe throughout a number of European nations and cultures, demonstrating that the question regarding Europe is not the privilege of one such nation. Furthermore, what all these essays reveal is that Europe is not a monolithical thing. It is not an essence in the common sense but the lively debate about what constitutes Europe itself. In order to bring the aliveness and liveliness of this debate to the fore, the book does not force the different reflections into a linear argument that develops in an integrated fashion across the book in view of some unifying thesis. On the contrary, the multiple ways in which Europe is reflected upon—whether as a figure, a concept, or an idea—should be understood as inhabiting a plane on which they mark as many different entries. In a way, one of the figures of Europe discussed in the book—the archipelago, as a figure of a plurality defined by its relationality—could be said to structure the different parts of the book, thus respecting the singularity of the various entries on Europe rather than unifying them in one idea. But if this book honors the contributions of various thinkers about Europe by keeping the uniqueness of each attempt to meet the challenge posed by a theme that calls for constant renewal, this does not exclude structuring these contributions and asking questions. Rather than presenting them in historical order, or even by the philosophers here considered, the chapters of this book are organized conceptually. Indeed, what links all the essays concerns the question regarding the representational status of Europe. Is it a figure, a concept, or an idea? Can the thought of Europe as described so far content itself with any of these representations, or does it rather compel its thinkers to rethink again and again its representational status? If Europe corresponds to a kind of thinking that resurrects, are its current representations as a figure, a concept, or an idea of equal significance? Or is there one representation in particular that harbors greater potential for being recast in response to the contemporary configuration of Europe? Which representational form is the most promising to think about the future of Europe? In all evidence, to answer these questions requires establishing, first of all, what it means to represent Europe as a figure, a concept, or an idea.

But before turning to the different ways in which it has been represented as a figure, a concept, or an idea, some further preliminary reflections are warranted.

As I already noted, the title of this book suggests that Europe is not, or not simply, a geographical location: a place where, in spite of the notorious difficulty of assigning it exact borders, a specific culture arose that for several centuries dominated the world in a hegemonic fashion. This dominance was made possible to a large extent through the superiority of the techno-sciences developed in Europe, its systematic exploration and colonial expansion into the non-Western world, and its military strength. But if, according to the questions raised by the title of this book, Europe might also be a figure, a concept, or an idea (before determining whether it is one, or the other, or all together), it is because Europe might also be something other than just a place identifiable in geopolitical terms and a culture whose particularity is just as particular as all other cultures, even though it has until recently been able to force it on the rest of the world. At first glance, what the question regarding Europe's representations as a figure, a concept, or an idea intimates is that it is *more* than just one geographical and cultural entity, a claim that will be considered as perhaps the climax of its imperialist arrogance. Given its history—and, furthermore, its historical claim to represent humanity itself—such a judgment is certainly not without reasons. Indeed, after the loss of its former political and cultural superiority, for Europe to claim for itself the status of representations such as a figure, a concept, or an idea, suggests an even more offensive or ridiculous self-aggrandizement, especially since, in this case, it is a claim made on seemingly spiritual grounds. Needless to say, it is not possible to simply ignore such suspicion.

But Europe's self-identification as a figure, a concept, or an idea also implies that it is *less* than a geographical and historical reality: that Europe has never been itself, and that unlike other parts of the world or other cultures, it cannot identify itself on territorial grounds and by a specific ethnic culture that emerged from its particular topography. Even in mythological terms it is lacking: it has not sprung from the earth; it is not rooted in a soil; it cannot lay claim to anything autochthonous whatsoever. Regarding its physical geography, it has famously understood itself as a cape, a promontory, or headland of the Asian continent extending westward beyond itself into the waterways. Lacking cultural origins that would be properly its own, Europe has, in contrast to what is the case with other cultures, a borrowed identity. This is a point forcefully made by Rémi Brague in *Europe, la voie romaine*.[10] Here let me only remark that, in terms of its temporal origin, Europe has identified itself with a historical culture and a world that, in essential ways, differs from itself, the Greek world from which it is separated by an "unbridgeable gulf," to quote Georg Lukacs, and religiously, according to Georg Wilhelm Friedrich Hegel, with a faith that is also properly foreign to it, namely Christianity.[11] It follows from this that when Europe posits itself as a figure, it is always only an image of something that it is not but that it seeks to resemble; understood as concept it is something against which it constantly must be measured and with respect to which it always falls short; and as an idea it is clearly not yet what it strives after in an endless attempt of approximation. For these reasons Europe has also persistently been referred to as a dream, a utopia, a project; in short, as something, perhaps, to come. It is always less than what its representations encapsulate. Its exceptionality is thus that, unlike the identity that other cultures can claim, it is not what it is.

It is obvious that to conceive of itself in terms that imply a fundamental willingness to self-questioning and self-criticism, is a strength. Such radical self-criticism has thus also been interpreted as indicative of the imperial undercurrent present in all of Western philosophical thought, and as a sign that even when Europe has lost all its former glory in the world it still seeks to retain and to demonstrate its superiority. Yet even though this contention may occasionally hit the mark, the claim that such self-criticism is per se still a form of superiority is disingenuous, to say the least, because rather than acknowledging that self-questioning and criticism are the signature marks of thinking as such, the critique of radical self-criticism makes of critical thought a predicament. It even contains a verdict regarding thinking itself and thus invalidates its own critical thrust. Even if it is the case that self-criticism can be self-serving, it remains a strength, in particular when relentlessly vigilant of all the temptations that it may face.

With this question regarding the representational status of Europe, this book focuses on an issue that I did not address in an earlier work on Europe.[12] Apart from featuring a variety of thinkers from within the phenomenological tradition whose work on Europe I have not engaged before, such as Hans-Georg Gadamer, Karl Jaspers, Karl Löwith, and others, this book focuses on a wealth of determination of the philosophically most significant representations of Europe. Is Europe a *figure* such as the archipelago, the horizon, or indistinguishable from light as thinkers as diverse as Alberto Savinio, Massimo Cacciari, Jean-Luc Nancy, and Jan Patočka have argued; or is it a *concept*, identifiable as the power of conceptuality as Gadamer has claimed, thus intimately linking Europe to the structures of the Indo-Germanic nature of the Greek language? As a philosophical concept, what is Europe's precise indebtedness to Greek as a language that, as Martin Heidegger holds, is no longer idiomatic; to a language that is from the start categorematic and universal? In this new work, I am particularly interested in exploring the identification of Europe as an *idea*, as well as the question of how "idea" is to be understood in this context; whether Europe is to be understood as an idea primarily in the Kantian sense. Conceiving of Europe as a figure, a concept, or an idea are not innocent gestures since these notions serve to prejudge *what* and *how* one is thinking when thinking about Europe. Broadly speaking, as a figure Europe is a schema, or image of intelligible nature, or structure, rather than a thing; as a concept it is the fully determined representation of the entity in question; and as an idea—that is, the philosophically highest representation of it—Europe is held to be a task to be accomplished, one that does not exhaust its cognitively determinable nature. It is, in particular, this identification of Europe as an idea that undergirds all the distinct essays collected in this volume, which also feature studies such as the intrinsic interweaving of the notion of Europe with the question of responsibility to the other, primarily Europe's responsibility toward its twofold (and aporetic) heritage of Greek and Christian and Judaic thought. The overall thrust of the essays is to explore the potential, and especially the limits that the representation of Europe as an idea carries with it, since an intrinsically Greek notion is here raised to articulate the demand for rationality and universality. It is in the last chapter of this volume that this question is explicitly taken up and addressed. Such questioning of the limits of the notion of the idea in identifying Europe aims at delineating the rudiments of a thinking about Europe in view of a conception of Europe beyond the idea.

Notes

1. Maria Zambrano, *Der Verfall Europas*, trans. C. Frei (Vienna: Turia & Kant, 2004), 61.
2. Maria Zambrano was a student of Ortega y Gasset, the limitations of whose rationalism she sought to overcome with a theory of what she calls "poetic reason," and Miguel de Unamuno. For a brief account of her career as a thinker "in the male-dominated intellectual milieu in which [she] lived, studied, and worked in the pre-War era to a more

female-centered life in the post-War period," see Roberta Johnsson, "The Context and Achievement of *Delirium and Destiny*," in *Delirium and Destiny. A Spaniard in Her Twenties*, trans. C. Maier (Albany, NY: SUNY Press, 1999), 219.

3. Zambrano, *Der Verfall Europas*, 70.

4. Zambrano, *Der Verfall Europas*, 70.

5. Zambrano, *Der Verfall Europas*, 79.

6. Zambrano, *Der Verfall Europas*, 41.

7. Zambrano, *Der Verfall Europas*, 42. For an in depth discussion of this statement, see Rodolphe Gasché, "A Ghost and Its Resurrection: Maria Zambrano on the Agony of Europe," *Research in Phenomenology*, 50 (2020), 351–69.

8. Georg Wilhelm Friedrich Hegel, "Introduction," *The Philosophy of History*, trans. L. Rauch (Indianapolis: Hackett, 1988), 90.

9. For this very reason, there is a history of philosophical thought to begin with, in fact, an extremely rich history.

10. Rémi Brague, *Europe, la voie romaine* (Paris: Criterion, 1993).

11. Georg Lukacs, *The Theory of the Novel: A Historico-Philosophical Essay on the Forms of Great Epic Literature*, trans. A. Bostock (Cambridge, MA: MIT Press, 1971), 31; Georg Wilhelm Friedrich Hegel, *Early Theological Writings*, trans. T. M. Knox (Chicago: University of Chicago Press, 1948), 146. Needless to say, only a transformation of the Old Testament through figural interpretation, as a result of which from a book of laws and a history of a people foreign and remote, it became part of a universal religion of salvation and a vision of history, could guarantee its reception by the Celtic and Germanic peoples. See Erich Auerbach, "Figura," in *Scenes from the Drama of European Literature*, trans. R. Manheim (Minneapolis: University of Minnesota Press, 1984), 52.

12. Rodolphe Gasché, *Europe, or the Infinite Task: A Study of a Philosophical Concept*, (Stanford, CA: Stanford University Press, 2009).

ACKNOWLEDGMENTS

THE ESSAYS CONTAINED IN THIS BOOK HAVE BEEN published previously, though several of them have been slightly revised or abridged. Chapter 1, "Archipelago," has been published previously under the title "Zur Figur des Archipels" in *Figuren des Europäischen. Kulturgeschichtliche Perspektiven* (Munich: Fink Verlag, 2006), 235–245. © 2006 Wilhelm Fink Verlag, an imprint of Brill Group (Konniklijke Brill NV, Leiden, The Netherlands; Brill USA, Boston MA; Brill Asia Pte Ltd, Singapore; Brill Germany GMbH, Paderborn, Germany). Chapter 2, "Without a Horizon," was previously titled "Alongside the Horizon" and was published in *The Sense of Philosophy: On Jean-Luc Nancy*, ed. D. Sheppard et al. (London: Routledge, 1997), 140–156. Chapter 3, "In Light of Light," appeared first under the title "In Light of Light: On Jan Patočka's Notion of Europe" in *The Politics of Deconstruction: Jacques Derrida and the Others of Philosophy*, ed. M. McQuillan (London, UK: Pluto Press 2007), 116–136. I thank Pluto Press (www.plutobooks.com) for the permission to reprint this essay. Chapter 4, "The Form of the Concept," is a reprint of "Europe, or the Form of the Concept" from *Europa: Stier und Sternenkranz. Von der Union mit Zeus zum Staatenverbund*, eds. A. B. Renger and R. A. Issler (Göttingen: V&R unipress, 2009), 609–624. Chapter 5, "Axial Time," appeared as "Unter dem Zeichen des Anderen. Jaspers' Blick zurück auf den Ursprung Europas in der 'Achsenzeit,'" in *Grundordungen. Geographie, Religion, Gesetz* (Berlin: Kadmos Verlag, 2013), 233–255. Chapter 6, "Eastward Trajectories," was included under the title "On an Eastward Trajectory Toward Europe: Karl Löwith's Exiles" in *"Escape to Life": German Intellectuals in New York: A Compendium on Exile after 1933*, eds. E. Goebel and S. Weigel (Berlin: De Guyter 2012), 305–330. Chapter 7, "Feeling Anew for the Idea of Europe," is a slightly revised version of "Feeling the Debt: On Europe," published in *Future Crossings: Literature between Philosophy and Cultural Studies*, eds. S. Deane and K. Ziarek (Evanston, IL.: Northwestern University Press, 2000), 123–146. (Copyright © 2000 by Northwestern University Press. Published 2000. All rights reserved). Chapter 8, "An Idea in the Kantian Sense," is an abbreviated version of "Is 'Europe' an Idea in the Kantian Sense?," published in *Europe Beyond Universalism and Particularism*, eds. S. Lindberg et al. (New York: Palgrave Macmillan, 2014), 33–65. Chapter 9, "Responsibility, a Strange Concept," appeared first in French under the title, "L'étrange concept de responsabilité," in *La démocratie à venir. Autour de Jacques Derrida*, ed. Marie-Louise Mallet (Paris: Galilée, 2004), 361–374. Chapter 10, "The Immemorial Remainder of Europe," was originally included under the title "An Immemorial Remainder: The Legacy of Derrida" in *A Companion to Derrida*," eds. Z. Direk and L. Lawlor (Malden, MA: Wiley Blackwell, 2014), 207–227. A part of chapter 11, "Beyond the Idea," was first published as "Patočka on Europe in the Aftermath of Europe," in *European Journal of Social Theory*, 2017, 1–16.

LOCATING EUROPE

1

ARCHIPELAGO

In contrast to Edmund Husserl's reference in the Vienna lecture from 1935 to Europe as a concept and, indirectly, as an idea—that is, as characterized by one unifying distinguishing trait, project, or telos—the notion of Europe as a figure suggests a plurality of individual patterns through which Europe became historically effective.[1] The belief that there are distinctly European figures not only suggests that what is proper to Europe is displayed or laid out in an array of distinct figures but also that Europe's essence may be intimately linked to the order of the figural (and hence, perhaps, to be less unified, as a concept or idea of Europe would have it). If the essence of Europe is made up of a plurality of figures, could it be that what is proper to Europe has an intricate relation to the figural? In any case, the recourse of figures to speak of what is European implies that Europe is only properly what it is by differentiating and spreading itself out in the manifold of these figures. One may even consider the possibility that Europe is such literal *Selbstauslegung*—that is, first and foremost, the spatial and temporal display of itself by way of a variety of figures—that it makes Europe what it is to begin with. Europe is, possibly, nothing other than a group, chain, or constellation of figures, all clearly distinct from one another, that only enters into a constellation when these figures are drawn into relations and thus made to interconnect. To speak of what is European in terms of figures would thus seem to clash with its formulation as a concept or idea. But when it comes to defining Europe or what is European, can one cast the difference between concept and idea, on the one hand, and figures, on the other, in terms of the One and the manifold? Indeed, I would like to consider the possibility that, in the precise case of what is European, it may not be possible to neatly hold apart the conceptual and the figural. While it may be impossible to elaborate on the figures of Europe without an anticipation of sorts of what Europe means, the unifying concept of Europe may harbor such structural features that necessarily give rise to a manifold of figures. Conversely, the unity of the concept may depend on such ways by which Europe's distinct figures are made to relate, that prevent this concept from ever having the unity of the One. This problematic relation of concept and idea, on the one hand, and figures, on the other, will guide the following investigation of one particular figure of Europe: a figure that is, perhaps, the mother of all its figures; one, moreover, that in itself is already inherently manifold.

Before taking up this figure itself, I wish to discuss briefly the concept, or rather idea of Europe, not in the context of Husserl's philosophy but in that of Italian writer and essayist Alberto Savinio's reflections on Europe. In *Sorte dell'Europa*, a collection of essays written between 1943 and 1944, Savinio contends that in order to create a unified Europe from the separate nations that at that moment made up Europe, Europe must free itself from a Ptolemaic—that is, theocratic and hence imperialist—conception of the world and enter the Copernican, or democratic age. Any attempt to unify Europe by imitating the Roman Empire, in other words, by centering it around one power or one person, is Ptolemaic in nature. Savinio opposes such a unification on the basis of an idea. He writes, "Only an idea can 'make' Europe. Idea: this 'human thing' par excellence."[2] The idea of Europe is thus not a Ptolemaic, theocratic, and imperialist unification principle. Although one, this idea is not centralizing but democratic. It is not a principle of subordination and subsequent totalization. Nor is it an abstract principle whose relevance would have little or no relation to the concrete European realities. Rather, it is the "'human thing' par excellence," Savinio claims. He thus characterizes ideas in general as follows: "Ideas must be easy to handle, and be portable. They must have the 'practical forms' that the Greeks gave to their temples, objects, and forms of spirit. The ideas themselves must have handles, or handholds."[3] Equipped with handles, the idea of Europe is a unifying principle that, unlike an abstract concept, lets itself be handled by everyone. It is a unifying principle on a horizontal rather than vertical plane.[4] What then does this idea imply? How can it be a unifying principle without being totalitarian? In order to answer these questions, I turn to the entry "Europe" in Savinio's *Nuovo Enciclopedia*, whose entries were written between 1941 and 1948. Here one reads that "*Lo spirito europeo odia il grumo.*" In English, "The European spirit hates that which is lumped together." As Savinio explains, "The European intellect [*intelligenza*] has a very singular function. It divides and separates."⁵ Its natural aim is the disintegration of everything coagulated, agglutinated, of "all social lumps," and of all "totalitarian tumors," which are anti-European by definition.⁶ What unifies Europe and constitutes it as an idea is this constant breaking up of all possible grumes, clots, clods, and lumps. "According to the Copernican conception, union is an error; it is a resistance to the natural order, and an obstacle to the perpetual course of life and its unlimited mutations."⁷ In contrast to the Ptolemaic mind-set, "the European intellect divides the union, and polytheizes [*politeizza*] God," the ultimate unifying power in the Ptolemaic conception of the world.⁸ As a result of this opposition to unification on the basis of a totalizing principle, the idea constitutive of Europe cannot be a form or an instance of the One. Savinio writes "that no idea can be put into the center of all that exists, and be considered the truest, the most beautiful, the best. Such is the 'democracy' of the ideas."⁹ This idea of Europe—the principle of disintegration of anything coagulated rather than a totalizing principle—is Greek in origin, Savinio contends. "The most pure Europeanism is to be found in pre-Socratic Greece: the most European condition of Europe."¹⁰ The names that Savinio invokes in this context are Thales, Heraclitus, and Empedocles.

Any disaggregation of lumps requires their dissolution, liquefaction, and fluidization. Is it not remarkable that, according to the first school of Western philosophy, the school of Miletus, water is held to be the substance that subtends all things and from which everything originates. What is decisive about this answer to what underlies all things and all change is, as Jeanne Hersch has observed, "the *direction*, the orientation toward something liquid, something fluid, that can transform itself into all things without disappearing."¹¹ Of the many philosophers who, like Thales, conceived of water as the medium in which things lose their fixity, I mention Immanuel Kant, who writes in *Critique of the Power of Judgment*: "The fluid is, to all appearances, older than the solid."¹² But above all I would like to evoke Hegel and his geophilosophical reflections on the Mediterranean Sea in *The Philosophy of History*. As the heart of the old world, the Mediterranean is said to be "the uniting element, and the centre of World-History," the "forum, where all came together."¹³ The Mediterranean has enjoyed this privileged role solely thanks to the very liquidity of its substance. As Hegel writes, "Only through the fact of being a sea, has the Mediterranean become a centre."¹⁴ Some of his reflections on "the principle of the sea" are of particular interest here.¹⁵ The sea, he writes, "gives us the idea of the indefinite, the unlimited, and infinite; and in feeling his own infinite in that Infinite, man is stimulated and emboldened to stretch beyond the limited."[16] The sea—in Greek, *pélagos*—as the watery expanse confronts us with the apeiron and hence invites us to overcome all dependence on the land, the soil, and the clod. By venturing out onto this treacherous surface of water—onto an element that is all the more dangerous as it is "yielding"—not only the limitations of the land, and all dependence on it, are overcome but also what had been fixed comes into movement and turns fluid. As Hegel remarks, "The activity to which the sea invites, is a quite peculiar one: thence arises the fact that the coast-lands almost always separate themselves from the states of the interior although they are connected with these by a river."[17] In the old world, the Mediterranean is thus the element that links the three parts of the world. Such linkage implies that they separate from the fixed soil on which they were located. Greece, "the focus of light in History"; Jerusalem, the "centre of Judaism and of Christianity"; and Mecca and Medina, the "cradle [*Ursitz*] of the Mussulman faith" enter here into relations thus loosening the dependence on their Ursitz.[18] By way of the waters they become detached from their terrestrial anchorage. They turn into so many interconnected islands, as it were, in or around the liquefying expanse. One of these "islands" is the group of islands of the Aegean Sea—the archipelago. With this I have reached the singular European figure that I wish to discuss.

In the preface to the German translation of his book *L'Arcipelago*, Massimo Cacciari asks, "Does Europe still remember the originary [*arché*] sea, the sea of the many islands related in 'astral-friendship' (Nietzsche)? Or more precisely, can Europe still be Mediterrean, can its thinking still be a thinking at midday?" To accomplish such Mediterraneity, the European—and, according to Cacciari, the German spirit, in particular—must recover the ability of "thinking itself in relation again, in *harmony* with the archipelago."[19] Repeatedly Cacciari refers to the archipelago as a figure of Europe, however, as the translation of the Greek term—"the originary [arché] sea"—intimates it is also an originary figure, comparable to what Hans Blumenberg calls an absolute metaphor. Considering the fundamental nature of this figure, Cacciari asks the radical question, "Did the archipelago ever exist? Or does it belong to a beginning more fundamental and more originary than even the first words of the European destiny?"[20] Possibly older than the first words of European destiny, the archipelago may be indicative of a beginning of Europe anterior to all historical and linguistic articulations of its destiny, anterior also to figures of speech and figures of thought, image, and concept. Not only that, the archipelago being a beginning older than even the first words of European destiny may refer to a beginning of Europe that is specifically European precisely in that it is *not* European—a beginning that, from the outset, sets Europe in relation to the non-European. In any case, from the start, Europe has, as Cacciari has shown in *Geo-Filosofia dell'Europa*, a "destinal relation to the fluid."[21] Linked to a shift of power from land to sea, the European character is in every respect determined by a relation to what is different from it that is mediated by the sea. But rather than the factual realization of the figure of the archipelago—the "islands related in astral-friendship"—Europe, during its history, may have excelled only in the hubris associated with the thalassocracy. According to Cacciari, it follows from this that "the idea of the archipelago is not one of a return to origins, but rather that of a 'new beginning' or also of a counter-stroke against the history and the destiny of Europe." Consequently, the question arises, "Could Europe (still) be an archipelago? Or, rather, is this its very *impossibility*? . . . Could it be that in the face of Europe's experience, after it has made land and sea *pervii*, it must come to a halt before this question, *aporos*—or that the antic sea-archipelago only existed in order to be 'betrayed' by the fantastic flights that have entirely covered it over?"[22] Before I inquire into the major characteristics of the figure of the archipelago, the preceding reflection on its status warrants several remarks. If it is a European figure, the archipelago is one that may never have achieved the sensible shape of a figure. Although Cacciari also refers to the archipelago as an idea, it has neither found an articulation as concept. The archipelago then is only a latent possibility of Europe, whose figurality and conceptuality is still to come, unless it represents a beginning whose sole function consists only in being covered over by the figures and concepts of Europe. Now, as a figure of a beginning that is more fundamental and originary than even the first words of European destiny, the exposition of the archipelago—that is, the outline of what this notion implies—may not be possible except conceptually. Indeed, as an originary figure, the archipelago may also be an originary concept or idea—more fundamental than figure and concept alike; a template, as it were, for both.

The archipelago, the originary sea of Europe, is, writes Cacciari, "the place of relation . . . of the dialogue, the standing over against each other of the islands that inhabit it: all of them distinct from the sea and all tied to the sea; all of them nourished by the sea and all of them exposed to the risk of the sea." He remarks, "The movement of the sea [*salos*] is immanent to the city of the archipelago; the sea does not come to a stop before its shores, but resonates in the voices on the agora."[23] In other words, none of the different islands is present in the archipelago by virtue or on the basis of the immediacy of its peculiar truth. But neither are the individualities of the manifold islands hegemonically subordinated to the One principle. "The space of the archipelago is by its very essence recalcitrant to subordination and hierarchical gradations. No island within it is in the position of a firm axis capable of structuring the archipelago in its entirety in the form of a *state*."[24] In fact, the movement of the sea is immanent to the different islands to such a degree that all are drawn by its expanse to leave the *oikos*, or home, for another island and, ultimately, for a homeland that all lack. Although free of hierarchy, this state is not, however, to be mistaken for one from which all violence would be absent. The uprootedness (*Entwurzelung*) and deterritorialization (*Entlandung*) of the islands (to use the terms that Carl Schmitt employs to describe the elemental turn to the sea in Europe), which makes the space of the archipelago possible, is not possible without the violent tear by which the islands transcend themselves.[25] Cacciari continues, "The singularities of the archipelago belong to each other in the moving and changing space of self-coordination and living-together, because none of them has in itself a center point specifically its own: and this because the center point is in truth only the drive which forces each of these singularities to transcend themselves by way of their journey toward the other, and all together, by way of their journey toward the absent homeland."[26] Within the archipelago the center is everywhere, or rather, the center is made up of the uprooted island's effort to reach out to the other islands. Given that such extending out to the other presupposes an exit from one's singularity, this self-transcendence consists in a movement of conversion (*anabasis*), of an ascent to light from out of the Platonic cave, as it were, toward a being together of the individual islands in uprootedness. As I said, this archipelagic conversion is not without violence; neither does it come without risks. In Cacciari's words, the harmony of the archipelago—or of Europe, if, indeed, the archipelago is its most fundamental figure—is "*dia-logos* and *polemos*: a tragic dialectic." Because no visible and stable center or axis structures its space, the being-with of the singularities of the archipelago is always exposed to two dangers. It can either result in a complete dissolution or be tempted by the subordination to one permanent center. However, as Cacciari emphasizes, the archipelago would not be what it is without this double danger: "This double danger is constitutive of its essence. In the archipelago there is no road without a Scylla and a Charybdis, Symplegaden. The cessation of the danger would amount to the cessation of the *poros*, the way of Europe, its *ex-periri*, its ex-perience."[27]

Before I take up the question of the constitutive dangers inherent in this European figure, let me delve briefly into the nature of the islands that make up the archipelago and the movement of the sea immanent to each one of them. As Cacciari writes, "The love that drives one into the expanse, and by way of which one gets to know the archipelago, is truly *a-oikos*."[28] The separation and parting from all terrestrial rootedness—from one's home and ethos—this is the basic and unifying trait upon which the archipelago is founded. However, such distancing from the oikos does not imply per se that the urge to travel that dominates the archipelago is to become wholly uncoupled from the land (as would be the case in utopia), or that it necessarily leads to a complete loss of oneself (suffering shipwreck). Rather it is an exit from oneself with a view to a determination, a decision, concerning who and what one is. All travel within the archipelago, however reckless, carries within itself an inner reference to the oikos. Cacciari remarks, "One originates in something 'inner,' and to find a way back to it, one must leave all those behind whom one meets—and that from which we originate, can never be found again. But the open in which one moves is constantly renewed by way of this origin."[29] Without the audacity to travel (and its inherent dangers), how could one know who or what one is? At the same time, such travel lets one know who one is only in relation to others, never as one had been before beginning the journey. One does not return from the journey to an unspoiled origin but to one that is marked by its exposition to others. The undoubtedly violent opening of themselves by which the islands turn to the open sea leads them to establish their identities not simply on their difference from others but also with respect to what they departed from. Until the islands of the archipelago relate to one another as absolutely different, they form only ephemeral lumps. An island achieves such absolute difference solely on the condition that it is involved in incessant sea travel contra-versus other singular islands. Its difference depends on the discovery that the manifold forms and logoi experienced in the travel to other islands also divide its own difference from within and that, consequently, each island cohabits with its own alter.[30] Cacciari writes, "How could the island know that it is an autonomous individual if it did not discover in its logos the *Cum* that connects it to the other island, and that, at the same time distinguishes it from itself?"[31] This *Cum*, or *Xynon*, that unifies harmonically the archipelago is thus nothing but the drive a-oikos in view of possible decision, by each of its islands, concerning its own singular individuality.

In *L'Archipelago*, Cacciari stresses repeatedly "the terrifying responsibility" that comes with the islands' determination of their form through a departure from their oikos. Indeed, the force that compels the islands to extract themselves from lump-like indeterminacy derives from "our ontological incapacity to stop . . . our incapacity not to strive toward the 'too much.'" The will to exit from oneself in order to decide on the singular form of one's individuality is grounded in the "*hubris* of this will."[32] The danger that is immanent to the archipelago is double at least. On the one hand, it is the danger of the hubristic attempt to radically cut all ties to the oikos in order to achieve unconditional and limitless absoluteness (and hence to suffer shipwreck); on the other, it is the threat that comes from efforts to remedy the hubris immanent to the archipelago by annulling it (in utopia). Cacciari adds that "from the same root that generates the *Pluriversum* of the archipelago, its 'catastrophe' consisting in becoming One can also take shape—its becoming a universal form a priori (which destroys every *topos* within it); the becoming of uniform and indifferent space in which the domination of the average has priority."[33] In any case, as we have seen, these dangers are not possible accidents that Europe can incur; they are constitutive of the figure of the archipelago as a figure of what is European. What this means is that Europe can only properly be the archipelago if it incessantly confronts its inherent dangers. Any attempt to cure the risks in question amounts to the annihilation of the archipelago itself as a community based on difference (rather than on a common substrate). Cacciari concludes, "In the archipelago there is no journey 'at midday' that does not reveal plenty of aporias; no light that does not clearly and in irreducible fashion delineate its own shadow. Every journey, and each of its thoughts is here *agon* and *polemos*. And every city which exposes itself to the proximity of the danger of the sea is in this way *twofold*."[34]

The archipelago as a figure of what is European is the figure of a *societas* in which the departure of each member from itself toward the others is the common ground, the idea that unites them. According to the figure of the archipelago, this drive to leave the oikos is produced by the infinite expanse of the sea—the pélagos—(and therefore also by the recognition that one is only a part among other parts). Although the sea as *pontos*, that is, as a bridge, enables each island to enter into a relation with other islands, the sea is also the most treacherous medium to fray passages and to construct bridges. Apart from the fact that "the bridge is the most dangerous and necessary of all ways that human beings have cleared," the sea itself is "the most necessary and dangerous of all bridges."[35] Indeed, as Hegel points out, yielding to the pressure the waters give way, so to speak, and this precisely constitutes its dangerousness. The sea invites the hubristic act of seeking to cut off all relation to the land (and to search for a land free from all dangers). But the sea is treacherous in still another sense, in that each of the passages that it permits to be cut and each bridge that it allows to be built, once frayed, once built, closes upon itself and must be recut again. As a result, the departure from the oikos and the subsequent travel to the other islands is not something that is achieved once and for all. The way to cut through the expanse of the sea must always be rediscovered and cut anew, while facing the dangers immanent to the archipelago. With this we touch on what I believe to be the essence of what is European according to this figure/concept. The figure of the archipelago suggests that Europe is an infinite task. It is the task not only to separate oneself from the oikos and to open a relation to others in order to construct on this very separation a community but also to relentlessly perform this task. Furthermore, since the way to the other can only be found by confronting the dangers immanent to the archipelago, this way must not only be cut each time anew but it is also always a necessarily singular way: Europe's proper, distinctive way. In other words, what the figure of the archipelago spells out with respect to Europe, is that Europe's task is the Impossible—that is, the task of incessantly departing from oneself and fraying an always new passage through to the other. This is not an impossible task but a task to accomplish the Impossible.

Let us recall that in heading for the open sea in order to encounter others, one must cut ways through the treacherously yielding elements and face each time anew the dangers immanent to this enterprise. Cacciari writes, "In the archipelago there is no road without a Scylla and a Charybdis, Symplegagen." The archipelago is thus aporos—the dangers are such that no way out exists—that is, from the seduction of hubris and the attempt to annihilate the dangers of shipwreck and utopia. As a figure of what is properly European, the archipelago stipulates that a way to the other must be cut precisely because there is no way. This figure suggests that there is a way only if all passage is barred. Only then is the way that has been cut a way in the first place, a way on which one can be underway to the other.

What the figure of the archipelago suggests above all is that solely a decision can decide about Europe, about its ways, and about whether these ways make a difference.

As Cacciari notes, the archipelago may have never historically existed, or it may belong to a beginning more fundamental and originary than the first words of European destiny. Although a figure/idea of what is properly European, but to which Europe during its history has never lived up to, the archipelago may have to be thought of as a conception of being together in uprootedness that is European only to the extent that it articulates such being together in such a way that this conception could as well have originated in other, non-European cultures. Paradoxically, the archipelago is a conception of what is properly European precisely because it names a conception of togetherness whose origin, descent, and belonging can no longer be attributed to it. It is therefore no longer a figure or an idea of what is European. Older than figures and older than ideas, the archipelago has been begotten by Europe only to defy all genitival attribution.

Notes

1. Edmund Husserl, *The Crisis of European Sciences and Transcendental Phenomenology*, trans. D. Carr (Evanston, IL: Northwestern University Press, 1970).
2. Alberto Savinio, *Destin de l'Europe*, trans. L. Chapuis (Paris: Christian Bourgois, 1990), 34.
3. Savinio, *Destin de l'Europe*, 50.
4. Savinio, *Destin de l'Europe*, 34.
5. Alberto Savinio, *Encyclopédie nouvelle*, trans. N. Frank (Paris: Gallimard, 1980), 161.
6. Savinio, *Encyclopédie nouvelle*, 169.
7. Savinio, *Encyclopédie nouvelle*, 162.
8. Savinio, *Encyclopédie nouvelle*, 165.
9. Savinio, *Encyclopédie nouvelle*, 165.
10. Savinio, *Encyclopédie nouvelle*, 164.
11. Jeanne Hersch, *Das philosophische Staunen. Einblicke in die Geschichte des Denkens* (Munich: Piper Verlag, 1981), 10.
12. Immanuel Kant, *Critique of the Power of Judgment*, trans. P. Guyer and E. Matthews (Cambridge: Cambridge University Press, 2000), .223.
13. Georg Wilhelm Friedrich Hegel, *The Philosophy of History*, trans. J. Sibree (New York: Dover, 1956), 87. Translation modified.
14. Hegel, *Philosophy of History*, 90. Translation modified.
15. Hegel, *Philosophy of History*, 101. Translation modified.
16. Hegel, *Philosophy of History*, 90.
17. Hegel, *Philosophy of History*, 91.

18. Hegel, *Philosophy of History*, 87.
19. Massimo Cacciari, *Der Archipel Europa*, trans. G. Memmert (Köln: DuMont, 1998), 6.
20. Cacciari, *Der Archipel Europa*, 31.
21. Massimo Cacciari, *Gewalt und Harmonie*, trans. G. Memmert (Munich: Carl Hanser, 1995), 62.
22. Cacciari, *Der Archipel Europa*, 32.
23. Cacciari, *Der Archipel Europa*, 11–12.
24. Cacciari, *Der Archipel Europa*, 17.
25. Carl Schmitt, *Land and Sea: A World-Historical Meditation*, trans. S. G. Zeitlin (Candor, NY: Telos Press, 2015), 81.
26. Cacciari, *Der Archipel Europa*, 17.
27. Cacciari, *Der Archipel Europa*, 18.
28. Cacciari, *Der Archipel Europa*, 20.
29. Cacciari, *Der Archipel Europa*, 37.
30. Cacciari, *Der Archipel Europa*, 26, 28.
31. Cacciari, *Der Archipel Europa*, 26.
32. Cacciari, *Der Archipel Europa*, 27.
33. Cacciari, *Der Archipel Europa*, 26.
34. Cacciari, *Der Archipel Europa*, 22–23.
35. Cacciari, *Der Archipel Europa*, 9.

2

WITHOUT A HORIZON

In "Euryopa: Le regard au loin," a short and dense text written in 1994, Jean-Luc Nancy approaches the philosophical question of Europe by way of an investigation of Europe's vision, look, glance; sight (*regard*).¹ Europe, Nancy writes, "is the particular way of looking whose singular sighting [*visée*] is the universal as such" (*EU*, 8). His concern throughout the essay is with Europe as "an idea of a vision": with the particular way of looking that this idea implies, with this vision's limits, as well as with the limits of vision itself.

Nancy's starting point is the admittedly questionable etymological meaning of Europe, *Euryopa*—originally an epithet of Zeus, meaning, according to Liddell and Scott, either "wide-eyed," or "far-sounding," that is, "thundering." *Der Kleine Pauly* renders it as "far-sounding and looking far into the distance," and goes on to mention another possible but equally questionable etymology, to which Nancy also has recourse, namely the Semitic, pre-Greek *ereb*: obscurity.² According to this origin, the name *Europe*, to cite Nancy, "would mean: the one who looks in the distance (or, as well, the one whose voice is far-sounding)" (*EU*, 5). But Nancy also brings to bear the other possible etymology on the meaning of the word, thus determining Euryopa's glance as a "look far into the obscurity, into its own obscurity." Whether or not these etymologies are correct is of no concern here. Indeed, Nancy does not use them in an etymological sense to authoritatively prove or to make a point by explaining the concept and the "thing" called Europe according to its roots. Rather he means these derivations to incite thought and response to what they could possibly indicate about the direction that a renewed assessment of the idea of Europe could take, as well as a response to the tension that exists between both etymological derivations. Indeed, independently of what the word Euryopa suggests, would anyone wish to contest that Europe looks into the distance, far ahead of itself? "It belongs to the essence, or idea of Europe that it faces the distant, that it is this headland of the continent that advances towards the remaining world, and from which the conquest, the invasion of the world, or the making of the world world-wide has started," Nancy writes (*EU*, 5). In his essay, he focuses on this way of looking, on this very idea of looking, as well as on its continuing realization; and, furthermore, on whether it is possible for Europe to look farther than that glance, farther than the distant horizon of universality within which it unfolds and at which it aims.

Undoubtedly, Europe's characterization as a look into the distance has become a historical reality in the form of the world market and the internationalization of the global community. But what makes Europe's identity as a look into the distance distinct from the pure and simple sighting of the "universal market," and hence what makes it truly an idea, is that it points at the universal, as Nancy holds, as such that is "evidently, the focus point, the aim, and the theme of the look of *Euryopa*." Thus understood, Europe is in essence a look at, and a conception of "'the world' as such: Europe has the universal in view, it has the world in view as universal" (*EU*, 6). But, Nancy will ask, given that there is no other idea than Europe, no other Idea of Europe, can an Idea be the Idea of a world to begin with? Can a world be the object of a vision, a sighting, at all; something, in other words, that one takes aim at? To answer these questions one must look more deeply into the look into the distance, into the ideal vision of universality that characterizes Europe. This deeper look, of course, is that of Euryopa's look into its own obscurity.

Still, one must continue to wonder whether it is at all possible to ask further questions about the look into the distance; questions that would go beyond an inquiry into the stakes of universal vision, the idea, or philosophy, and whose response would not be determined by the horizon of the universality into which they are to take a deeper look. What would it mean to look farther ahead into the distance than the distant; farther than and beyond universality? Would such a look into the distance still be a look, a vision, a sighting? In any event, before envisioning a response to these questions, one must first take a good look—an analytical look—at *looking* itself: that is, at the look into the distance, the look at what is universal.

As Nancy points out, Europe is the idea not only of a vision but of a vision characterized by a special way of looking. It has a form of its own, and it targets one and only one "object"—the universal. "Europe is thus inevitably the idea of an idea—form and vision, in the language of Plato," Nancy adds (*EU*, 8). Moreover, this idea of a look, and of an ideal form of that look itself, is the idea of a look that exposes and unfolds itself in accordance with a mode of exposition, or a language, of its own. *Logos* designates the language of the idea. Nancy explains the resulting implications for the idea of European vision, if it must expose itself in the medium of logos, as follows: "The idea expresses, formulates, and exposes itself according to the *logos*: this is to say, according to the law of autonomy, the law of what grounds itself upon itself, of what develops and verifies itself through itself, and what returns to itself, in and for itself. *Logos* is the language of the idea insofar as it is its 'reason.' The principal 'reason' of the idea is to be the essential form, essential to the extent that it forms itself, and thus *sees itself* in everything that it makes visible and intelligible" (*EU*, 8–9).

Consequently, since Europe as the idea of a look includes this idea of a special form in which that look is realized and exposes itself, it is a look that sees itself seeing and thereby sees what it sees. "The idea is the 'seeing-oneself-seeing' of vision and what it aims at," Nancy writes (*EU*, 9). The way the look into the distance (the look at what is universal) is modeled, as a look shaped in such a way that it is able to return to and into itself and thus to become its own ground, makes this look a look that owns itself, that is its ownmost self. At the same time, thus shaped, the vision at the heart of Europe—a vision that sets it apart—gathers its difference into itself, into a self properly closed on itself.

Nancy draws several consequences for the idea of Europe from this form of "seeing-oneself-seeing" that Europe's vision espouses insofar as the logos is the medium of its exposition. One of these consequences in particular requires our attention here: owing to the formal "reasons" of the idea in question, the look into the distance—the look at universality and the look that sees its own vision—is also a look that leaves itself behind. It leaves itself behind in dissolving and sublating itself. This means that as many times as "Europe" will have taken place,

> as many times it will have figured, configured, and represented itself as the privileged identity of the vision of the universal until Europe sees itself outside itself as a new subject, until it reengenders itself as 'Occident', as 'occidental civilization'—as a result of which, curiously, it exits itself, goes farther than itself all the way to the end of the world and, at the same time, it sees itself as an other, an other than itself insofar as it is not the *Orient*, not the birth of a world, but rather is the world occupied in totality, shaped in totality, and which comes back to itself as its *end*. (*EU*, 9)

The moment Europe shapes itself into the figure of the "Occident"—that is, as the figure of the totalization of the world, pursuing that totalization as a purpose until its end, until the world as purpose (*Zweck*) has become this end (*Ende*)—it leaves itself behind in the figure of a fulfillment that is not only a figure of exhaustion but is also one that, in its distinction from the "Orient," is necessarily a limited figure of its own self. Demarcating itself from itself, Europe, at this point, becomes the look at its own dissolution and disappearance. "The Occident—or the Erebus—is essentially and structurally a self-dissolving and self-alienating notion: it is the day that sees itself ending" (*EU*, 9). In this figure of itself, Europe—the look into the distance, the look at universality—leaves itself behind. Yet, seeing itself leaving itself behind, its demarcation from self is also its self-demarcation. In other words, the disappearance is a loss in which losing is not lost; on the contrary, by this loss the look returns into itself. It does so at the end of the look and by thematizing its end: by reappropriating that end as the dark spot that is necessarily presupposed by the look itself. Nancy concludes his discussion of this self-overcoming of the glance of universality as follows: "In this way, the universal that is the theme of its vision . . . returns to itself as the blind spot of its eye" (*EU*, 10).

Inevitably, any attempt to distinguish oneself from the look into the distance, which is a look at the universal, is already a preprescribed movement, and one that will become reinscribed into that look itself. To set oneself apart from the universal, and from the world shaped in accordance with it, is to obey the very logic of the look itself. It is to execute this look's *own* execution by which it transforms its end into a constituting limit of itself. As a result, one faces the question of whether it is at all possible to keep one's distance from a universal vision such as the one named *Europe*. Nancy thus wonders whether each effort to distance oneself from the look into the distance is not inevitably bound to produce just "one more turn of this return into self, in a turn each time more *archeo-logical*, which would only make us come back to the principle of Europe in order to better confirm the night of the universal into which this principle makes us enter" (*EU*, 10). However, this is also for Nancy the moment to suggest that at the very pole where universal vision achieves its most extreme degree of self-inflection, one might, perhaps, also touch on—and it will, indeed, be a question of touch—something that leads to this vision's outside, an exiting in which vision would no longer have any part, and hence would no longer be a part of vision itself. And so Nancy writes: "It is not one more dialectical turn, not one more *Aufhebung*. Rather it is of the order of an additional affirmation, one more step forward. Instead of taking the form of a return, it is to go farther in front of us. Farther, that is, deeper into the night, deeper into the blind spot. Deeper into the look of *Euryopa*" (*EU*, 10). But what is it that remains to be seen in this step that affirms the look of Euryopa, the look in the distance, by going deeper into its look? It is, I recall, to be a look into that end, or dusk of universal vision, at the moment the telos of this vision has been realized by Europe's worldwide expansion, and when this vision returns to and reappropriates "the blind spot of its eye" (*EU*, 10). Advancing deeper into the blind spot of universal vision, the look that goes farther into this blind spot, while not distinguishing anything in particular, not even itself ("the subject of the look itself") in the darkness, sees the night itself, Nancy holds. The eye that thus advances into the night of the blind spot at the heart of vision, and that sees itself not seeing, achieves a strange proximity to itself. "It is closest to itself" at the very limit of itself, not yet seeing, but merely a seeing that it does not see (*EU*, 10). It is not even a seeing that could already see *itself* as *not yet* seeing; no self-objectivation occurs here, nor does its nonseeing become thematic to any seeing. It is a seeing that before having the power of sight, "sees" seeing nothing. It is seeing affected by itself in advance of all "itself," and, hence, before all seeing that sees something particular.

Nancy writes of this eye that "it sees *at itself* [*à même soi*] and not in itself" (*EU*, 10). Against the possible objection that such a determination of the eye that sees itself not seeing is an identifying determination, one by which even this seeing-not-seeing becomes reappropriated and launched back as the ultimately first moment onto a dialectical circumference, Nancy draws on his analysis in *La remarque speculative* of Hegel's use of the expression *an sich—à même soi*, "at itself"—in which text he argued that "'at itself' is in Hegel the only undialectical word."[3] Thus, in keeping with this earlier analysis, everything hinges on the mode in which the nearness to itself of the eye that sees itself not seeing is thought. As Nancy submits, this eye, rather than looking outside or inside, looks "at (*à même*) the limit of seeing" (*EU*, 10). In other words, it does not thematize the limit of seeing. The eye that ventures a step farther into the constitutive blind spot of universal vision is not a seeing that sees a more essential condition, an even blinder spot of vision that becomes meaningful in view of what it makes possible. Rather, it is a seeing that, without seeing anything, is just seeing: a seeing without a subject, without a vision, without a horizon—absolutely finite seeing. Rigorously speaking, it is, therefore, not a seeing anymore, but a singular "awareness" at the border, or on the limit, of the dialectic of the particular and the universal. This "awareness" of seeing *an sich*, or at itself, is, however, not *of* the limit, insofar as the limit would be that of universal vision. It is the awareness of seeing prior to seeing *itself*. It is, says Nancy, a touch. "One ought to say that it [the eye] *touches* rather than that it sees" (*EU*, 10; italics mine).

Yet, what is it that is touched by the eye? According to Nancy, "It touches at itself as at the infinite of its vision. It is touched by itself, affected by itself as the infinite of vision. What is nearest is the most distant; in truth, there is no 'near' nor 'distant' anymore: there is a 'self-touching' that is the absolute distance at the heart of the abolishment of distance, comparable to the touching of the eye by the eyelid that closes upon it. There is a finite touching of the infinite—or, more exactly: this touching is the infinite of finitude" (*EU*, 11). As Nancy himself admits, this passage, which concludes his analysis of the step farther into the blind spot of universal vision and hence into a trait of seeing that is not shaped into a condition of possibility of the horizon of universality, would require lengthy elaborations on an ontological plane. But this, at least, can be said: next to the eye, on the bare surface of it, a seeing takes place, which is not mediated but which is not, for that matter, immediate. It consists of the singular touch by the eye at itself. What is touched in this singular look of bare seeing is the infinity of vision; in turn, the infinite of vision touches it. This moment of intimacy of self-identity at its most profound—this self-affection of bare seeing by its infinite possibilities—is also the place where seeing is most distant from itself. In its invisibility, it is a seeing from which the polarities of nearness and distance are still absent and not yet anticipatable as such. What the singular, finite touch touches, is seeing's openness to determinations to come, to the infinite of its possibilities. As such, this touch is also an infinite touch: the infinite of the singularity of that touch, which proceeds from nothing that it might have been given to see.[4]

Setting aside the question about the ontological presuppositions of this touch, or "nocturnal vision," as it is also termed, "Euryopa: Le regard au loin" limits itself to exploring the touch's ethical implications. If, indeed, "Europe conceived of and presented itself above all as an ethics" (*EU*, 11), then a touch that touches seeing, and that occurs in the reappropriated blind spot of universal vision, must have a necessary bearing on Europe's self-understanding; and this means also on the accompanying conceptions of the world and of the ways in which to inhabit it. As Nancy remarks, the values of universality, and of a world shaped accordingly, have become obscure as a result of the historical process in which the universal has turned into "the world launched into the space of the universe." These values are no longer worth anything. This obscurity and loss of value, which follows precisely from Europe's successful expansion into the world, is the context for Nancy's statement that "the entire world has become alienated by the value of the universal and the universal of value" (*EU*, 11). In becoming worldwide, extending as far as the world goes and stopping only at the limits of the universe itself, the world linked to the universal—hence, the world *of* the universal—has become entirely suspended from the universal. In this suspension, it has given up something of itself and has become estranged from itself; it has been made other than and foreign to itself by the universal. "Alienation" is an eminently dialectical term and suggests initially that the effects of the ideality-constituting-difference of Europe on the world can, and even should, be undone. But by framing Europe's difference from and to itself in terms of alienation, Nancy clearly gestures not only toward a concern eminently his own—a concern with thinking the world on this side of universality—but also gestures beyond the dialectics of the particular and the universal. Nancy's aim is to secure a notion of world prior to the world of universality: one not alienated by the universal but, as the terminology suggests, free from the universal; and this aim shows him to construe the universal as merely an oppressive and repressive gown thrown by a particularity upon the world. It is an abstract gown, and since it coincides with ascendancy of one part of the world over the whole world, up to the very limits of the universe, its universality is only disguised particularity. Hence, this gown's intrinsic violence. The difference that it makes is to inhibit the world from being itself. A violent prohibition to be itself, it forces the whole world, Europe included, into being other than itself. Nancy can, therefore, write: "Europe, or the *Entäusserung* [exteriorization] and the *Entfremdung* [alienation] of self in the other, of self as other" (*EU*, 11). It would thus seem that Nancy wishes to repudiate the concept of universality (and, in the same breath, also of Europe) altogether. But what, then, is this world, on this side of universality? Does it still deserve to be called "world"? Is there nothing universal about it at all, in no possible sense of "universality"? A world, by definition, is a world in common! Can this commonality of the world not be accounted for at all by means of the category of the universal? Or is the point, perhaps, that the world in question is not the world simply and finally freed from the tenacious grasp of the universal, but rather, in a strange way, one that has never been and will never be under the power of universality? And is it for this reason that this singular world cannot ever, as far as its singularity is concerned, be thought from—whatever the complexity of the renegotiated term might be—a notion such as the universal?

At this point, I wish to recall a statement made by Nancy in *The Inoperative Community*, concerning the declaration by Sartre that communism is contemporary community's unsurpassable horizon. After having argued that communism is no longer that horizon, Nancy remarks that this is "not because we have passed beyond any horizon. Rather, everything is inflicted by resignation, as if the new unsurpassable horizon took form around the disappearance, the impossibility, or the condemnation of communism."[5] Yet, at this precise moment in his argument, Nancy adds: "It is the *horizons* themselves that must be challenged. The ultimate limit of community, or the limit that is formed by community, as such, traces an entirely different line."[6] Even though I cannot, in the present context, discuss Nancy's thoughts on community and on the limit that is entirely distinct from a horizon that characterizes the community, I wish to bring this demand to "go farther than all possible horizons" to bear on the issue of a world severed from universality.[7] Understood from the Greek verb *horizein* (to divide, to separate from, or, as with a border, to mark out by boundaries, to delimit, to determine, to define), the universal—or Europe, for that matter—is a horizon, and more precisely, the horizon of the world. I do not need to recall this notion's origin in elementary optics and astronomy, nor its venerable philosophical history from Neo-Platonism to phenomenology. In the interest of brevity and focus, I shall limit myself to an extremely succinct exposition of the Husserlian phenomenological conception of the horizon. If I single out the Husserlian conception of horizon, it is, first of all, because in Husserl's theory of perception, world and universal horizon are so intimately interconnected that a world without horizon appears as a sheer inconceivability. By contrast, Nancy's proposition to challenge the horizons themselves is exactly what it claims to be: an attempt to think a world not enclosed within a horizon.

The Husserlian conception of the horizon emerges in the process of constitutional analyses, which is to say, of analyses that seek to determine being of all kinds through the accomplishments of transcendental consciousness. Rather than being a geocentric spatial framework for ordinary perception, "horizon," in Husserl, is "a title for what is phenomenologically exhibited in pure consciousness."[8] In order to uncover transcendental subjectivity and to open up the field of transcendental experience, a phenomenological reduction is required, in which everything that does not properly belong to the acts of consciousness qua acts is "bracketed." Such a reduction starts out from the fact, established in a preliminary description, that every individual act of experience, whether it is one of perceiving worldly objects or ideal possibilities, already implies a consciousness of the world—a consciousness of horizons. Each single act, with its particular horizon, always has *the* world for its *universal basis*. But in the natural attitude, the world presupposed by all positing acts is a world held to exist. This is the all-embracing doxic basis of all individual acts. Therefore, in order to reach the transcendental field of experience, and hence the phenomenal concept of the horizon, it is necessary not only to depart from the individual acts, and from the doxic belief in the being of objects, but also to suspend the doxic positing of being that affects the consciousness of the world present in any single act of perception. In setting all presupposed objectivity out of action, both for the correlate of the individual acts and for the correlate "world," or "horizon," phenomenological reduction shows all acts of consciousness not only to include their objects qua meant objects, but furthermore to be founded on a "consciousness of horizons . . . a consciousness which is ultimately consciousness of the world as the total horizon."[9] It is the consciousness of the world as ultimate horizon, rather than a world behind the world in its factual existence for us, that sustains the ways in which we always already experience the world and that makes a real understanding of the world possible; that is, makes possible an understanding of the (doxic) way in which the world is, and will always be, given for man as man. The constitutionally clarified world, the world as total horizon, thus names the transsubjective understanding of "world," of what is always meant by "world" whether it is our own or an alien world.

For Husserl, then, the world has a horizonal structure. Although the horizon is rarely thematized as such, to live in a world is to live within its particular horizon and, ultimately, within the total horizon. World and horizon are inseparable. As Ludwig Landgrebe notes: "It is essentially impossible to find men in any 'pre-wordly' state, because to be human, to be aware of oneself as a man and to exist as a human person, is precisely to live on the basis of a world."[10] Undoubtedly, this statement would require a detailed commentary, especially regarding the "humanist" underpinnings of the concepts of world and horizon. These underpinnings are thrown into even stronger relief in the following statement by Cornelius A. Van Peursen: "The world without a horizon is unimaginable. The world would lose its framework, along with the horizon, thereby making it entirely different. The world, as a human world, is even impossible without the horizon. . . . To eliminate the horizon is to remove man."[11] If I stress the inextricable interconnectedness of Husserlian world and horizon, it is precisely because of Nancy's call for engaging the horizons. The stakes are high, given that to attack the horizon is to attack the world. Indeed, what can it mean, therefore, if it means anything at all, to contend against the horizons, particularly, if a world without horizons, and without a universal horizon, would seem to be unthinkable? Unthinkable, also, because it would seem to mean the destruction of the scope of human space. Should it thus only be a question of forcing existing horizons to recede and of forcing them to open up to the "horizon of the horizon?"[12] Since a horizon, even a limited one, is an openness—and in the case of a limited horizon, a finite openness—does Nancy only wish to argue for a limitlessly open horizon? He would then be saying the same thing that Husserl has already said. For the latter, as Landgrebe puts it, our own world and alien worlds stand

> in a nexus of possible continuous (direct or indirect) experience with our own, in such a manner that all such 'worlds' combine to make up the unity of the all-embracing world. Accordingly, the world cannot have for us the sense of being a self-contained world . . . we must take it to be a world unlimitedly open on all sides. In this openness it provides free space for all the different home-worlds of the most diverse human communities. It becomes the infinitely open universe as the whole of existence, the completely open horizon in which, ideally at least, our experiences can always be extended *ad infinitum*.[13]

But did Nancy not call precisely for a contestation of the horizons themselves, and for going farther than all possible horizons, hence also farther than a world unlimitedly and infinitely open? Given the way we have seen him to understand universality as the extension of one particular humanity to the outer limit of the entire (real) universe—in other words, as a universality that is not only repressive of particularity but one whose infinity belongs to what Hegel called "spurious infinity"—it is certainly safe to say that he wishes to go beyond that world's unlimited openness, beyond its total horizon. In what remains of my commentary on "Euryopa: Le regard au loin," I will seek to clarify a bit of what it could mean to abandon the concept of horizon altogether.

The world of Europe, as we have seen before, is the world within the horizon of universality. Europe has alienated itself into this world, and this has prompted Nancy to speak of it as the name for an essential, or structural, alienation of self in the other, of self as other. But, he argues, although Europe sees itself thus defined as "the *Selbstanschauung* [self-intuition] of *Selbstentfremdung* [self-alienation]," it is as well "the *Entfremdung* [alienation] of *Anschauung* [intuition]" (*EU*, 11). What does this mean? As a glance at the universal, a glance that is a "glance into the distance" (*regard au loin*), Europe looks at itself as other than itself, as alienated from itself. But, as Nancy suggests, this look at itself is a look no less alienated. Europe is alienated from intuition—namely, from all perception that is unmediated by the universal—hence it is alienated, first and foremost, from the immediate perception of evident and self-present truth, that is, ultimately the truth of itself. Consequently, Europe must also be understood to name an alienation of the possibility of intuiting the other as other, and the self in its "immediacy." In other words, Europe also stands for an essential structural inhibition of the self to close itself to the other (itself included) as other, and to a world whose common denominator would be the self and the other's otherness. This negative openness, however, precedes by right the emergence of Europe as the world subjected to universality and horizonality. Nancy acknowledges as much when he writes: "Europe opens up the world, as its other self, but it carries it away in its alienation" (*EU*, 11). Europe, in short, opens up the "world" in the sense just alluded to, namely as a place constituted by an intuiting of self and other that would not be mediated; but it blocks it out at the very moment it launches it onto the road to universality; that is, at the moment it alienates itself in the value of universality. Nevertheless, since alienation is an eminently dialectical concept,

> alienation always ends up bringing to light that which is inalienable, and which makes alienation itself possible: the alterity that the "self" is not, and to which it cannot get through, but that it only encounters, that comes towards and against it, and that is the other "self"—not the "self" as other, but the other of the self that is "self," being absolutely and irreducibly other, infinitely resisting the universal reduction of "self" to "self." The inalienable of the other is, henceforth, what Europe finds everywhere, in front of itself and in itself, since the world is, henceforth, at once what Europe has in front of itself and that into which it has alienated itself, alienating the world itself through its universal vision. (*EU*, 11–12)

The inalienable is the other self, insofar as it is not a self carried along by the universal self. The inalienable is the world of these singular "selves," the world before universal horizonality. But both harbor within themselves the possibility of alienation, in that they are structured so as to be beside-before-beyond-oneself—beside-before-beyond-"self." Even as extroverted selves, as it were, they inherently carry the possibility of alienation into the universal self; and yet they themselves remain irreducible to the universal reduction. They and their world remain on, and at, the margin of the alienated world to which they give rise. The world is hence at least double. It is what Europe encounters outside and inside itself as irreducible to itself, but it is also that into which it has lost itself, the horizonal world in which the world has been lost. Once the European universal vision experiences the world both as that which it faces and as the universal world estranged from the world of alterity, "the universal itself has taken on the strangeness of a dark night," Nancy continues (*EU*, 12). In other words, the world alienated in universal vision has itself become strange, no longer familiar as before, uncanny like the obscurity of the night.

Once the universal is no longer recognizable as that which is most proper to us, the incumbent task is not to seek to reanimate it by calling upon values, but rather "to look, without looking away, at what thus happens to us" (*EU*, 12). Nancy writes: "One must reaffirm again the *ethos* of the look—not by turning one's eyes toward a firmament spangled with values, but by facing straight ahead into the obscurity" (*EU*, 12). From everything we have seen so far, the way this ethos is to inhabit the world is different from that of the ethos of European universal vision. There can no longer be a question of a look arising from a world that is *its* world, and embracing the horizon as the horizon of horizons. Rather the look into the darkness of universality is, in Nancy's words, to be "a finite look into the infinite. As a matter of fact, what we currently see is nothing other than the infinite. It is no longer the universal, as the gathering and the *Anschauung* [intuition] by a subject of the world, but its [the world's] *ethos* having become infinite" (*EU*, 12). I recall that Nancy has described the probing of the gaze of Euryopa as a glancing into its blind spot, into the night at the heart of universal vision. By looking deeper into this night—a process in which seeing is shown to touch itself, in a finite touch that is a touching of the infinite—universal vision has itself become as strange, or uncanny, as the night itself. By touching "itself," seeing opens upon the infinite of seeing, of a seeing no longer dominated by a totalizing horizon: that is, on a world that is infinite rather than universal. With the nocturnal vision in which seeing "sees" itself touching itself before it sees, and even before it sees that it does not see, it "sees" the infinite of vision. This is the finite touch that Nancy has called, "the infinite of finitude" (*EU*, 10). In short, what such a glance into the blind spot of universal vision reveals, if one can still speak of revelation in this case, is the world as an infinite place of dwelling: that is, a place of finites, of singularities. At the extreme border of the horizon, the world appears in its horizonless infinity, a finite world, and hence an infinite one. Needless to say, it would be necessary to ponder here how the infinity of a world is to be thought in view of its lack of horizon and of everything that horizonality implies. But, for the moment, let me continue to follow Nancy's lead concerning what it means for the world's ethos to have become infinite.

"The *ethos* (and the *logos*) which are incumbent upon all, and which bring us all together into the world," are "existence, and truth," Nancy writes. Given that Nancy understands existence as being "separated (*absolutum*) from all essence and all fulfillment of essence,"[14] it follows that existence, not unlike its Heideggerian homologue, is not so much an (im-mutable) value as what is at stake for all finite beings as beings within an infinite world. "Existence and truth are *what is at stake* [*ce qui est en jeu*], and there is nothing else at stake. . . . One and the other are *sighted* [*visées*, related to, aimed at] by something that is not exactly a looking, by a mode of sighting that Europe and the West have called 'love'—as if to give it the name of the impossible" (*EU*, 12). If it is love—something that is "not exactly a looking"—in which existence and truth are being aimed at, and not a look, glance, or vision, it is precisely because both existence and truth are not, to quote Heidegger, "to be construed in terms of some concrete possible idea of existence."[15] Or, following Nancy, if existence and truth are correlates of love it is because existence is not a positively identifiable reality, nor truth something that could be cognitively appropriated. If existence is absolutely separated from all essence, and truth, by eluding the possibility of anamnestic rediscovery, something wagered, existence and truth are infinite. Nancy writes: "'Existence' and 'truth' mean the infinite. They mean the infinite alterity that are 'existence' and 'truth': one and the other, and both together, are always absolutely and infinitely other. Differently put, that which is other in the other . . . and which from its own infinite alterity comes to meet the 'self,' is always existence and truth as such" (*EU*, 13). Yet because existence and truth are infinite, only a finite look that touches them, at their bare surface as it were (*posé sur lui, à même lui*) (*EU*, 12), is the appropriate look in their case. In other words, existence and truth demand an ethical mode of relating, given that the ethical, for Nancy, is a relation to the infinite; that is, to a finite that is infinitely finite because it is always exposed to alterity. Love, understood otherwise than "the unappeased tension of desire or the communal fusion of Christian love" (*EU*, 12), is such an ethical "relation."

Love faces the infinite: it is a finite look, a look that gazes into the infinite. If this finite look that rests on the alterity of existence and truth does not perceive or reveal any idea, form, or figure of the infinite, it is because this look is not out to render the infinite intelligible. It does not, in an idealizing gesture, duplicate this infinite in an attempt to make it truly itself. Through this look, the infinite is not alienated from itself in an attempt to universally establish its identity. Just in resting its glance on the mere surface of the infinite, the finite look lets it be the infinite; hence it "sees at one stroke right to the end, as it were, of the infinite." Nancy writes:

> The finite look is not a look deprived of the infinite, a look that would not go far enough—on the contrary, it is the look that comes to rest on the infinite as such. It does not see anything. It does not behold any Idea, any Form or Figure in need of a presentation or a production. But this look sees at one stroke right to the end [*d'un seul trait jusqu'au bout*], as it were, of the infinite. It sees that it is existence and truth, their common alterity, that are henceforth the infinite stakes of a finite world. (*EU*, 13)

But looking at one go right to the end of the infinite also means seeing its limits: in short, seeing that it is the infinity of finitude, an infinity that is infinitely finite. Nancy, therefore, continues: "This world is finite because it is entirely given back, or restored, to itself. This world no longer opens on other worlds, be they new, ancient, celestial, or infernal worlds. It is not topped by values and Ideas that float above it. It is *the world* that is only world" (*EU*, 13). Clearly, the idea of the world is, for Nancy, what prevents a world from being a world. He writes: "The Idea of a world is still beyond all Idea. The Idea of the world has no figure that would incarnate it, no project that would contain it, no ideal that would measure up to it, no universal that would constitute its *arkhe*, or its *telos*, no *reason* (in the sense of a *ground*) to account for it" (*EU*, 14). To say that the world cannot be the object of an ideal sighting implies not only that it cannot be a vision *by* Europe, and *of* Europe, "as if in Europe such a sighting had its place and seat," but also that such a sighting would not be that of a world (*EU*, 14); a further implication being that a world cannot really be visually sighted. "A world," Nancy contends, "is a space for the infinite of truth and existence, of all existence—and is not something on which one can properly set one's sights [*cela ne se vise pas proprement*]. It is not the *Angeschaute einer Anschauung* [the intuited of an intuition]" (*EU*, 14). What Nancy calls *world*, which is the "object" of the finite look closer to love than to vision, is a world free of a horizon. If it does not open onto other worlds such as new, ancient, celestial, or infernal worlds, it neither opens onto *the* world, the "total-horizon" supposedly shared by all particular worlds. No universal consciousness of the world, no transsubjective understanding of what world qua world means, pervades this finite world. And because no horizon-consciousness overhangs, or is immanently implied by the finite world, no universal meaning or essence alienates itself into particular worlds, alienating them in turn; and furthermore, no one single world can maintain the pretense of being more than just itself. In the finite world, no glance into the distance, or sighting of universality, permits a particular world to gain ascendency over all others. If the finite world is without a horizon, this is primarily because it does not rest on visual perception, but rather on what Nancy has called the finite look, which is a look that is not essentially of the order of vision.

For Nancy, the finite world—the world that is infinitely finite and infinitely exposed to its lack of a total and universal horizon—is *the world* that is merely world. Having established this much, Nancy concludes by way of a return to the question of the way in which Euryopa sees. I recall that Euryopa's glance, in addition to being a look into the distance, or the universal, is also a glance deep into universal vision's blind spot; a glance, furthermore, that does not *see* so much as it *touches* seeing, as it were, at its bare surface. He thus holds that the finite world "is *the world* that is just world, become world by means of the expansion of the sighting of Euryopa from out of itself, and return to itself—which does not find *itself* in this world, but which finds itself carried away, altered in it, beyond itself" (*EU*, 13). As has been previously shown, the glance of Euryopa is a glance at what infinitely makes the world finite—its lack of an essence, an idea, a horizon, and so forth. By probing into the darkness of universality, Euryopa's glance touches on infinity, rather than on universality. Now the finite world, not unlike the universal world, is constituted by a glance that expands beyond the particular and that returns to itself. But rather than achieving an identity with itself, this glance that returns to itself returns only to discover the otherness of its own being. The world that emerges by way of Euryopa's glance is a world infinitely exposed to the lack of horizonal meaning and also to its own otherness. It is thus a world that is no longer Euryopa's own world but instead a world in which it itself, and the vision it represents, have become altered and othered.

Undoubtedly, the finite world on which Euryopa's glance rests is, because it is horizonless, a world unlike the idea of the world that Europe has stood for. It is no longer a human world: not inhuman, though, but a-human. Rather than of humans, this world is one made up of beings for whom existence and truth are the stakes. Unlike humans, whose essence is determined by their gaze at a universal idea of what the human being is (and for whom this idea is of a universalized particularity), these beings that make up the finite world are infinitely exposed to existence as a nonessence. They are thus finite beings, or singular beings who are not, for that matter, noninfinite beings. Rather, these singular beings that make up this finite and horizonless world—a world infinitely finite, hence infinite—these beings are as many finite looks, exposed to the otherness of what is both before them and in themselves. No horizon that would ensure the scope of human space is tied to these looks as their absolute limit. Rather, these looks touch the infinite; and this tangible infinite is the infinite of the finite beings' exposure to the constituting absence in their existence, of an eventual fulfillment of essence: in short, to the infinity of the world.

Notes

1. Jean-Luc Nancy, "Euryopa: Le regard au loin," in *Contributions*, a prepublication (in French and German) of the proceedings of a conference at the University of Leipzig (May 11–14, 1994), 5–15 (hereafter cited in text as *EU*), on "La philosophie européenne de la culture et le projet 'logos' de 1910." The essay has also been published in *Terra Lingonna*, nr.00 (Langres: Lycée Diderot, January 1995).

2. *Der Kleine Pauly. Lexikon der Antike*, eds. K. Ziegler and W. Sonthheimer (Munich: Deutscher Taschenbuch Verlag, 1979), 2:447.

3. Jean-Luc Nancy, *La remarque spéculative* (Paris: Galilée, 1973), 110–118.

4. Let me recall here that, for Nancy, finitude is not to be confused with classical "finity." Finitude is infinitely in excess of itself. Speaking of human finitude, Nancy writes: "*Finitude* does not mean that we are noninfinite—like small, insignificant beings within a grand, universal, and continuous being—but it means that we are *infinitely* finite, infinitely exposed to our existence as a nonessence, infinitely exposed to the otherness of our own 'being' (or that being is in us exposed to its own otherness). We begin and we end without beginning and ending: without having a beginning and an end that is *ours*, but having (or being) them only as others', and through others." Jean-Luc Nancy, *The Birth to Presence* (Stanford, CA: Stanford University Press, 1993), 155–156.

5. Jean-Luc Nancy, *The Inoperative Community*, trans. P. Connor et al. (Minneapolis: University of Minnesota Press, 1991), 8–9.
6. Nancy, *Inoperative Community*, 8–9.
7. Nancy, *Inoperative Community*, 8–9.
8. Elizabeth Ströker, *Husserl's Transcendental Philosophy*, trans. L. Hardy (Stanford, CA: Stanford University Press, 1993), 90.
9. Ludwig Landgrebe, *The Phenomenology of Edmund Husserl: Six Essays* (Ithaca, NY: Cornell University Press, 1981), 93–94.
10. Landgrebe, *Phenomenology of Edmund Husserl*, 140.
11. Cornelius A. Van Peursen, "The Horizon," in *Husserl: Expositions and Appraisals*, ed. F. Elliston and P. McCormick (Notre Dame: University of Notre Dame Press, 1977), 184.
12. Van Peursen, "The Horizon," 184.
13. Landgrebe, *Phenomenology of Edmund Husserl*, 137.
14. Jean-Luc Nancy, "Our History," *Diacritics* 20, no.3 (1990): 103–104.
15. Martin Heidegger (1962), *Being and Time*, trans. J. Macquarrie and E. Robinson (London: Harper and Row, 1962), 69.

3

IN LIGHT OF LIGHT

In *The Crisis of European Sciences and Transcendental Phenomenology*, Edmund Husserl claims that Europe, rather than being a merely geographical entity, is an absolute idea. This claim consolidates philosophical and secularizing notions of Europe's spiritual determination, the endpoint of a process that begins in the seventh century, when Western Europe first defines itself as *sacrum imperium*. Husserl thus raises the notion of Europe to a conceptual level unheard of until that date. But this claim, as well as the conceptual effort devoted to clarifying the idea of Europe, sounds strange today. To pair words such as *Europe* with *idea* sounds odd at a time when, despite the active integration of the European nations into a unified economic and political zone, intellectual vitality seems to have migrated elsewhere. The coupling of the two words thus appears questionable for reasons of cultural and historical dynamics. But apart from these reasons, to identify Europe as an absolute idea has also been challenged on moral and political grounds. Gérard Granel, in his controversial preface to his 1976 translation of *Crisis of European Sciences*, calls Husserl's conception of Europe "completely outdated," describing it as an "ancient scene of an ancient theater." Although he recognizes Husserl's courage, particularly in the "Vienna Lecture," in standing up to Nazi barbarism, Granel nonetheless questions how Husserl's philosophy bears on the historical context in question, and finds it morally reprehensible that the sole solution it offers for putting an end to the rise of fascism and the crisis of humanity is to invoke the idea of Europe and the concomitant notion of the "'self-responsibility' of humanity." Husserl's attempt, in *Crisis of European Sciences*, to "reawaken (and accomplish once and for all) under the form of absolute transcendental phenomenological philosophy the reason that is immanent in man and which defines his humanity," thus shows itself, Granel concludes, as "the purest example of Western 'theoretical' paranoia."¹ But even though he holds morality and politics to be more important than philosophy, Granel also objects to Husserl's definition of Europe as an absolute idea on purely philosophical grounds. His objections are most evident in a lecture titled "L'Europe de Husserl," presented in 1987 in Lima on the occasion of a Franco-Peruvian philosophy colloquium, where he references Karl Marx, Martin Heidegger, Ludwig Wittgenstein, and Jean-Toussaint Desanti in order to criticize Husserl's characterization of Europe as a spiritual figure, or absolute idea. Granel suggests that Husserl may have projected onto the Greek conception of science an ideal of science that is essentially of modern origin. More importantly, he holds that because of the rise of the United States and its American ideology to world hegemony, every aspect that makes up the concept of Europe as an absolute idea, and which, according to Husserl, must be traced back to the Greek conception of a rational science, has lost all possible pertinence—including the idea that the sciences unfold according to a logic specific and internal to themselves, as well as the Greek model of political existence. Marx and Heidegger are invoked in order to argue that, in the present, the Greek model of political existence has been entirely replaced by a life in the service of capitalist production. Wittgenstein and Desanti serve Granel to explain that the sciences are no longer in need of justification and have become autonomous such that they can do entirely without philosophy. Furthermore, they no longer obey the logic of unitary development. Concluding his demonstration of Husserl's completely obsolete conception of the "absolute idea" of Europe, Granel exclaims: "American end of 'Europe.' Metaphysico-scientist end of logicity. Total extinction, at the horizon of our future, of the light in which the clarity of the Greek days still reverberated."²

If the concept of Europe as a spiritual figure, or absolute idea, is passé and if this conception no longer has leverage nowadays, why bother taking up this notion at all? If, indeed, to suggest an ideational content to the notion of Europe is the outrageous expression of Europe's arrogant self-representation, is one not contributing to Europe's self-delusion if one is to take up this issue, even if only to criticize it, at a time when the complete obsolescence of this idea is plain to all? Or could it be that when it comes to dealing with the notion of Europe, things are even more complex, intricate, if not perverse? Granel, who foresees the "total extinction, at the horizon of our future, of the light in which the clarity of the Greek days still reverberated," claims to take note of a fact. But significantly enough, this statement also mourns the disappearance from our horizon of the light that still reflected Greek clarity! Why such mourning? Since we may certainly exclude nostalgia in Granel's case given that he views the disappearance of Europe as an entirely positive event, what reason could make such mourning inevitable? Could it be that without the clarity of the Greek day, even when it is said to have completely faded, it is impossible to notice the alleged extinction of the light at our horizon to begin with? Could it not be that without such clarity, it is not even possible to make others see that the light has faded from our horizon?

Before continuing such questioning, let me briefly recall how Husserl conceives of the idea of Europe. This idea, which is said to originate in Greece and which unifies European history, is not something given positively to Europe but, rather, constitutes a task to be accomplished. In essence, it is the idea of a universal rational science. Considering the current suspicion that the concept of anything "universal" would be a hegemonic, abstract idea oblivious to difference, whose role is one of dominion, I will sketch out in some very broad strokes what is meant by *universal science*, bringing out in relief some of the implications that come with this notion. The idea of a universal science—not in the modern but in the Greek sense, that is, as philosophy from which the various sciences have branched out— marks a break not only with the prescientific world of myth but also with everything on the order of regional traditionalisms, customs, beliefs, and even linguistic idioms.[3] Husserl, therefore, can contend that this science is an expression of "humanity struggling to understand itself."[4] With this, one beholds the first reason why such an idea is universal: it reaches out toward what unifies the whole of what *is*. However, to appreciate the specific sense in which universal is to be taken here, it must be distinguished from the unmistakably universalist aspirations of the world views, and conceptions of the human and the divine, in pre-Platonic Greece, or other civilizations, for that matter. Husserl, for one, clearly recognizes a "world-encompassing interest" in "Indian, Chinese, and similar 'philosophies,'" and notes that this interest has led to a universal knowledge of the world. But, according to Husserl, the universal direction of interest is fundamentally different in Greek philosophy. He argues that the theoretical attitude that emerges in Greece not only reaches toward that which, beyond all particularities in the natural and human world, unifies the manifold but is also an attitude that, rather than being merely theoretical, takes shape as a practical attitude, that is, as a "vocation-like life-interest," and commands life in terms of what is universal.[5] To the extent that this philosophical science aims at freeing itself from all particularities, it conceives of a philosophizing subject who transcends the specificities of nation, race, or culture. It consequently implies as well the positing (and minimal recognition) of the human "other" as an "other" notwithstanding differences. Thus, a second dimension of this science's universality comes to light. A science that makes universal claims is a science that is structurally open toward the other. When science turns to the other, the other is torn from the obscurity of anonymity, or from his or her state of foreignness. A science that is universal thus inscribes within itself an essential responsiveness, and thus responsibility, to the other. To call the object of the idea in question a science in the sense of a philosophical science, suggests, in addition, that "science" is the idea of a mental disposition, or cognitive paradigm that is conscious of itself as an interpretation of the world and distinct from myth. With this, the third, and, especially, crucial, sense in which this science is said to be universal, shows itself. This form of science's self-consciousness as a science, as an interpretation of the world, requires it to sustain, ground, and justify any claims it makes. The idea at the heart of Europe is the idea of a mental or cognitive paradigm (in a very broad sense) that imposes on itself the burden to justify itself, in short, to identify itself on the basis of criteria and minimal rules of argumentation that can be held to be universally shareable. The very mode of exposition, that is, the argumentative, or discursive nature of this science, is an intrinsic part of its universality. It is a science that attends to its responsibility to the other by seeking to be accountable for any of the propositions it may advance.

Even without further elaborating on the universality of this science, or philosophy, it should be clear that this idea cannot be relinquished easily, or only at a very high cost—tribalism, the denial of all humanity to the other, and the abandonment of any obligation to account for one's words and deeds. Still, to point out that to part with the exigency of universality is to condone the worst, does not imply that this exigency is without problems and does not exclude the possibility that, ultimately, it may need to be rethought. What is true of universality is true of Europe as an idea. As the idea of a rational science, a life of reason, and public responsibility, it cannot be surrendered in the blink of eye. From what I have sketched out so far, it should also be evident that if such a surrender is to be argumentative, and hence subject to a method and rules that any other could comprehend, it presupposes the very rationality that it seeks to overthrow. Evidently, all partial questioning of the conception of Europe discussed earlier (and thus of philosophy, or universality) is destined to fail since inevitably it makes use of rationality as it has been defined by this conception. By critically opposing this or that theme that is woven into the idea of Europe—the theme, for instance, of mankind's self-responsibility, or of a rational, and universal science—and be it in the name of the exalted theme of the other of Europe, one remains tributary to the idea in question as a whole. But is it possible to challenge the whole concept in any judicious way? This can certainly not be achieved by having recourse to any of the historical variations on the basic tenets of the idea of Europe, for example, by referencing Marx, Heidegger, or Wittgenstein, in whose names Granel thought to challenge Husserl. Nor can it be accomplished by making an about-face toward the non-Western, the Oriental, the absolutely other, primitive, or irrational. For by turning to the other of Europe on the basis of preprogrammed oppositional patterns such as the non-Western, one remains indebted to what one turns away from (the Western), and performs a turn toward the irrational, in short, toward the rational in the shape of the other of the rational. If, furthermore, such a turn away from "Europe" seeks universal assent, it yields again to what is specifically a European idea. As Nancy notes, "all confrontation of other ways of looking *than* that of Europe, or of other ways of looking *at* Europe itself, must face this particular fact, namely that the 'universal' as such, its category or point of view, is of European extraction."[6] In order to present, assert, and justify themselves, all ways of looking other than the European gaze remain inextricably bound to the rationality by means of which such presentation, assertion, or claims can be made in a way that, in principle at least, could be intelligible to all.

At this point it may be useful to distinguish between these contestations of Western thought, which either substitute one formulation of Western philosophy for another or invert this conception as a whole along with differences and oppositions laid out by this conception itself, from what I would like to call rewritings (I do not say reconceptions) of Western thought. These latter attempts do not seek to abandon Western thought's universalist bent. Rather, they inquire into the structural limits that inhabit the unrelinquishable idea of universality. They seek the enabling limits whence universality comes into being, understanding that these limits also inscribe a certain finitude into it.

Undoubtedly, there is today a deep malaise and discontent about everything Western, about a thinking and looking named "European." To the cosmological, biological, and psychological blows to human self-love that Sigmund Freud distinguished, a new blow has been added. It is the deep-seated disillusionment with philosophical thought and its universalist thrust.[7] As said before, the attempts made to step outside the conception of Western thought by continuing to rely on what precisely they seek to escape—argumentative rationality and preprogrammed operating systems—are, undoubtedly, clear failures, which, rather than overthrowing Western thinking, continue to pay homage to it. And yet they are also unmistakably symptoms of a malaise with philosophical thought. But it remains that this malaise is also a symptom of misunderstanding. And hence attempts to overcome Western philosophical thought are heavy-handed and fall short of their goal. In fact, these attempts constitute the malaise itself and are symptoms of an inability to command the resources of the philosophical for a radical interrogation and rewriting of philosophy's legitimate demands. To all the reasons I have pointed out that make these attempts to exit from Western thought unsuccessful, I need to add another, more formidable one. This reason concerns the category of the step outside, and of a farewell altogether to Western thought. Deeply rooted in the Platonic myth of the cave, the figure of the step outside is intimately linked to the thought of universality itself. Indeed, it is the opening gesture toward truth and universality. The very goal of reaching beyond Western thought is thus still dependent on the resources of Western thought itself. Distinct from these efforts to overturn Western thought, however, are those rewritings of philosophy, or of "Europe," that articulate a new and singular experience, or feeling, of what philosophy, or "Europe" imply. Beyond the alternative of either full acceptance or total rejection of the idea of Europe, beyond the urge to shore this idea up, or set off to altogether new shores, are those writings on Europe and the idea of universality by contemporary thinkers who, by tapping unrealized resources of the concept of Europe, proceed to rethink this concept's internal relation to the non-European. In addition, these writings are also attempts to open Europe up to the other in general and, more precisely, to an otherness not yet constituted, or precalculated in terms of existing difference—an otherness to come. I am thinking, of course, of Jacques Derrida's *The Other Heading*, and Jean-Luc Nancy's "Euryopa. Le Regard au Loin" among others.[8] In what follows, however, I will focus on drawing out further implications that come with the idea of Europe, less obvious perhaps than those of rationality, universality, responsibility, but no less essential, as we will see, for a debate intent on reconfiguring the idea of Europe.

Martin Heidegger was the first in the phenomenological tradition inaugurated by Husserl to reinterpret the latter's conception of Europe. Whereas Husserl identifies "Europe" with a theoretical attitude (and philosophy as episteme) inseparably bound up with a life-interest in raising mankind above all of its particularities to the higher state of humanity as such, Heidegger conceives of philosophy, and "Europe," as a being attuned to being, that is, in terms of a state of mind, still pretheoretical and more akin to the pragmatic, as some have it, world of Dasein. A second major rearticulation within phenomenological thought of the idea of Europe takes place in Jan Patočka's work. I will be concerned hereafter with his reworking of the notion of Europe.

Patočka's *Plato and Europe* is a series of lectures delivered in the context of a private seminar in Prague in 1973 (which preceded the writing of *Heretical Essays*), whose aim is to inquire into whether the European heritage contains something that could also work for mankind east of Europe, as well as for those who come after Europe, after its decline. The central argument of these lectures is that "care of the soul is the central theme around which . . . the life plan of Europe crystallized."[9] Since Patočka's interpretation of this motif from Plato's aporetic dialogues is very much tied to his own understanding of phenomenology, I need to linger for a moment on what sets his thought apart from Husserl.[10] Undoubtedly, Patočka subscribes to Husserlian phenomenology as a science of the phenomenon as phenomenon and of the essence of appearing, as a science in search of the fundamental structures of possibility that determine the way things show themselves. But the world is not only made up of phenomenal structures alone, Patočka argues. There are also "things" that show themselves. Husserlian "phenomenology, the science of the phenomenon as such, show us not things, but rather the *way of givenness* of things" (*PE*, 31). Distinct from the nonobjective structures of phenomenality, there are thus the structures of the things themselves, as well as of those beings to whom they show themselves, the human beings. By centering on how things, and especially human beings, are codetermined by the structures of manifestation, and by inquiring into the relations between phenomenon and being (or beings), Patočka wishes to draw attention to the metaphysical consequences of the phenomenological analysis of the phenomenon qua phenomenon. In contrast to Husserlian phenomenological analysis, Patočka's approach lays claim, therefore, to being "already a certain *phenomenological philosophy*" (*PE*, 32).

For the Czech philosopher, the Husserlian systematic exploration of the phenomenon qua phenomenon, that is, of appearing as such, is only the most radical continuation of philosophy's discovery, continuing from its inception in Greece, that being as a whole, or the world, is manifest to the human in its totality. Yet for the Greeks, the appearing of being, as totality, to the human being implies that appearing is the privilege of the human being. It is his destiny since it is destined to him, but also because he can choose to encounter or refuse the encounter with what shows itself to him. If this is so, then this privilege may also bring with it an obligation, the obligation to embrace what shows itself—appearing, clarity in the world, the phenomenon as such. However, once embraced by the human being, the nonreal aspect of the universe, appearing as such, becomes real and acquires effective actuality. It becomes real in the shape of what Plato calls the tendance of, or care of, the soul (*tes psyches epimeleisthai*). Admittedly, Patočka's phenomenological philosophy is a metaphysics, for it subordinates and brings to bear the phenomenological analysis of the structures of appearing as such, upon the being to whom appearing is destined.

As I mentioned already, the idea of a care of the soul is, according to Patočka, the unique core of the heritage bequeathed upon Europe by the Greeks. The soul is what properly distinguishes the human being; that precise instance in us to which the totality of being shows itself, hence becoming phenomenon. Patočka writes: "The soul is that to which things are revealed as they are, or that and what they are. Our own being has to show itself to us by that, that the call, which is encompassed within this situation, becomes for us also the impulse to that, so that our own essence, our own being, our own being in that which is its own, is revealed to us" (*PE*, 36). Indeed, as the sole addressee of the phenomenon, the innermost, or principial, possibility of the human being as human being, a possibility that presents itself precisely by the fact that being manifests itself in totality to him, depends on his response to manifestation as such, and on assuming responsibility for and to it. If Greek philosophy has become the foundation of European life it is because it derives, as Patočka ascertains, "*a plan for life* from this situation" (*PE*, 35). He writes: "The Greek idea is the following: in just this situation it is shown that man has *various* possibilities on the basis of this original situation [i.e. that things appear to man]. Only then, in this situation, he has to prove himself; only then he has to show himself as a creature who really does make phenomenon, that means clarity, *truth the law of his life*, and with the help of this law in every domain in which man is involved. *Given certain circumstances, man could make at least the human world a world of truth and justice*" (*PE*, 36). As Patočka stresses, such a thing is possible only "as long as we make this clarity, the phenomenon as such, the phenomenalization of the world, the placing into clarity—the program of all of human life. All this from looking-in [*nahlédnuti*]. Like in our thinking, so in our deeds, always to act with clarity" (*PE*, 35). Because of the originary situation that makes the human being the addressee of the manifestation of the world in its totality, the human being has the possibility "to realize himself as a *being of truth, a being of phenomenon* . . . How this can be achieved is the very subject of the care of the soul" (*PE*, 36). Out of this concept, Patočka argues, "grew not only classical Greek philosophy but also Europe and our history" (*PE*, 36–37).

From what we have seen so far, it should be evident that the manifestedness of being, the phenomenon, or appearing as such, of which the human being, or the soul that, for the Greeks, defines the human being in essence, becomes aware, and by which it is summoned to respond, corresponds to the realization in wonder that it is in light, in the clarity of the day, that things show themselves to us. With this realization Greek philosophical thought comes into being and departs from myth. Patočka remarks, "there is no amazement in myth; myth is not in wonder about anything, it knows everything beforehand. Just for philosophy it is symptomatic that it *is amazed*. It is not in amazement about particular real things but rather about this primeval reality. This clarity is clarity about the fact *that* things are there, that the manifest actualities are in the world before us" (*PE*, 59). In so far as the Greek heritage that makes up the idea of Europe is tied to the idea of the care of the soul, the concept of Europe is thus connected, even synonymous with, a concern with light, clarity, lucidity, limpidity. This concern with clarity translates into the practical demand of a life from which all obscurity is banned, a life of transparency, a life of truth.

At this point I would like to quote a lengthy passage from C.M. Bowra's *The Greek Experience*. While explaining the various reasons that have contributed to making Greece a unique civilization, particularly the fact that its people were ethnically mixed and that each of their city-states maintained distinct local traditions, Bowra also comes to speak about "the influence which the Greek scene had on the eye and the Greek mind."

After evoking the commanding beauty that forces itself slowly and unforgettably on the traveler who approaches Greece from the North or the West, he writes:

> What matters above all is the quality of the light. Not only in the cloudless days of summer but even in winter the light is unlike that of any other European country, brighter, cleaner, and stronger. It sharpens the edges of the mountains against the sky, as they rise from valleys or sea; it gives an ever-changing design to the folds and hollows as the shadows shift on or off them; it turns the sea to opal at dawn, to sapphire at midday, and in the succession to gold, silver, and lead before nightfall; it outlines the dark green of the olive-trees in contrast to the rusty or ochre soil; it starts innumerable variations of color and shape in unhewn rock and hewn stonework. The beauty of the Greek landscape depends primarily on the light, and this had a powerful influence on the Greek vision of the world. Just because by its very strength and sharpening the light forbids the shifting, melting, diaphanous effect which give so delicate a charm to the French or the Italian scene, it stimulates a vision which belongs to the sculptor more than the painter, which depends not so much on an intricate combination or contrast of colors passing into each other as on a clearness of outline and a sense of mass, of bodies emphatically placed in space, of strength and solidity behind natural curves and protuberances. Such a landscape and such a light impose their secret discipline on the eye, and make it see things in contour and relief rather than in mysterious perspective or in flat spatial relations. They explain why the Greeks produced great sculptors and architects, and why even in their painting the foundation of any design is the exact and confident line. Nor is it perhaps fanciful to think that the Greek light played a part in the formation of Greek thought. Just as the cloudy skies of northern Europe have nursed the huge, amorphous progeny of Norse mythology or German metaphysics, so the Greek light surely influenced the clear-cut conceptions of Greek philosophy. If the Greeks were the world's first true philosophers in that they formed a consistent and straightforward vocabulary for abstract ideas, it was largely because their minds, like their eyes, sought naturally what is lucid and well defined. Their senses were kept lively by the force of the light ... Just as Plato, in his search for transcendental principles behind the mass of phenomena tended to see them as individual objects and compared his central principle to the sun which illuminates all things in the visible world and reveals their shapes and colors, so no Greek philosophy is happy until it can pin down an idea with a limpid definition and make its outline firm and intelligible. That the Greeks were moved by some such consideration may be seen from their use of the words *eidos* and *idea* to mean "notion" or "idea." Originally they meant no more than "form."[11]

The passage quoted from Bowra clearly resonates with the tradition according to which the distinctive clarity of Greek light is the birthplace of Western philosophy. The topos of the light, and its relation to the peculiar civilization of ancient Greece, especially to Greek philosophy, pervades

Western philosophical reflection at least from the eighteenth century to the present. From the heliotropic pull of ancient Greece expressed in Hölderlin's "In lovely blueness . . . ," to Heidegger's evocation, in his address to the Academy of the Sciences and the Arts in Athens, of the "unique" and "strange" light of Hellas, the light of Greece is understood not only to enjoy a very special brightness but also is associated with the origin of a culture of clarity that itself has stood as a model for Europe.[12] Upon his return from his voyage to Greece, Heidegger comes back to the question of "the enigma of the much-mentioned light of Greece" of which he spoke in his address. He writes to Erhart Kästner: "This sea, these mountains, these islands, this sky—that here and only here *a-letheia* could open up, and that the gods could, or had to, settle in its sheltering light; that here Being as presencing occurred and founded human dwelling; this is today more amazing, and more unthinkable [*unausdenkbar*] to me than before."[13] I cannot take up the issue of philosophical geography itself, in which the features of the landscape are eloquently described in terms borrowed from the conceptual implements of the type of thinking that these geographical features are supposed to explain, and which is only further testimony to the primacy of the light of the philosophical over the geography that is believed to influence it. Rather, I present this passage to highlight the concern with clarity that characterizes the thought of Western philosophy—a concern central to the type of thought that from Hegel to Heidegger is consistently said to have *dawned* in Greece. It is a mode of thinking that relies on sight and on the discipline of the eye, that is to say, on a vision that submits itself to a disciplinary rigor equal in sharpness to that which presents itself within clear, distinct outlines in a light so strong as to prevent any blending of forms. This clarity and precision permeates as well conceptuality and rules for defining terms, not to mention Greek language, as Bowra asserts, whose "elaborate syntax is a testimony to [the Greeks'] desire to say things shortly and directly without circumlocution or ambiguity," but which the Greek thinkers, significantly enough, did not hesitate to bend and manipulate, in short, to de-idiomatize, whenever clarity was needed.[14] As we have seen, this clarity is not limited to the theoretical, but as our elaborations on Patočka have evidenced, it also bears on the practical and does so even in a privileged fashion. The Platonic notion of a tending, or care of the soul, which spells out a life project for which clarity is the determining law, serves Patočka to make the point against Husserl (although as the first chapters of *The Crisis* demonstrate, and even more so the "Vienna Lecture," he also acknowledges a practical dimension of the Greek heritage) that what constitutes the idea of Europe pertains to a life project that is not primarily theoretical.

According to the Husserl of *The Crisis* and the "Vienna Lecture," the absolute idea of Europe is the rational idea of a universal science and of a form of existence that takes its rule from pure reason. Certainly, clarity is intimately and essentially tied up with the idea of reason. Still, to conceive of the guiding idea of European thought, in terms of clarity rather than of reason, could have the strategic advantage of forestalling the dominant prejudice against "reason" as the common substrate of humanity and the instance of universal appeal. How can one object to the demand to be clear and lucid, except in the name of obscurantism? But by privileging clarity as the essential demand of Greek philosophy, Patočka seeks, in fact, to shift emphasis from the theoretical to the practical, a practical in which the *bios politicos* is no longer subservient to the *bios theoreticos*, as is the case with Greek thinkers, even including Aristotle. More precisely, to highlight clarity means to recognize a responsibility in terms of life that derives from the fact that the human is the sole addressee of appearing, the phenomenon, or manifestation. To tend to the soul is not done merely for the sake of clarity but for the sake of justice. This practical framing of clarity as the essential component of the idea of Europe by Patočka must remain present to us, as we now question whether the universal request for clarity is problematic, and whether the idea of Europe can be dispensed with inasmuch as it is the incarnation of such a request. As I suggested before, to name "reason" one of the few things that humanity, or rather the various humanities, share has lost some of its credibility. Light, and its demand for clarity and lucidity, seems to be more difficult to do away with, even though, after all, it is the same as reason. As Derrida noted in his response to Emmanuel Levinas, "it is difficult to maintain a philosophical discourse against light."[15]

It now needs to be pointed out that after having asserted the primacy of light and the aspiration toward clarity over its opposites as the defining character of philosophy, Patočka remarks: "Philosophy wants clarity, and as far as possible a radical one, yet radical clarity leads it to see *limits* of this clarity and that man lives in this equivocacy, in this peculiar polarity" (*PE*, 139). If light and clarity have limits, it is because light and clarity have the distinctive power to bring these limits to light. Within the light achieved by, or as, philosophy—that is, Greek thought—certain strictures of light come into visibility. As is well known, in his reflections on the Greek motif and founding conception of Europe, namely, the care of the soul,

Patočka not only finds fault with this conception's emphasis on the necessity to *know* the good (*agathon*) in order to act responsibly, but also with the Platonic demand for clarity, self-transparency, and accountability for one's words and deeds in the public space. This critique is exercised in the name of an essential Christianity that seeks to purge all traces of Platonism from the hitherto existing forms of Christianity in Christian Europe. According to this essential Christianity, it is not knowledge of the Good, but the *mysterium tremendum*, that is, the unseen gaze of an absolute selfless Goodness (i.e., God) who shakes the individual soul insofar as it is unable to ever adequately respond to such a gift, which opens up the demand for genuine responsibility. But rather than pursuing here Patočka's rebuttal of philosophy's demand for light in the perspective of a Christian conception of responsibility based on secrecy and a refusal to account in the open for one's words and deeds, I wish to pursue another facet of his attempt to establish the limits of light.[16] Indeed, a reference in *Plato and Europe* to Eugen Fink's *Metaphysik der Erziehung im Weltverständnis von Plato und Aristoteles* suggests that Patočka's recognition of the limits of clarity that become visible within light itself owes some debt to Fink's work. Patočka refers to Fink when he writes that Plato has been said to be "the philosopher of radical clarity, that in him all obscurity finally disappears and that important is the sun which shines its rays into ever greater and greater darkness. But darkness is there; the cave does not cease to exist" (*PE*, 139).

Before formulating the specific point Fink wishes to make in the abovementioned work, it is necessary to recall that Fink holds that with Plato, "an interpretation of the world that seeks to conceive of the universe in a fundamental manner from the mundane moment of the 'sky' becomes victorious for two millenary. 'Sky' signifies the gathered appearing of the many things into a space of light. Sky is the luminously opened 'open' of an all-encompassing clarity. Within it, the individual things show themselves. Within this clarity they have their appearance and outline, a character and a figure."[17] Taking its clues from the mundane phenomenon of light, and from the distinctions and articulations grounded in this phenomenon, the Platonic-Aristotelian interpretation of being dominated for many centuries the Western conception of being, and in the same breath, the field of philosophy. Fink writes: "Light makes appearing, shining possible. It brings clarity and brightness. It puts into relief, and brings out figures, sights, within the sharp edges of their characters. Light accentuates the limits of individual things, gives them independence and a fixed self-standing.

But light also illuminates the interconnections between things, and the field in which they exist together; it shows the interconnected foundation from which they emerge, the ground that they cover and cover over, but to which they nonetheless belong . . . Light 'sets apart' and gathers the sharply and clearly separated within its encompassing brightness" (*ME*, 316). This conception of light, which achieves world-historical ascendance with Plato and Aristotle, and on which, as Fink demonstrates, the Western model of education and the very notion of politics rest, is a conception intent on radically breaking with the tragic vision of the world. But as Fink argues, the victory of philosophical, or metaphysical, thought, as a thinking that proceeds from light and in the name of clarity, rests on a hypostatization of one singular mundane moment. All the conceptual tools that metaphysics uses to transcend the realm of phenomena are taken from this one mundane moment (*ME*, 306). From the outset, metaphysics is thus rooted in "a *one-sided* fundamental decision by which one moment of the world is rendered absolute, as it were" (*ME*, 33). As Fink remarks: "The *one* mundane moment of light, of reason, of individuation is the sole one that thinking takes into consideration" (*ME*, 303–304). By "overemphasizing and exaggerating the moment of light" (*ME*, 319), the Platonic vision of the world is thus "cosmically onesided" (*ME*, 303).

Having described the one-sidedness of light, Fink gestures suggestively toward the need "to put into question the central world model of 'lighting,' to search it for implications, to monitor it for hidden presuppositions, to recognize the interlockedness of the medium of light with other elementary media, and to contest onesided interpretations that have achieved for centuries undisputed domination" (*ME*, 320). But the persistent (yet by no means sole[18]) objection that Fink expands on in this critique of the metaphysics of light, of the world model of "lighting" by means of which nascent philosophy overcomes the tragic vision, is that it no longer seeks to think "the night from which we all originate and into which we all sink back—from which all things arise and in which they return again, this night of *Pan*, of the one indivisible foundation of being which undergirds all individuation, and sustains it" (*ME*, 304). Against the one-sidedness of the mundane moment of light, Fink recalls the tragic insight that "all rising into clarity comes from a figureless motherly night where all is one" (*ME*, 21). His critique of the model of intelligibility peculiar to Western metaphysics amounts to recalling the truth of the tragic world vision, the vision of an originary *polemos* of day and night, light and darkness.

Yet, is it sufficient, or rather, is it possible, to counter the metaphysics of light by speaking of light as a *moment*, and thus, accuse it of one-sidedness? Can the metaphysics of light be put into question in the name of another mundane moment, the night, especially, if the latter is conceived as the opposite of light? As Derrida has observed, "light has perhaps no opposite; if it does, it is certainly not night."[19] Indeed, if it is so difficult to mount a discourse against light, is it not because everything that could be objected, or opposed to it, becomes visible within, and is conceivable only from, the lighting? The limits of light can only come from light and become clear in light itself, or with respect to light, that is, still in light. But if this is true, light is not a moment against which other moments could be opposed. Rather, it is the medium in which opposites come to make their stand. Fink, at one point, comes close to recognizing this. In the context of a discussion of the parable of the sun in the sixth book of the *Politeia*, he remarks that light is the realm that is home both to the real things and their unreal reflective images and shadows—a realm that harbors, therefore, the very distinction between what is real and what is only a shadow, or a simulacrum. Fink writes:

> The realm of light is in itself already separated into the real and that which is of the order of the shadows. The correspondence at home in the realm of light between reality and the order of shadows becomes [for Plato in the context of the *Politeia*] the model that serves to characterize the relation of the illumined realm of the visible things to the dimension of the pure powers of being, the 'ideas,' and finally to that which is in an eminent way, the *agathon*. That is to say, this thought takes off from the phenomenon of shadowing and reflection present *in* light in order to explain the whole sphere of light with all the so-called 'real' things, including their shadows that are within it, as, on the whole, a shadow of a lesser being compared to a more authentic being. *The models and categories that serve to devalue the sphere of light are thus taken from this same sphere; it provides the conceptual means to ontologically condemn itself*, as it were. (*ME*, 36–37)

This passage on the Platonic problematic of the good *epekeina tes ousias* would, of course, require a lengthy commentary. I must content myself with pointing out that rather than radically putting light into question, the limits of light that become visible in the sphere of light lead us to the conception of a light of a higher order than mundane light. The devaluation of light that occurs in the parable, by way of a schema borrowed from the sphere of light itself, concerns only sensible light and takes place in view of the *agathon*, the source of all good, intelligible light. The thought of the epekeina tes ousias complicates the metaphysics of light for it gestures toward a kind of shining forth and an opening that is no longer of the order of light in either a literal or a metaphorical sense, a shining forth in which light and its others become meaningful to begin with. To quote Derrida again, the agathon is "the light of light beyond light."[20] Compared to the intelligible light, the sensible sun is only the shadow of the agathon. This devaluation—which is also a form of making intelligible since qua shadow, the sensible light, is given a determined meaning from, and in view, of the source of intelligibility—takes place by applying the intramundane distinction between light and shadow to the difference between the sensible and the intelligible. This is thus a distinction that becomes visible, and meaningful, only within the intelligible light. As a consequence, the shadow, and the whole illumined realm of the sensible world, cannot be turned against the realm of the light of intelligibility.

The possibility of invoking other moments as the very limits of light is one that thus originates only within mundane light. If this possibility depreciates the sphere of sensible light it is only to better highlight intelligible light. Therefore, by turning to other moments of light, moments that stand in a relation of opposition to it such as the shadow, or the night, Fink's attempt to unseat the "one-sidedness" of light, that is, of that on which Greek, and subsequently, European thought, set all its hopes for overcoming myth and the tragic vision, must necessarily fail. But as we have seen, Fink also conceives of the moment of the night that he opposes to that of light as the night of Pan, or the motherly night from which everything originates only to return to it again. The night is thus thought of here as the womb of light itself. Rather than setting limits to the one-sidedness of mundane light, the night of origination and subsequent destruction to which Fink resorts, is meant to counter the primacy of Plato's intelligible light. The pre-Socratic tragic worldview is thus thought to set boundaries to the domination that light has enjoyed since the inauguration of Greek philosophical thought. But, does not the very attempt to reinscribe light into the night draw on the intelligibility that only light can provide? Does not the thought that light returns into darkness as into its motherly womb continue to conceive of light as a moment, and hence, as *sensible* light? If this is the case, the Platonic light remains untouched. And the very meaningfulness of the limitation of light by the night of Pan remains dependent on light as the realm of intelligibility.

Yet, if light cannot be confronted with the night to limit its one-sidedness because nothing can be opposed to it, and in particular nothing that appears within its luminous opening, and if furthermore, its intelligibility cannot be challenged by recourse to the tragic vision, this does not mean that the indisputable superiority of light over darkness would not imply complication. But if it should prove possible and necessary to relate the principle at the core of Western thought, and the idea of Europe, to a certain darkness, in no way is this to be taken as a return to what Fink terms "tragic vision." Such a return is to be avoided at all cost. The fundamental decision by which philosophy and the principle of light come into being, a decision against tragic vision, cannot be overturned or rescinded, except at the price of the greatest violence. What can and must be demanded, however, is that the principle of light open itself up to a reflection on what Fink has called for, namely, the implications, hidden presuppositions, and the essential interlockedness of the medium of light with other elementary media. The task that must no longer be avoided consists in spelling out the unthematized structural implications that are inextricably linked up with the concept of light. To inquire into these structural implications of the principle of light is not to do away with it. It is to reconfigure it, or rather, to use a Derridian term, to reinscribe it.

The very possibility that the limits of sensible light come into sight in light itself, does not depreciate sensible light in favor of intelligible light. The possibility in question indicates that the shining forth of light and its subsequent limitation by shadows and darkness presupposes the opening of a more originary Open in which both illumination and darkening can occur. As Heidegger remarks, "light is capable of illuminating what is present only if what is present has already unfolded into an open and a free region in which it can spread out. This openness becomes illuminated by light, but it does in no way bring it about, or form it. For even darkness requires this openness without which we could not cross or traverse it."[21] With this, thinking faces a limit of light that cannot become visible in light itself, an irreducible limit to light, because it is one from which it shines forth. It is a limit to intelligibility as well since without this limit the process of making intelligible could not even begin. Taking up the question of the enigma of the much-mentioned Greek light, Heidegger writes that its mystery "rests in the unconcealedness, in the dis-closure that holds sway within it. This dis-closure belongs to concealedness, and conceals itself, but in such a manner that by way of this withdrawal it surrenders to things their stay [in the Open], a stay which comes into appearance from limitation."[22] There is thus a limit to light and to its intelligibility that is a limit in a double sense, for it enables and at the same time sets an end point to light. Any attempt to pursue the question raised by Patočka concerning the limits of clarity constitutive of philosophy and, by extension, of the idea of Europe needs to take as its starting point Heidegger's meditation on the constituting dependence of light on the unconcealing openness that withdraws again into concealedness. But to conceive of the limit of light in terms of the origin of light and its endpoint is to conceive of only one of many sides of such a limit. However, the meaning of "limit" as beginnings and endpoints does not provide just any limitation.

Whereas the phenomenological reflection on the idea of Europe has always sought to counter deep European crises, in which Europe appeared to sense its own ending, Granel, a thinker deeply indebted to phenomenology, declares such a reflection to be worn out, given that Europe has come to a final end with "the total extinction, at the horizon of our future, of the light in which the clarity of the Greek days still reverberated." Indeed, all of phenomenological discourse about Europe is intrinsically tied up with the conception of an end. If this is so, it is, first and foremost, because the idea of Europe is bound up with the idea of light, clarity, and lucidity. As the idea of light, Europe signifies the end of obscurity. It is therefore also necessarily haunted by the specter of an end of light. For this reason, it would seem that it is impossible to extricate all reflection about Europe from the concern with finality. In fact, to do so would mean to have given up all concern with light and clarity from the start. Yet if it is not possible to gesture toward ends when speaking about the idea of light, all ends are therefore not equal. They can, and do, represent diverse desires and stand for various agendas, among others, agendas that actively take an interest in extinguishing light. Faced with these desires and agendas, and having to acknowledge the ineradicable inscription of an orientation toward an end in the discourse about light and clarity, it needs to be emphasized that only the desire to end in clarity can decide on the ends, or limits, of light. After having recalled that it is in the name of an *Aufklärung* that Immanuel Kant undertakes to demystify an overlordly tone in philosophy, Derrida writes, in his "On a Newly Arisen Apocalyptic Tone in Philosophy":

> We cannot and we must not—this is a law and a destiny—forgo the *Aufklärung*, in other words, what imposes itself as the *enigmatic* desire for vigilance, for the lucid vigil, for elucidation, for critique and truth, but for a truth that at the same time keeps within itself some apocalyptic desire, this time as desire for clarity and revelation, in order to demystify or, if you prefer, deconstruct

apocalyptic discourse itself and with it everything that speculates on vision, the imminence of the end, theophany, parousia, the last judgment. Thus each time, we intractably ask ourselves where they want to come to, and to what ends, those who declare the end of this or that, of man or the subject, of consciousness, of history, of the West.[23]

To inquire into the limits of clarity, that is, to the idea bound up with the concept of Europe, cannot possibly mean to seek to bring clarity to an end in the sense of terminating the demand for transparency. Curtailing this demand would open the doors to the worst, to a violence so much greater than the violence that inevitably comes with the demand for transparency and the request to account for one's claims and deeds. If the limits of light are to be brought to light, it is in order to infinitely resist what in light itself may be accomplice to the worst. Indeed, blindness toward the limits of lucidity makes light side with the forces that seek its termination. The bounds of light are thus to be taken on in view of the never-ending task of securing, and of increasing, clarity. Indeed, if light has limits, light is not a given. It is not given once and for all. To inquire into the boundaries of light, where light comes to an end, is to seek out the limits from which it can shine forth, from which light thus becomes visible as an infinite task. To consider the end of light means, therefore, to seek out in light that which, precisely, incites us to work in light of light. By thinking the limits of light, thinking thus assumes the infinite responsibility of making light shine forth from those limits, be they the invisible limits due to the Open presupposed by light, or those that become only manifest in the illuminated realm of what is present.

Notes

1. Gérard Granel, preface to *La Crise des sciences européennes et la phénoménologie transcendentale*, by Edmund Husserl, trans. Gérard Granel (Paris: Gallimard, 1976), v–vii.

2. Gérard Granel, "L'Europe de Husserl," in *Écrits logiques et politiques* (Paris: Galilée, 1990), 55.

3. As is evident at least from the *Logical Investigations*, language for Husserl is essentially language in its logical use. In *What is Philosophy?*, for example, Heidegger's elaborations on Greek language show that it is not a language like others. It is nonidiomatic. Greek is a language that transcends its own idiomaticity. Indeed, have not many of the Greek words become philosophical concepts, and have they not remained so throughout the centuries? If deconstruction can be characterized as an attempt to both capitalize on the semantic and syntactical potential of singular idioms while writing at the same time against them, in its own complex way, it continues this concern with a language that would be universal.

4. Edmund Husserl, *The Crisis of European Sciences and Transcendental Phenomenology*, trans. D. Carr (Evanston, IL: Northwestern University Press, 1970), 14.

5. Husserl, *Crisis of European Sciences*, 280. See also 283–284.

6. Jean-Luc Nancy, "Euryopa: Le regard au loin," in *Contributions*, a prepublication (in French and German) of the proceedings of a conference at the University of Leipzig (May 11–14, 1994) on "La philosophie européenne de la culture et le projet 'Logos' de 1910," 7.

7. This malaise with philosophical thought brings to a conclusion the retreat of philosophy in the face of the natural sciences and of those human sciences that have acceded to a level of scientificity. Limiting itself to the secondary role of critically assessing the achievements of the sciences in the name of meaning, values, ethics, and so forth, philosophy has self-destructed. It has become a cultural commodity like any other. More fundamentally, philosophy itself has turned its constituting idea of universality into a norm, or value, where it has not simply relinquished it. However, as a norm, or value, universality invites disbelief, at least, a profound unease.

8. See chap. 2, "Alongside the Horizon," for a detailed discussion of the essay by Nancy, and chap. 8, "Feeling again for the Idea of Europe," for Derrida's *The Other Heading*.

9. Jan Patočka, *Plato and Europe*, trans. P. Lom (Stanford, CA: Stanford University Press, 2002), 15 (hereafter cited in text as *PE*).

10. To Heidegger, Patočka objects that "the problem of showing is deeper, more fundamental, more primary than the problem of being. Just because I can only get to the problem of being through the problem of showing" (*PE*, 177).

11. C. M. Bowra, *The Greek Experience* (New York: Praeger, 1969), 11–12.

12. Martin Heidegger, "Die Herkunft der Kunst und die Bestimmung des Denkens," in *Denkerfahrungen* (Frankfurt/Main: Klostermann, 1983), 138.

13. Heidegger, *Denkerfahrungen*, 148; Martin Heidegger and Erhart Kästner, *Briefwechsel 1953–1974*, ed. H. W. Petzet (Frankfurt: Insel Verlag, 1986), 51.

14. Bowra, *Greek Experience*, 14–16.

15. Jacques Derrida, *Writing and Difference*, trans. A. Bass (Chicago: Chicago University Press, 1978), 85.

16. A fuller, and considerably more refined discussion of Patočka's conception of Europe based on a rejection of Platonism, and in view of a fundamental Christianity, is found in Rodolphe Gasché, *Europe, or the Infinite Task. A Study of a Philosophical Concept* (Stanford, CA: University of Stanford Press, 2009).

17. Eugen Fink, *Metaphysik der Erziehung im Weltverständnis von Plato und Aristoteles* (Frankfurt/Main: Klostermann, 1970), 32 (hereafter cited in text as *ME*).

18. For further suggestions by Fink on how to put the metaphysics of light into question, see *ME*, 321.

19. Derrida, *Writing and Difference*, 92.

20. Derrida, *Writing and Difference*, 86.

21. Heidegger, *Denkerfahrungen*, 147.

22. Heidegger, *Denkerfahrungen*, 148.

23. Jacques Derrida, "On a Newly Arisen Apocalyptic Tone in Philosophy," in *Raising the Tone of Philosophy: Late Essays by Immanuel Kant, Transformative Critique by Jacques Derrida*, ed. P. Fenves (Baltimore: Johns Hopkins University Press, 1993), 148–149.

4

THE FORM OF THE CONCEPT

THE ESSAYS COLLECTED IN HANS-GEORG GADAMER'S *DAS ERBE Europas*, which were by and large written for specific occasions, pose the question of the significance and task of Europe in a changed world, in a world in which Europe sees itself reduced—politically and in many other aspects—to a very modest player in the shaping of the world. In posing this question, Gadamer is mindful of the fact that there are now several centers of world-shaping, and that the inhabited world—the *oikumene*—rather than separate from the rest of the world, that is, the world of barbarians, now extends to the whole planet. He wants to redefine Europe's role and task given the reality of diversity and globalization.[1] For Gadamer, the answer to the question of what Europe could mean in these circumstances is first and foremost predicated on "Europe's spiritual unity [which is] a reality [*Wirklichkeit*], as well as a task, which has its deepest foundation [or reason] in the consciousness of the manifold of this, our Europe."[2] In other words, it is in light of the spiritual (rather than political) unity that Europe has achieved in spite of (or rather, because of) its own intrinsic diversity that we must rethink its role and task in a global and diversified world.

To ask this question about Europe is also to ask what philosophy has to offer at a moment in history when the world is in crisis, and Europe is irremediably involved in this crisis of global dimensions. First, it will be necessary to achieve some clarity about the nature of philosophy and about why philosophy—"in our sense," as Gadamer writes—is intrinsically connected to European civilization (*EE*, 13). After all, we sometimes use the Greek word *philosophy* to refer to the great answers to the questions of humanity that the high civilizations of East Asia and India have provided because these are the questions "that in Europe have been repeatedly asked by philosophy." But the concept of philosophy cannot, in good faith, be applied to them.³ To do so would be to force a Western concept onto the achievements of others. Now, as Gadamer writes, "In our Western civilization, philosophy is from the outset connected with the emergence of science. This is the novel thing which has created the unity of Europe" (*EE*, 13). For not only does science come into being at the same time as philosophy, science endows philosophy with the power of unifying Europe. We should not lose sight of the fact that Gadamer refers to "science" in the singular. He thus unmistakably refers to philosophy as *episteme*, as the one unifying science, rather than to the manifold sciences, which, as empirical sciences (*Erfahrungswissenschaften*), originated in the seventeenth century and brought philosophical *Gesamtwissen* to a close. In the same way as philosophy "in our sense" is "science as it has been developed in Greece which makes up the distinctive character of the world-civilization that originated in Europe" (*EE*, 103). Although, as Gadamer admits, the advanced civilizations of antiquity had stimulated and enriched Greek thought, "the figure of science [*Gestalt der Wissenschaft*] . . . received its proper formation [solely] in Greece" (*EE*, 103). In Europe alone did the figure of science "develop into an autonomous and dominant cultural formation." In fact, and, according to Gadamer, it is an axiom (*Grundsatz*) that "the figure itself of science literally defines Europe. Science has given form [or figure, Gestalt] to Europe, to its historical essence and becoming, yes, literally to the limits within which something can be called European" (*EE*, 37).

Undoubtedly, there has never been a civilization that has not known something like "sciences" developed from experience and taught intergenerationally. But "there has also never been a civilization which with all its multitudinous cultural creations that has been dominated by science to such an extent as Europe" (*EE*, 38). Indeed, "culture does not necessarily have to take its lead from science and its potential—and did so nowhere else [aside from Europe]. It is the specificity of Europe to have gone down this road" (*EE*, 14). But, as Gadamer forcefully argues in *Das Erbe Europas*, such a predominance of science in the formation and unification of Europe is also concurrent with an unheard of differentiation between, and within, the various cultural creations. It is differentiation that calls for science, but it is the unifying power of science that allows differentiation to take place from within. Whereas in other high civilizations it is almost impossible to decide whether a cultural creation belongs to philosophy, poetry, science, or religion, "one of the fundamental distinguishing traits of Europe is the distinction between philosophy, religion, art, and science. This distinction originated in Greek culture and has formed the Greek-Christian cultural unity of the Western world" (*EE*, 39).[4] So, whereas the figure of science gives form to Europe, the unity of this form implies internal differentiation, and this differentiation is as specific to Europe as the predominance of science. Gadamer writes that "it is highly significant that it is in Europe alone that such a deep differentiation and articulation of human knowledge and of the will to knowledge as it is represented by the concepts of religion, philosophy, art and science took place. Nothing corresponds genuinely to this in other civilizations, not even in other high civilizations" (*EE*, 38). The conceptual differentiation in question represents a thoroughly European way of thinking. As a consequence, when we use these terms to refer to cultural creations by other civilizations we make a preliminary decision (*Vorentscheidung*) by means of which we miss these civilizations' self-understanding (*EE*, 38). This differentiation of the spiritual activities characteristic of Europe is the condition for philosophy's demarcation of itself from art and religion, the condition for it to achieve in the figure of science a unifying hegemony in, or as, Europe. Gadamer sums this up as follows: "Thanks to the scientific step taken by the spiritual becoming of Europe, a differentiation of forms of predication and forms of thought developed as it never existed before in the cultural life of humanity. I am referring to the fact that here science and philosophy make up an autonomous figure of the spirit which is distinct from religion and poetry. Yes, it has even lead to the demarcation of religion from poetry, and has assigned to art a specific though precarious function in the formation of truth" (*EE*, 106–107).

The specificity of Europe derives from its differentiating between the various forms of creative force, and Europe's Gestalt is also owed to the "powerful tensions" (*EE*, 14) that erupted between these forms during its history. We should think of the clash between philosophy and science, in particular. But these powerful tensions are not limited to the differences between philosophy, religion, art, and science.[5] Gadamer avers: "There are other distinctions that contribute to a further differentiation of European civilization" (*EE*, 39). First and foremost, there is the distinction between East and West—that is, between the two separate Christian churches (the Greek Orthodox and the Roman Catholic Churches).This differentiation within Europe into a Western and an Eastern part has created a lack of equilibrium within Europe. The reason for this disequilibrium lies primarily with the cultural world of Western Europe. Certainly, this disequilibrium finds its explanation in "the increasing importance of overseas world trade, which, glancing at the globe, makes Western Europe look like one gigantic landscape of ports, compared to the enormous landmass of Eastern Europe, and it looks virtually open for exploration journeys to other worlds" (*EE*, 40). However, the more fundamental reason for this disequilibrium resides in the deepening of the Western European process of differentiation. Gadamer refers, in particular, to the considerably higher differentiation and separation (*Auseinanderdifferenzierung*) of languages in the West compared to what allegedly is the case with Slavic languages. There are many other examples of this extended differentiation: the antagonism between church and empire in the West, the schism in Western Christianity, the development of a multitude of art styles, and so forth. Now, let me point out that the greater differentiation of languages that occurred in Western Europe, and which is a major reason for the lack of balance within Europe itself, also harbors the possibility of overcoming the disequilibrium in question. This is an overcoming that Gadamer characterizes as one of the tasks that lie with Europe.

The disequilibrium between Eastern and Western Europe itself is a task that Europe will most certainly have to address in the future, but the question of the significance and of the future task of Europe arose primarily with the awareness of the loss of Europe's hegemony in a changed world. In the wake of colonialism and the emancipation of the members of the British Empire, the most pressing type of disequilibrium on a global scale that Gadamer evokes is the imbalance within the newly emerging independent national states between two tendencies. On the one hand, they have a tendency, inherited from the West, toward uniformity of their world-picture and a relation to the world that corresponds to the increasing mobility of today's human society. On the other hand, they have a tendency toward recovering and deepening their innermost identity. Furthermore, there is the additional problem that arises from the multiplication of sovereign national states—namely, the problem of how to relate to one another without surrendering the identity that one has finally achieved. These problems, along with the forms of disequilibrium in a world that Europe no longer dominates, make Europe decisive again. Gadamer avers that, faced with a global situation in which "so many old countries begin to take new routes, and in which new countries search for the old ways, Europe seems to acquire a new relevance [*Aktualität*], since it has the richest historical experience. Indeed, in a highly constricted space, Europe enjoys the greatest diversity and a pluralism of linguistic, political, religious, ethnic traditions with which it had to cope for many centuries" (*EE*, 58). According to Gadamer, "Europe's linguistic plurality, this neighborliness of the other and the equality of the other in a constricted space," is a "true school" of life, not only for the unity of Europe as a political entity but, in particular, for "learning together what we calculate our European task to be in view of the future of mankind as a whole" (*EE*, 31). Indeed, thanks to its linguistic plurality, what Europe has to offer, in light of the current problems faced by mankind as whole, is a way of finding common ground, points in common, or commonalities (*Gemeinsamkeiten*). This ability of finding "true commonalities" (*EE*, 32) in the face of diversity and plurality—a task (and accomplishment) for which Gadamer credits Europe—constitutes its current relevance for the world as a whole. Let us point out right away that the task of finding true commonalities is not to be understood as the production of consensual temporal agreements around common interests. This does not mean, however, that the true commonality to be discovered would be of the order of an eternal and immutable substrate, or a truth beyond the realities of the practical world of humans. In order to grasp the precise sense of what one has in common and of the modalities of finding it, we will need to briefly broach Gadamer's elaborations on the notion of the *other*, thus also his ideas of hermeneutic experience, which are inextricably linked to the question of the other. As a practical experience, however, hermeneutic experience only yields probable truths, no certainties.

Let us begin with some of Gadamer's general remarks about the other. The core of the experience of the other is that "the other is encountered, first of all, as other. The other is not my dominion, nor my territory" (*EE*, 28–29). To encounter the other as other—that is, as not under my rule—implies that I do not dominate him, have no power over him, and that he does not belong to what I own, to the household within which I am dominus, master, father, and sovereign. At the same time, the other is inseparable from me. To speak of the other as other is to acknowledge an irreducible relation to the other. As other, the other is set off against myself; he is experienced and conceptualized by me in relation to myself while, at the same time, I see him as determining me as an identity distinct from his own. Speaking, at one point, of nature as the other, Gadamer asks, "is she not inseparable from us, the other of ourselves, in the way the old languages tell us when rather than saying the one and the other, they say, the other and the other?[6] Is not even the absolutely other—the famous definition that Rudolf Otto proposed of the divine—in spite of all the emphasis on absolute otherness, the other of ourselves, and does this not extend to the neighborly other, to you and to everything that is yours? Is there even anything other, that is not the other of ourselves? At least not anyone who is an other—that is, who is also a human being" (*EE*, 29). It is more than doubtful that by conceiving of the other as being there in mere relationality to myself, Gadamer can avoid what Max Scheler has qualified as "the naive illusion," namely, the illusion that the self is an absolute reality and that the other, who is experienced in such ontic and egocentric relationality, is the "ultimate and absolute reality" of the other.[7] In any case, if the other, according to Gadamer, is essentially the other of ourselves, it follows that at any moment every human being is confronted with a "truly gigantic task," the task of making sure "that the other does not become invisible or remain invisible" (*EE*, 29). For if the other is the other of ourselves—hence, inseparable from us—then "the fundamental human task" consists "in living, as the other of the other, with the other" (*EE*, 30). This requires "learning to come to a stop [*haltmachen*] before the other," and to show respect for him (*EE*, 34, 30). Such respect is owed to any other if the other is the other of ourselves (as a kind of respect that I owe myself). For Gadamer, the other is not simply—perhaps, not even primarily—the human other. As will become clear later on, the other is first of all the other language. What is other is also nature, which, as Gadamer remarks, should no longer be considered as merely an object of exploitation. "In all her forms of appearing, she must be experienced as a partner, and that means she must be understood as the other together with whom we live" (*EE*, 28). Hence, whether the other is nature, another language, a different civilization, or simply the human other, we have to experience the other and the others as the others of ourselves—that is, as intimately linked to ourselves—and, ultimately, "in order to participate in one another [*um aneinander teilzugewinnen*]" (*EE*, 34).

But if the other is essentially the other of ourselves, the further consequence is that the other can also make something about ourselves known to us. The encounter with the other as other represents an opportunity for an encounter with oneself. Gadamer writes: "The otherness of the neighbor is not only an otherness that is to be shied away from or to be avoided. It is also an inviting otherness, one that contributes to one's own self-encounter" (*EE*, 30–31). If the other extends an invitation, it is an invitation not only to encounter the other in his otherness but also to encounter oneself in, or through, the other. In addition to letting the other be the other, the encounter with the other, who is by definition the other of ourselves, can become a self-encounter if "we learn to recognize in otherness what we have in common [*in der Andersheit das Gemeinsame erkennen zu lernen*]" (*EE*, 125). Obviously, it requires a self and an other to find something in common. But Gadamer's point is perhaps a bit more complex. Indeed, in the self-encounter made possible by an encounter with the other, I must recognize a "mineness" that I have in common with others, something of mine of which I was not aware before the encounter, a mineness in advance of what I thought to be mine, which I share with the other. That commonality, which is recognized through the encounter with an other as an other of myself, is not something new that is produced in the encounter; rather, it is something that is recognized, refound, and rediscovered. Unlike agreements through consensus, "true commonalities [*wahre Gemeinsamkeiten*] proceed essentially from a "re-cognition [*Wiedererkennung*] of oneself, a re-encountering [*Wiederbegegnung*] of the other" (*EE*, 32), hence from a re-membrance, or recollection, of what the self and the other always already had in common. Not a (Hegelian) recognition (*Anerkennung*) of the other, but his recognition (*Wiedererkennung*) is the ground from which true commonality emerges. Defined as the other of ourselves, otherness—whether it is that of nature, or other languages, civilizations, or human beings—is the occasion of an anamnestic discovering of a part of myself that I have in common with others, a part that is more fundamentally my own than any identity based on prepossession. Hermeneutic experience, according to Gadamer, is an experience based on the encounter of the other both as other and as other to myself; it is, in essence, the experience of remembering a commonality with the other that is the substrate of my individuality as a self. It is Gadamer's contention that at this juncture of history, where the problem of the relation of the self and the other poses itself on a global scale, Europe—because of its history of differentiation and, in particular, its multilinguism—is in a privileged situation to remind not only the European but also "those who think and choose differently [*den anders Denkenden und anders Wählenden*]" of the task of achieving "participation in what we have in common, a participation which is our human destiny" (*EE*, 135). For, indeed, "Europe's special privilege . . . is that it, more than other countries, has been able, and has had, to learn to live with others even though the others are other" (*EE*, 30).

But before further elucidating Gadamer's conception of the new relevance of Europe, let me first return to the founding differentiation that sets Europe apart from the rest of the world: the sharp differentiation between art, religion, science, and philosophy that has made it possible for philosophy and science to gain a cultural momentum that exists nowhere else in the world. Gadamer writes: "The form of science and the form of the concept, on which the philosophical penetration of the cognition of the world rests, these are obviously particularities, advantages, but also tasks, which have given European civilization alone its special character, as well as to the world once Christianity absorbed and assimilated them" (*EE*, 14). What characterizes Europe are not only the clear-cut differentiations and tensions within European civilization, as well as the predominance of at least some of the differences that are produced by these tensions (philosophy and science), but also what Gadamer refers to as "the form of science" and "the form of the concept," both of which originated in Greece. How is one to understand these terms? Gadamer evokes the development—made possible thanks to the specific structure of the Indo-Germanic languages—of a concept of *substance* in Greek thought, which is distinct from what belongs to it (its accidental, nonessential qualities). This is a distinction that severs the natural unity of word and thing (*Sache*), and which is characteristic of natural linguistic self-understanding. Given this specificity of Indo-Germanic languages, Gadamer concludes in *Das Erbe Europas*: "A linguistic family like ours, which, because of the grammar that is specifically its own, is based to such an extent on the relation of the verb to the substantive, and of the predicate to the subject, was literally predisposed to dissolving the unity of word and thing— and thus to 'science'" (*EE*, 110).[8] We can see that, linking in this manner the possibility of the formation of science to the grammatical possibilities of Indo-Germanic languages, Gadamer understands "form," first and foremost, as grammatical form. It is grammatical form that enables the "comprehending articulation of reality" by the concept—that is, the subsumption of, or application of, a concept to a given thing. Given this structure it is safe to assume that Gadamer borrowed the notions of "the form of the concept" and "the form of science" from Johannes Lohmann, who, in his 1965 work titled *Philosophie und Sprachwissenschaft* and in a review article of Gadamer's *Truth and Method*, which appeared that same year in *Gnomon*, places the origin of the grammatical form of the concept in the linguistic form, which is specific to the Indo-Germanic languages. As Lohmann puts it in his review article, the concept that emerges in Greece as an explicit form (together with the form of the thinking subject) engages "the task of rendering conscious the [unconscious] 'understanding of world' as 'effective history' which has taken place in natural language since it came into being—that is, of rendering it conscious by way of a reflection on the 'metalinguistic' function of world-interpretation which in every natural language unconsciously accompanies language's object related function of reproducing the world." The form of the concept, which originates in the old Indo-Germanic grammatical form of the inflexion of the radical (*Stamm-Flexion*), and which finds its clearest expression in the copula, made it possible for the Greeks "to subsume the world as 'theory' under the concept," in other words, to develop "the form of 'science' in the European sense."[9] From this form of the concept in the shape of the copula "derives the possibility of theory as the Western World's ownmost creation," Gadamer remarks approvingly.[10] Distinct from the image, and thinking in images, which is always concrete rather than discursive, the form of the concept allows for the intuition of the general and universal, and, as Hannah Arendt remarks, such thinking in words or concepts "traveling through an ordered train of thought" makes it possible to "give account of itself [*logon didonai*]."[11] In sum, the discovery of the form of the concept is Europe's most distinguishing trait. It is that which makes up Europe's Gestalt, what gives it a Gestalt in the first place, and hence, if one radically extends Gadamer's and Lohmann's thought, something that perhaps no other civilization can claim.

If the form of the concept enabled the creation of theory and science in the Greek sense, this is because this form, which rests on the discovery of the h‌ypokeimenon, or *subjectum* as the lasting foundation for varying predications and contents of judgments, makes it possible to combine differentiation and unification and mediate between the two. Two major ways in which Europe in the form of the concept has found expression are philosophy in the shape of metaphysics, and, in the wake of the development of the modern sciences in the seventeenth century, philosophical system-building as an attempt to bring together in harmony what falls apart (*Zusammenbringen von Auseinanderfallendem*) (*EE*, 19). After the positivism of the nineteenth century, after the prevalence of epistemology in philosophy, and after various efforts by "outsiders" (a reference to Schopenhauer, Marx, and Nietzsche—the creators of the so-called worldviews) to address the metaphysical desire for an answer to the question of the meaning of the whole that positivism had left unanswered (*EE*, 20), the human sciences, Gadamer argues, have taken up, more or less consciously, the great inheritance of metaphysics as first science (*EE*, 45).

Animated by the spirit of Romanticism, the human sciences emerged in Germany, where they found their unique epiphany in the school of the historical sciences. Protestantism with its traditional emphasis on the freedom of Christian man further contributed to the triumphant progress of the human sciences in Germany throughout the nineteenth century (*EE*, 45). This new scientific cast of mind that originated in Germany—"the land of Romanticism's origin"—spread through the entire European cultural world (including Russia), but "in a spectacle of its own kind," the "particular foundations of the traditions of the European peoples" gave rise to a diversification of this scientific cast of mind in the different countries of Europe (*EE*, 45). Indeed, as Gadamer underscores, the human sciences are characterized by an indelible relation to tradition and to historical being (*gewordenes Sein*) (*EE*, 49). This differentiation of the human sciences manifests itself, according to Gadamer, not only in the plurality of the names that these sciences received, such as moral sciences, humanities, letters, and so forth (*EE*, 46), but also, and more profoundly, in their historical variations, which are closely connected to the individual traditions of each country, and involved in "the historical and social formation of the modern territorial and national states" (*EE*, 46). In each case, they contribute to the foundation of the inmost identity of each particular political entity on the basis of its unique historical past. Yet the role of the human sciences has not simply been limited to bringing the particular traditions to bear on national and cultural identity formation, and thus to foster diversity. Within the multifaceted landscape of Europe, they also have a unifying function. In the essay "Die Zukunft der Europäischen Geisteswissenschaften," from *Das Erbe Europas*, Gadamer claims that the special role that the human sciences play in Europe as a whole "is one that forms a common ground of the highest degree. Not least, this common ground consists in the fact that Europe is a multilinguistic whole, one that is made up of manifold national linguistic cultures" (*EE*, 35). The common ground that these human sciences represent is necessarily tied to linguistic diversity in Europe, to its natural languages, which, apart from being the inevitable source of prejudices, are also "an offer [*Angebot*, invitation] to recognize oneself [*sich wiederzuerkennen*], and to make all the knowledge that has been deposited in language—that is, in poetry, philosophy, historical narrative, religion, law and custom, in everything thus that constitutes a culture—recognizable [*wiedererkennbar*] for us" (*EE*, 33). Gadamer adds that "the plurality of Europe's national languages is most intimately at one with the fact of [the existence of] the human sciences and with its function in the cultural life of humanity" (*EE*, 36) because the human sciences are closely related to "the otherness that demands recognition," which manifests itself first and foremost in the natural languages (*EE*, 32). Apart from their role in fostering national self-identity, the human sciences shared by the manifold European cultures also render conscious the different and other ways of understanding the world that occurs in other languages, against the backdrop of other traditions, by giving it the form of the concept. Incarnating the spirit of Europe—that which gives the continent its current spiritual Gestalt—the human sciences are the media in which the other is experienced as the other of ourselves, and in which we recognize a mineness that we share with the other. In sum, the human sciences that are common to Europe unify the disparate national cultures of Europe by manifesting themselves precisely in the diverse forms that they take within the different linguistic idioms. The human sciences are the common ground of Europe, a ground that manifests itself exclusively in diversity.

The relevance and task of Europe in a planetary world, in which it no longer enjoys its former hegemony, is, therefore, closely tied to the European human sciences. Indeed, as Gadamer argues, the "thoughtful experiments [*Denkerfahrungen*] which modern Europe has performed, have become interesting on a planetary scale" (*EE*, 47). Here we should remember the disequilibrium within Europe itself, between East and West, which, according to Gadamer, explains why, "in distinction to the manifold Western cultures of Europe, Eastern Europe has not gained the same scientific presence in our human sciences." One can assume, Gadamer continues, that "in the future Europe will work at this disequilibrium and that it is in particular the human sciences, which will contribute to diminishing it" (*EE*, 40). *Das Erbe Europas* does not go so far as to state that the new relevance and the tasks of Europe's human sciences are a function of the truly global field of tasks for human coexistence on the planet, but only that the pluralistic interconnection of mankind poses ever new tasks on the human sciences themselves. However, this collection of essays makes clear that the human sciences offer a model for meeting these new global tasks because they consolidate experience and knowledge in a certain way. But let us first try to understand what the new relevance of the human sciences may be for a Europe that confronts a changed world. As we have seen, the human sciences are tied to particular traditions and histories. In the face of the worldwide danger of an expansion of a uniform world-civilization that levels all differences (a civilization that has its roots in Europe), the human sciences (which equally well originated in Europe) acquire a new relevance. This is because of their sharp eye for "the forces of inertia [*Beharrungskräfte*] in the cultural life of human beings," that is, for what persists and continues in lived life and which signals the inner limit of such expansion (*EE*, 61). By bringing the elements of tradition and of historical being into relief, the human sciences have, therefore, been from the start a counterforce to the disequilibrium produced by the ascendency of the natural sciences in Europe. As Gadamer remarks, "in the competition and exchange of various cultures, the fact that Europe keeps the essential specificity of its lived traditions consciously alive is the most obvious sign of life and of a profound spiritual breath by which Europe becomes aware of itself. Furthering this process, this seems to me to be the lasting contribution which the human sciences have to accomplish, not only for the future of Europe but also for the future of mankind itself" (*EE*, 62). When compared to the "dreamlike changeableness of technological progress," history is, as Gadamer puts it, "the granite stone of our being" (*EE*, 105). Then "to defend the whole of our cultural riches, and, perhaps, to protect them from threats" is not only to work for the benefit of Europe but also to prepare oneself for the task that awaits humanity (*EE*, 21). Indeed, the role of the human sciences in today's world is also to provide a model for resolving problems worldwide. Let us remind ourselves again of the economic, human, and social, planetary disequilibrium between highly developed and undeveloped countries that Gadamer evokes. With the end of colonialism and the emancipation of the former British colonies, "many countries in the world are in search of a form of civilization, which would succeed in accomplishing the feat of combining their own tradition and the deeply rooted values of their forms of life with an economic progress regulated in European fashion" (*EE*, 48).Confronted with these problems, "the human sciences that have been developed in Europe cannot shirk a task, which, because of their very existence, they have already taken upon themselves" (*EE*, 47).

However, by construing Europe and its human sciences as a model for solving problems, such as the conflicts between past and future, tradition and the demands of economic and political progress in other parts of the world, Gadamer does not acknowledge that these problems are above all problems that Europe has created by Europeanizing the world.

Although "Europeanization" is, as Joachim Ritter put it in a 1956 essay devoted to contemporary developments in Turkey, an "ugly word" since, from the perspective of the people who have undergone it, Europeanization amounts to an assertion of the universal in everything particular and implies no continuity whatsoever with respect to the historically grown, it remains the case that Europeanization has also provided these people with the resources necessary to prepare for the future.[12] This is, however, a future that to a large extent has been of the making of Europe. If Europe faces tasks with respect to the rest of the world, is it not therefore because "by having Europeanized the world, Europe has stepped outside the boundaries of its history"? Undoubtedly, since Europe itself is responsible for the emerging world-civilization, it cannot "close itself off from itself and the role assigned to in relation to the people that have entered the process of Europeanization." But as Ritter also points out, "the history of Europeanization which points toward the future is in fact the continuation of Europe's history itself. As far as its very history is concerned, Europe relates to this history of Europeanization as to its own future history."[13] Does it not follow from this that the model that the human sciences offers for confronting burning issues in the non-European world, is a model that construes the world of the other in the perspective of, and in continuity with, Europe's own past and future, and that the solutions Europe offers to the other are primarily attempts to come to grips with itself, and what, by Europeanizing the world, it has accomplished for better or for worse?

In any event, according to Gadamer, the human sciences permit Europe to play a privileged role in a decentered world as a model for discovering true commonalities between self and other, a model that applies equally well to Europe's relation to itself, Europe's relations with the rest of the world, as well as its relations with each one of the newly emerging nation-states. At this point, however, we might allow ourselves another critical remark. As Jürgen Habermas has pointed out, the human sciences initially arose in a reaction to the natural sciences' explicatory subsumption of phenomena under universal laws. They meant to highlight the fact that, unlike the exact sciences that explicate (*erklären*) phenomena, the human sciences, whose focus is on the cultural specificity and the individuality of their objects, attempt to understand (*verstehen*) these objects. They also tried to emphasize understanding's proclivity (if not prejudice) for what is one's own, as opposed to what is foreign, or alien. In reference to Jacob Grimm's speech at the meeting of the Germanists in Frankfort in 1846, Habermas writes that the

> hermeneutical insight into the prejudicial structure of understanding is to express pointedly that we understand what is closest to us better than what is foreign. Like must be recognized by like ... This is evident as well in the case of "German antiquities." Understanding such historical documents of "the spirit of a people," which are removed from the present, is no neutral scientific operation; it is deeply rooted in the mind [*Gefühl*]. To understand truly is to bring the whole of one's subjectivity into play, a process of recognition whose ultimate goal is the enthusiastic self-re-cognition in the other.[14]

This emphasis on the same and one's self-recognition in the other provokes an important question about the nature and the status of what Gadamer calls the other, which, or who, is the other of oneself. In *Das Erbe Europas*, the historical sciences, which are, for Gadamer, the sciences that are most representative of this new scientific cast of mind, are said to arise from the Romantic critique of the Enlightenment, which took its impetus from a consciousness of "the otherness of everything past [*Andersartigkeit aller Vergangenheiten*]" (*EE*, 67). The historical sciences have made us sensitive to "the other of the past" (*EE*, 25), with the result that since then philosophy has adopted "a historical orientation" (*EE*, 45). However, this otherness of the past is primarily one's own past—more precisely, it is the past of Europe. Gadamer's emphasis on the classical past and the humanist past—particularly in *Truth and Method*—is a further indication that the past means, first and foremost, one's own past from which one has become alienated, and which has to be re-encountered in an encounter that, consequently, is a self-encounter. Undoubtedly, this model of coming to grips with the otherness that is part of one's own inheritance and tradition can become relevant to the solving of identity problems and the overcoming of imbalances in other parts of the world. However, since it is predicated on the relation to one's own past as other, it is difficult to see how this model could aid in relation to the past of the other—hence, to the past of the non-European. It is not clear either how this model could benefit the newly sovereign states that arose with the end of the British Empire—that is, it may be inapplicable to the relation of the non-European others among themselves. We must ask ourselves, first, whether Gadamer's concept of the other is an adequate concept of otherness to begin with, and second, whether a notion of otherness that is the otherness of ourselves is at all capable of diagnosing the current problems of Europe and the world, and last but not least, whether such a conception of the other does not think too little of what "the form of the concept" is, in fact, capable of comprehending.

Assessing the current state of the sciences, Gadamer asks whether "we cannot learn something from the Greek inheritance of our thinking, which, undoubtedly, bequeathed 'science' to us—not just any kind of science, but a science that remains incorporated into the human life-world, and subservient to the guiding concept of its thought, namely physis." What this inheritance—and, according to Gadamer, in particular, Plato's dialectic—can teach us is that "the task of philosophy is to awaken in our thinking that which in truth already lies in our experience in the life-world and in its linguistic storage, with the result that, as Plato put it, all cognition is a recognition" (EE, 119–120).[15] But Gadamer also acknowledges that "it would be a misunderstanding to believe that, in a changed world, a past way of thinking can be renewed as such. Rather, what is in question is using it as a corrective" in the understanding of the present situation and for the task of accomplishing "the primal belonging-together of all who live together" (EE, 124, 121). Yet, would such a task not have to consist in thinking's receptiveness to that which is not yet present and stored up in the life-world and in language, something that, nonetheless, binds those who live together, and yet is not recognizable? If Europe is, in essence, the form of the concept, and if, as such, this form is what gives it its relevance in today's world, is it not precisely because this Greek inheritance enables thinking to do what it has not done so far within the Western tradition, namely, to open itself to what is not recognizable, to what is still to come, and to an otherness that is not the otherness of ourselves? Finally, is Europe, as the form of the concept, not also the promise of another form of togetherness—a togetherness no longer rooted in a true commonality—but a togetherness in which diversity is no longer simply diversity within the One?

Notes

1. Hans-Georg Gadamer, "Europa und die Oikumene," *Europa und die Philosophie*, ed. H. H. Gander (Frankfurt/Main: Klostermann, 1993), 67. If the notion of *oikumene* originally referred to the Greek world as the only inhabited region distinct from the barbarian lands, can one simply assume that the reference to the non-Greeks and the barbarians has been eliminated from it once this notion begins, as in Aristotle, to include some non-Greek lands or when the oikumene is extended to the whole world?

2. Hans-Georg Gadamer, *Das Erbe Europas: Beiträge* (Frankfurt/Main: Suhrkamp, 1989), 62 (hereafter abbreviated in text as *EE*).

3. Gadamer, "Europa und die Oikumene," 68. See also Hans-Georg Gadamer, *Vernunft im Zeitalter der Wissenschaft* (Frankfurt/Main: Suhrkamp, 1976), 8.

4. Gadamer adds: "Who could dare say that Chuang Tse or any other of the Chinese sages was more of a religious, or more of a knowing figure, more a thinker, or more a poet?" (*EE*, 14).

5. As Dan Diner has recently pointed out, the separation of spheres and the fundamental institutional tensions that characterize the culture of the Occident—such as the separations between state and society, politics and economy, public and private—is the origin of the birth of freedom in Christian Europe. In distinction from Islam where "everything is subsumed into One—into God and His Law," and time is impregnated with the sacred to such a degree as to render anathema all historical conception of time, the perpetual conflict and discord that European man faces since the two authorities of the *imperium* and the *sacerdotium* competed in the heart of an uncertain and doubting human being in the Middle Ages—a conflict in which the individual is thoroughly left to himself, and by extension, exposed to the possibility of erring—is the very condition of possibility for cultural development in the Western world. Dan Diner, *Lost in the Sacred: Why the Muslim World Stood Still*, trans. S. Rendall (Princeton: Princeton University Press, 2009), 63–64. For the fertility of a life in contradictory polarities in Europe, see also Karl Jaspers, "Vom Europäischen Geist," in *Rechenschaft und Ausblick. Reden und Aufsätze* (Munich: Piper, 1951), 240.

6. Gadamer is thinking here of the Latin expression "*alius atque alius*," one and another; now this, now that.

7. Max Scheler, *The Nature of Sympathy*, trans. P. Heath (London: Routledge & Keegan Paul, 1954), 59.

8. Ultimately, the unity of Europe and its intense internal differentiation thus finds its schema in the structure of Indo-Germanic language.

9. Johannes Lohmann, "*Hans-Georg Gadamer: Wahrheit und Methode*. Grundzüge einer philosophischen Hermeneutik. Tübingen: Mohr 1960. XVII, 486 Seiten," *Gnomon* 37 (1965): 716–717.

10. Hans-Georg Gadamer, "Rhetorik, Hermeneutik und Ideologiekritik," *Gesammelte Werke*, (Tübingen: Mohr, 1993), 2:233.

11. In reference to China, "whose philosophy may well rank with the philosophy of the Occident," but whose writing and thinking is not conceptual and not of the order of reasoned speech, that is, discursive, Hannah Arendt writes: "What distinguishes us from them is not *nous* but *logos*, our necessity to give account of and *justify* in words. All strictly logical processes, such as the deducing of inferences from the general to the particular or inductive reasoning from particulars to some general rule, represent such justifications, and this can be done only in words." Hannah Arendt, *The Life of the Mind: Volume One, Thinking* (New York: Harcourt Brace Jovanovich, 1978), 100–102.

12. Joachim Ritter, "Europäisierung als europäisches Problem," in *Metaphysik und Politik. Studien zu Aristoteles und Hegel* (Frankfurt/Main: Suhrkamp, 1977), 336.

13. Ritter, "Europäisierung als europäisches Problem," 336.

14. Jürgen Habermas, *The Postnational Constellation: Political Essays*, trans. M. Pensky (Cambridge, MA: MIT Press, 2001), 6. Translation modified.

15. But, indeed, how is one to reconcile the reference to anamnesis when *truth* here is "merely" of the order of the practical, that is, probable truth, or in Aristotle's words, a truth that resembles truth?

5

AXIAL TIME

IN HIS CONTRIBUTION TO THE FIRST CONFERENCE ABOUT Europe organized by the Rencontres Internationales in Geneva in 1946, Karl Jaspers notes that humanism—faith in the progress of civilization through sciences and technology, in a society based on the political equilibrium of sovereign states, and in the vital spiritual power of the Christian churches, all of which had been the pillars that upheld the idea of Europe—in the aftermath of the two world wars, has lost our confidence.[1] In this talk, titled "Vom Europäischen Geist," Jaspers thus concludes that if "we wish to live on a European foundation, a more profound origin has to take effect [*dann müssen wir einen tieferen Ursprung wirksam werden lassen*]."[2] And, he adds, "We must delve deeper into our historical origins, there whence all these powers that now have become weak once drew their force."[3] The modalities of such a return to a deeper, and more fundamental, origin of the European spirit in response to the questions posed by the conference hosts—questions such as, What is Europe? What is Europe's role in the changed world? And, What is it that a European self-consciousness can make us will?—are what I would like to consider. The gesture of reaching back into the historical origins of Europe in order to overcome the current crisis is, of course, nothing new. Jaspers shares the humanistic watchword—*ad fontes*—with both Edmund Husserl and Martin Heidegger, who, before him, had sought to reconnect Europe with its proper origins in Greek thought and poetry. Yet from the start, Jaspers's emphasis on the Christian sources of the European spirit, for instance, signals that the idea of Europe is not, as with Husserl and Heidegger, to be retraced back to one single origin. But apart from a diversified conception of the origin of Europe—Jaspers speaks of origins in the plural—there is in Jaspers's conception a step back from the current loss of confidence in those great things that, until recently, buttressed European self-consciousness to the historical origins of Europe, a more significant difference. Since, in the writings on Europe that I will consider here, Jaspers's approach is, at first sight, primarily historical, the difference in question could be explained as a consequence of the merely empirical nature of such an examination. But the philosophical thread that runs throughout his writings on Europe considerably complicates the conceptual status of what Jaspers construes as Europe's profound historical origins.

In "Vom Europäischen Geist," the origins of the Occident, and more narrowly of Europe, are located in what Jaspers styles as the *Achsenzeit*, in English: the Axial Period, the Axial Age, or the pivotal age, a term and a conception that he refines at considerable length in his 1949 book *The Origin and Goal of History*.[4] How is the term *Axial Period* to be understood here? "Axial" pertains here to an axis defined as a line, or structure, about which something turns, rotates, or pivots, and thus the Axial Period is one in which a turn (*Wende*) occurs. As Hannah Arendt notes, the concept is Jaspers's "great historical discovery" (though it is a discovery that Jaspers admits is based on the work of several historians) and "the cornerstone of his philosophy of history."[5] But the mere term axial period simply refers to turns in history, that is, to turns in which history as it had been understood comes to an end and something new occurs.[6] However, although axial periods in general refer to "new origins" in history, Jaspers predominantly uses the term Axial Period for one such turn in history, namely, the greatest turn, the one with which history in a proper sense begins in the first place (*OG*, 237). Speaking of history in the genuine sense, that is, as world history, Jaspers holds that this new origin of history occurs through history's pivoting upon itself, causing it to annul time by "cutting across time," thus "lay[ing] hold of the eternal" [*Geschichte [ist] das Geschehen, das in sich, quer zur Zeit, in Tilgung der Zeit, das Ewige erfasst*] (*OG*, 233). The Axial Age is the happening in time of what unifies human history. It is the emergence within history of something universal that unites all the manifold histories of humankind. But, as Jaspers also points out, the axis in question is not meant as an ahistorical interiority of all historical manifestations. Rather than absolute and forever unique, the Axial Age and the universal that it represents are real occurrences in historical time, and, so far, the first and sole effective incarnation of an "ideal axis" that draws together around itself *being human*, in all its movements (*OG*, 262–263).

More profound than all the representations of what makes up the previously mentioned specificity of Europe, the Axial Age is the true origin of Europe. But, let me add immediately, that this origin, as is still to be seen, is not European itself. It is older than Europe, indeed foreign to it since it refers to an event that topologically occurred outside Europe. From what we have seen so far the Axial Period is not an ahistorical essence that informs all historical manifestations. Rather, it is of the order of a revolutionary empirical event that goes "to the roots of humanity itself" (*OG*, 231), and which, by cutting across time and thus blocking the continuity of time, amounts to the "awakening of the specifically human spirit" (*OG*, 5). In other words, as the historical occurrence of a modification of humanity—through the emergence of what is "*specifically human in man,*" that is, by the "*spiritualization*" of man (*OG*, 3)—the Axial Age, as the fundamental origin of Europe, is thus not of the order of an idea. In distinction from Husserl, for whom the idea of a rational and universal science that originates in Greece is the origin and telos of Europe, the Axial Age as the deeper origin to which one must regress in order to save Europe is not only a very concrete historical event, a fact indeed, but also a very strange one. This is not only because it is, as is still to be seen, topologically plural but also because it is raised, as it were, to the position of a "transcendental" fact. Furthermore, the conception of the Axial Period is not of the order of a vision in all senses of the word, that is, a utopian-prophetic visionary grand scheme that, even though it is discovered in the past, is also of the order of an anticipation, or simply an apparition, or phantasm. Rather, as will become clear, the Axial Period is an empirically evident formation of meaning that can be intuited by everyone and can be understood as a measure against which to judge history.

But before I pursue this line of thought, I must first describe that to which the Axial Period refers. Inspired by the work of historians such as Ernst von Lasaulx, Viktor von Strauss, Hermann Keyserling, and Alfred Weber, Jaspers locates the axis of history "in the period around 500 BC, in the spiritual process that occurred between 800 and 200 BC. It is there that we meet with the most deepcut dividing line in history" (*OG*, 1).[7] According to Jaspers,

> the most extraordinary events are concentrated in this period. Confucius and Lao-tse were living in China, all the schools of Chinese philosophy came into being, including those of Mo-ti, Chuang-tse, Lieh-tsu and a host of others; India produced the Upanishads and Buddha and, like China, ran the whole gamut of philosophical possibilities down to skepticism, to materialism, sophism and nihilism; in Iran Zarathustra taught a challenging view of the world as

a struggle between good and evil; in Palestine the prophets made their appearance, from Elijah, by way of Isaiah and Jeremiah to Deutero-Issaiah; Greece witnessed the appearance of Homer, of the philosophers—Parmenides, Heraclitus and Plato—of the tragedians, Thucydides and Archimedes. (*OG*, 2)

The Axial Period to which one must reach back if one is concerned with a renewal of Europe is a historical age in which extraordinary events become concentrated (*drängt sich Ausserordentliches zusammen*), events that happened more or less simultaneously but which, at the same time, also remained topologically separate. As Jaspers notes, everything implied by the names and the figures that the Axial Period invokes "developed during these few centuries almost simultaneously in China, India, and the West; without any one of these regions knowing of the others" (*OG*, 2). Undoubtedly, one may take issue with the alleged parallelism between these very different historical spaces of time, and argue that only an all-too-traditional interpretation of these phenomena would emphasize their identities over their deep differences.[8] But since I am primarily concerned with the structure of Jaspers's historico-philosophical argument, I will not take up this objection nor the possibility that historical evidence may put into question the contention that these world-regions were, indeed, without any communication between each other.[9] Indeed, if the Axial Period is construed as the ultimate origin of Europe, it is not only because during that period crucial things happened but also because they happened in isolation from one another and in three different parts of the world without relation to one another. Let me also underline immediately that although Jaspers highlights the emergence of philosophy in the Axial Period, not only is it juxtaposed to the equally valorized formations of literature and the emerging world religions but also philosophy is not seen to be, in essence, a Greek thing. One of the implications of the Axial Period as the most originary source of Europe consists in a seeming relativization of the specifically Greek origin of Europe and of its reinscription of everything commonly regarded as specific of Europe into a tripartite topological configuration of the origin. But if, as we will see, Greece is nonetheless accorded a special role in the formation of Europe, it is in a different capacity than simply the origin of rational philosophical thought.

Now what is it precisely that opened up at that time? As I have pointed out, the period in question is the event of a spiritualization (*Vergeistigung*) of humankind, an event in which "the spiritual foundation of mankind" is laid (*OG*, 23). But what does such spiritualization imply?

Jaspers writes: "What is involved in the Axial Period is . . . the common element in an overall historical picture, the break-through to the principles which, right up to our own time, have been operative for humanity in borderline situations" (*OG*, 9). In other words, what is new in the three separate worlds that constitute the Axial Period is that man, by way of reflection (*OG*, 2), reaches out beyond himself (*OG*, 4), and as a result "becomes conscious of Being as a whole, of himself and his limitations" (*OG*, 2). More specifically, this event implies a break with the mythical: it is the birth of rationality and the struggle "for the transcendence of the One God"; it is also the emergence of the individual person in the shape of the philosopher, the traveling thinker, the prophet, and so forth. "In this age were born the fundamental categories within which we still think today, and the beginnings of the world religions, by which human beings still live, were created. The step into universality was taken in every sense" (*OG*, 2). Let us bear in mind that this development occurs separately within three, and only three, areas of the world. Even though these three realms did not at first have any communication with one another, what irrupted here made possible "a *profound [bis in die Tiefe] mutual comprehension*" between them (*OG*, 8). Indeed, in the Axial Period was born everything that since then has been the common frame of historical self-comprehension for all peoples.

The radical breakthrough that occurs in the Axial Period can only be fully gauged under the condition that the spiritualization of humankind to which it gives rise in "a multiplicity of the same in three shapes" (*OG*, 10) is seen against the backdrop of the high cultures that preceded the event in question. All the millennia-old high cultures, or civilizations, "like those of Babylon, Egypt, the Indus valley and the aboriginal culture of China, may have been magnificent in their own way, but they appear in some manner unawakened," Jaspers claims (*OG*, 6). Refined though these civilizations were, however, the specific technological rationalizations that characterized them, such as "large scale organizations, writing, the dominant position of the scribe class," corresponded to an "unawakedness devoid of authentic reflection" (*OG*, 48). In short, these high cultures "are destitute of the spiritual revolution . . . outlined in our picture of the Axial Period and which laid the foundations for a new humanity, our humanity" (*OG*, 44). They are "brought to an end by the Axial Period, which melts them down, assimilates them or causes them to sink from view, irrespective of whether it was the same peoples or others that became the bearers of the new cultural forms" (*OG*, 36). Thus, when Jaspers avers that "the mystery of the simultaneous inception of the Axial Period appears to [him] to be situated at a much deeper level than the problem of the birth of the ancient civilizations" (*OG*, 36), it becomes clear that the mystery in question concerns the difference between high cultures and what originates within the Axial Period itself. This, consequently, may be something that can no longer be accounted for in terms of culture and civilization.

Although limited to only a small area of the world, the "new departure within mankind" (*OG*, 17) that occurs during the Axial Period lays the spiritual foundation for humankind insofar as in all their isolation from one another, each one of the areas undertakes a "step into universality," in every sense (*OG*, 2). Here, something is won that binds all men together and "acts as a *challenge to boundless communication*" (*OG*, 19). In Jaspers words, the leap that the Axial peoples took amounts to "a second birth, so to speak, and through it they laid the foundations of man's spiritual being and his history properly so called" (*OG*, 51). Undoubtedly, this leap takes place in continuity with the Chinese's, Indians', Iranians', Jews', and Greeks' past, but as a leap and a breakthrough it also clearly implies a radical departure from that past. From what we have seen, the high cultures and civilization that preceded the Axial Period lacked the spiritual revolution that characterized the latter. They are still destitute of that quality of reflection which transformed humankind, and thus not yet fully awakened. In other words, the leap that brings about the Axial Period is one by which the Axial peoples not only are carried right past the ancient high cultures but also transcend their own cultures as well. The difference between, on the one hand, primitive cultures and high cultures and, on the other hand, the Axial Period is that only the latter know history as an all-embracing happening (*OG*, 7). This fundamental historicity of the Axial Age is the index of a difference in kind—an ontological difference, as it were—between this age and all previous and later cultures, whether high or not. The way Jaspers describes the high cultures prior to the Axial Period, or those which were still flourishing while a breakthrough occurred in the areas in question, seems to suggest that cultures, all cultures, are still part of nature. Indeed, however magnificent they may be, a gulf exists between the Axial Period and the ancient high cultures and civilizations because of their lack of everything that came along with the breakthrough (*OG*, 52). As Jaspers does not tire to emphasize, those peoples and cultures that did not catch up with what occurred between 800 and 200 BC in three parts of the world remained at the level of primitive peoples (*Naturvölker*) (*OG*, 7–8). But even the high cultures, in spite of their sophistication, remain foreign to the Axial Age as formations that have not yet made the break with nature. The development of individuality, that is, of freedom from all *Naturgebundenheit* had been celebrated from the start as a major achievement of the three Axial peoples. Furthermore, in the context of a discussion of what is specific about the Occident, Jaspers points to the development by the Jewish prophets and Greek philosophers of selfhood, as well as to Roman statements concerning a "*conscious inwardness of personal selfhood*," arguing that this development "made it possible to break away from the matrix of nature and human community, to step into the void" of freedom (*OG*, 63).[10] Since all cultures high or low imply a distinction from nature, whose traces thus continue to inhabit it, the emergence of the universal in the Axial Period is no longer of the order of a cultural accomplishment. It implies a much more radical break with man's attachment to nature than that which cultures achieve.[11] The spiritual transformation of humankind that takes place during this period presupposes a break with the respective cultures in spite of the fact that this break occurs in continuity with them. More precisely, the spiritual revolution of the Axial Period is rooted not in a new form of high culture that, while transcending nature, remains linked to it, but rather in a difference of culture with itself. The accomplishment of the Axial Period as the simultaneous but unrelated emergence (*Auftauchen*) (*OG*, 70) of three peoples from all forms of attachment to nature is to have opened up within the three respective cultures and in difference from them, something that transcends the immanence of all particular cultures and that, by making it possible to turn back to them in order to shed a light on them, has a universal appeal.

Let me return once more to Jaspers's contention that the revolution of humankind in question occurs in the three distinct areas of the world more or less simultaneously, but in complete independence from one another. What unfolds in the Axial Period is not to be understood as the result of "a series of stages, either in time or in meaning," say, from China to Greece (*OG*, 10). There is no such thing as a course of history moving in relation to the cardinal points. Attempts to comprehend the course of history as a whole in this way are culturally bound. Jaspers remarks, "Seeing the road that leads from Babylon *via* Greece and Rome to the North, historians said that the course of history runs from east to west and made the prognostication that, pursuing that same direction, the road would lead on to America. In India, however, the road ran from the Indus region (early Vedic period) *via* the central area (period of the Upanishads) to the Ganges (Buddha and his period), that is from west to east. All such schemata are valid only from certain points of view for limited worlds, and even there only with reservations" (*OG*, 73).

Instead, the occurrence of the breakthrough of the Axial Period, a breakthrough that was "decisive for universal history" although it itself was not a universal occurrence, "was rather one of contemporaneous, side by side existence without contact. To begin with, several roads seem to lead from disparate origins toward the same goal. There is a multiplicity of the same in three shapes. There are three independent roots of one history, which later—after isolated and interrupted contacts, finally only a few centuries ago and properly speaking not until our own day—become a single unity" (*OG*, 10–11). Let me try to draw out some implications from this specific way in which, in the Axial Period, the breakthrough of something universal occurs. First, that the spiritual revolution of humanity is held to have taken place in three different areas of the world, more or less at the same time but in complete separation from one another, suggests that what breaks through in these three areas is something that, from the start, is a possibility of humanity shareable by all. If such a transformation effectively happened in three very different parts of the world at the same time, then the implication is that all peoples can undergo such a revolution. The emergence (*Auftauchen*) of axiality from nature and culture is a universal process. Second, since the breakthrough happens in three distinctly different areas of the world, the irruption of something universal here is not an ethnic or cultural formation, but on the contrary something that transcends culture and is the expression of a difference of culture with itself. Third, if the spiritual revolution of humankind occurs approximately at the same time in three separate areas of the world, this also suggests that the revolution in question can take place in a multiplicity of historical manifestations, or shapes, without each particular humanity having to give up its cultural specificity, or difference. Let us bear in mind that Jaspers bases his contention on historical, that is, empirical evidence. But from what we have begun to see, this empirical happening is also not without philosophical significance. Consequently, this might be the appropriate moment to inquire a bit into the nature and status of the factuality of the Axial Period.

Having drawn on the authority of Lasaulx and von Strauss to assert that the Axial Period is a fact—a *Tatbestand*—Jaspers takes on the possible objection that it "is not a fact at all, but *the product of a judgment of value*"

(*OG*, 9). Arguing that "in matters of the spirit, a fact can only be apprehended through the understanding of [its] meaning," he holds that

> though it rests empirically upon an accumulation of separate data, an historical construction [*Bild*] never comes into being through these alone. Only through an understanding do we arrive at our view [*Anschauung*] of the Axial Period, as of the spirit of any historical event. And this view involves understanding and evaluation at the same time; it includes the fact that we are emotionally moved, because we feel ourselves touched by it, because it concerns our own history and not merely as a past of which we can trace the effects, but as the past whose wider, more original effect, which is continually beginning afresh, is incalculable. (*OG*, 9–10)

Now, since in the Axial Period a spiritual transformation occurred through the breakthrough of something universal that "draws humanity into the single context of world history," this period becomes, Jaspers claims, "a yardstick with whose aid we measure the historical significance of the various peoples to mankind as a whole" (*OG*, 51). So I ask, what is the status of the Axial Period, of an empirical occurrence in humankind, which at the same time serves as a standard for all historical evaluation?

On the opening pages of *The Origin and Goal of History*, Jaspers acknowledges that for the Western world, and the history of philosophy that emerged there, "the appearance of the Son of God is the axis of world history" (*OG*, 1). At the beginning of this chapter I referred to Arendt's claim that the Axial Age is Jaspers's own original discovery. But from these beginning pages of his book, it is also obvious that the term *Axial Age* itself is indebted to a passage from Hegel's lectures on *The Philosophy of History*, which states that the goal and starting point of history, or the axis (*Angel*) of world history, is the Christian conception of the Godhead as a trinity in unity.[12] However, Jaspers' concept of the Axial Period is also clearly intended to overcome such a faith-bound interpretation of history in the name of a multiple origination of history. Christian faith, he emphasizes, is one faith among others, "not the faith of mankind" (*OG*, 1). But more generally, a universally recognizable axis of world history would have to be independent from all creeds. Jaspers avers: "An axis of world history, if such a thing exists, would have to be discovered *empirically*, as a fact capable of being accepted as such by all men, Christians included. This axis would be situated at the point in history which gave birth to everything which, since then, man has been able to be" (*OG*, 1). Needless to say, the insistence on the empirical nature of the axis is a function of the need to discover an axis that can be recognized and acknowledged by everyone, whatever his or her particular faith may be. Since, in distinction from faith, "experience is available to man as man," only something that can be experienced can also bind all men together (*OG*, 19). And this is precisely the case with what happened between 800 and 200 BC. The Axial Age is a fact that is available to all in an experience of intuition. Indeed, the centuries in question "are the empirically evident [*einsehbare*] axis of world history for all men" (*OG*, 19). Jaspers writes: "Really to visualize [*wirklich zu sehen*] the facts of the Axial Period and to make them the basis of our universal conception of history is to gain possession of something *common to all mankind*, beyond all differences of creed" (*OG*, 19). The "lucid humanity" of the Axial Period is, in his own words, a "*geschichtliche Anschauung*," that is, a historical intuition that itself throws "light upon the entire history of the world" (*OG*, 6). In short, the Axial Period is something like a phenomenological intuition by which the factual simultaneous occurrence in three unrelated and distinct areas of the world of a break with the still unawakened previous high cultures is understood as "a total universal parallelism on the plane of world history" rather than "merely the chance occurrence of particular phenomena" (*OG*, 12).[13] The Axial Period is the intuition of a parallelism within the threefold event that bequeaths the meaning of a spiritual revolution on it; more precisely, it is the new beginning of "an original community of meaning [*Sinngemeinschaft*]" (*OG*, 12). What raises the Axial Period to the status of a historical intuition is the nearly simultaneous occurrence, in always particular shapes, of new, no longer culture-bound humanities in unrelated areas of the world. The Axial Period is an empirical transcendental, as it were.

As the earliest and most profound source of all the now discredited self-representations by which Europe has lived, the Axial Period is "the historical fact of the threefold origin" (*OG*, 19). As the occurrence of the spiritual foundation of humankind, this is an origin that from the start is universal and to which no one can lay possessive claims. But if, in order to live on a European foundation, Europe must reach back to this deeper threefold origin, it must also be noted that this origin therefore does not belong to Europe alone, and certainly not primarily, in the additional sense that, historically and geographically, the Axial Period took place prior to what is known as Europe, and outside of it. On what basis, then, can Jaspers claim that Europe can and must reactualize the more profound ground of the Axial Period, if it was never actually part of it? As we have seen, what happened between 800 and 200 BC is, undoubtedly, the standard for all humanities since then. As Jaspers remarks: "*Until today* mankind has lived by what happened during the Axial Period, by what was thought and created during that period" (*OG*, 7). But that does not lay the question to rest. For indeed, Europe only becomes a world-historical player long after the end of the Axial Period, which was brought down by the reemergence of the imperial idea (*Reichgedanke*)—a heritage from the ancient high cultures and civilizations—that "originally constituted a culture-creating principle," but which now serves to stabilize the declining humanities and to lay them in their coffins (*OG*, 7). Only after the Nordic peoples "had come into contact with the Axial Period in the first millennium AD, a hitherto unreflected substance, which—vague as such notions are bound to be—is akin to the forces partially manifested in the Axial Period itself" (*OG*, 56–57) awoke in Europe. Through appropriation, working over, and transmutation of what is assumed from "a foreign source" (*OG*, 59), the Nordic peoples created a new beginning called "Europe." More exactly, Europe becomes significant in world-historical terms only with the late Middle Ages and the production of modern science, and, toward the end of the eighteenth century, the ensuing technological age. According to Jaspers, this scientific-technological age, which draws the whole world into "a single unit of communications" (*OG*, 24) is "the first entirely new development in the spiritual or material sphere since the Axial Period" (*OG*, 23). In fact, in a rigorous sense, it is "the beginning of world history properly so called" (*OG*, 24) since "there has been no world history until now, but only an aggregate of local histories" (*OG*, 24). Thus, the question arises whether the special character of Europe and the Occident correspond to a "second breath . . . being taken by mankind as a whole," in short, a "second Axial Period" (*OG*, 250). This question imposes itself all the more since "the developments issuing from the first breath in their manifold conformation look to us as though, as a whole, they would have come to naught if something new had not arisen in the West" (*OG*, 25). In other words, does the special character of the West rest on its being the direct inheritor of the Axial Period and on its turning of a happening that was only of universal significance into a truly universal event, namely the beginning of universal and planetary history and of "boundless communication"?

But before we pursue Jaspers's response to this question, it may be useful to remind ourselves that the step taken into universality by the three separate peoples during the Axial Age did not materialize in actual universal history. Indeed, since these areas remained without contact with one another, the possibility of boundless communication remained only just that—a mere possibility. For this possibility and, hence, for the universal significance of the happening of the Axial Age to become factually universal, something else was required—the advent of an actual encounter with others. It is here that Jaspers's elaborations on what, subsequent to the Axial Age, happened in the West are of crucial importance. But by way of preparation for Jaspers's response to the above raised question, let me first inquire into why, specifically, science and technology were created in the West, rather than in the two other great cultural zones. Jaspers wonders, "Can some peculiar element have already been present in the West during the Axial Period, which has only had these effects in the course of the last few centuries? Did that which finally manifested itself in science already exist in embryo during the Axial Period? Is there some quality specific to the West?" (*OG*, 62). The question, then, is whether an element was present from the start in at least some parts of the West that allowed a region like Northern Europe, that later became associated with it, to eventually create something new.

In order to construe the specificity of Europe, the lecture "Vom Europäischen Geist" highlighted the words *freedom, history*, and *science*. As the spiritual principle of the West, freedom in Europe takes on the twofold form of a life in polarities and in the face of extremes (*vor dem Aussersten*); history is understood as a process of struggling to realize such freedom; and, finally, the passion of science "as the unconditional, universal willing to know everything without exception that can be known" and as "merciless criticism" of fixed opinions, is called upon by freedom itself.[14] In *The Origin and the Goal of History*, Jaspers pursues this specificity of Europe by lining up nine pointers directing attention to the features that make up the quality peculiar to the West. Very briefly, these are: the extraordinary variety of its *geographical* features (as opposed to "the closed continental territories of China and India" [*OG*, 62]); its knowledge of the idea of *political liberty*; the pursuit without stay of *rationality*; "*conscious inwardness of personal selfhood*"; recognition of the impossibility of circumventing the world's reality, and thus the need to shape and transform the world; the realization of a universal that "*does not coagulate into a dogmatic fixity*" [hence, also the "perpetual disquiet of the West"]; distinct from, and in contradiction with this fluidity, "*the claim to exclusive truth*" by the three religions of the Book; "a *resoluteness* that takes things to extremes"; and, finally, "the amplitude of character, [and] autonomous personalities" (*OG*, 62–66). What all these pointers succeed in suggesting is that the specificity of the West is that of a world that is not circumscribed by any universal, or any creed. Precisely because in the West everything is taken to the extreme and thrown into clarity, the West is a world of disquietness and of tensions that never permit fixation and completion. This world is fundamentally a world of limits, and that means for Jaspers a world that experiences transcendence—a transcendence of immanence—in short, a world of existence at the limit of the world, a limit-world.[15] Only such a world could give rise to the European line of development that has ushered in the age of technology, and which "today gives the whole world a European countenance" (*OG*, 67). With Jaspers's question in mind, whether the world-historical preeminence of Europe owing to the specificity of "its" world is a function of the consequential unfolding of something that already existed in embryonic form in the Axial Age (solely "in the West during the Axial Period," or in all its the parts?), would one thus not have to wonder whether this embryonic kernel is not precisely the way of a life in limit-situations that constitutes the specifically Western world as a world at the limit?[16] At this juncture, however, it needs to be pointed out that, for Jaspers, the element that may already have existed in embryonic form during the Axial Period, and which may have been the origin of the sciences as they developed at the beginning of the 17th century in Europe, is not what led to the world-historical preeminence or planetary expansion of Europe. By contrast, the latter is seen as a consequence of technology made possible by the sciences. Undoubtedly, the rapid and almost limitless expansion of European technology across the globe is not unrelated to what it is that made the European sciences possible to begin with, but scientific spirit and the worldwide spread of European technological innovations are of a different nature. What the reasons and implications of this distinction are will only become clear in a moment.

In any case, whereas "by 1400 the overall life in Europe, India and China had reached a uniform level of civilization" (*OG*, 74), in the late Middle Ages a break occurred in Europe (as a part of the Occident) "that was unique in its importance to the West and, in its consequences, to the whole world; a break whose results make up our own situation and whose ultimate significance is still open" (*OG*, 74–75). For what follows, it is important to emphasize that what occurs in this break is a twofold development. On the one hand, the break in question is the emergence of the modern sciences, which, since the seventeenth century, distinguish Europe from all other cultures and which inaugurated the age of technology, and on the other hand, the extraordinary accomplishments of the spiritual creations between 1500 and 1800 that even outshined (perhaps because of their indebtedness to the classical age) science and technology (*OG*, 75). These latter accomplishments, in particular, make Jaspers wonder whether what happened in these later centuries is not the advent of a second Axial Period (*OG*, 75). But, as he notes, in spite of all of Europe's exceptional spiritual achievements, the difference with the first Axial Period is considerable. "Everything stands in the shadow of exacting traditions [hence, the break is not radical] and follows false roads; it is as if in spite of these false directions that the great figures, the solitary ones, find their way to the most miraculous successes" (*OG*, 76). As a consequence, the European developments lack "the purity and clarity, the ingenuousness and freshness of the worlds of the first axis." Furthermore, as Jaspers remarks, this period is not a new Axial Age because it is above all "a purely European phenomenon and for that reason alone has no claim to the title of second axis" (*OG*, 76). Indeed, by definition, axiality requires a plural topology. However fruitful these centuries may have been for the Europeans, "they do not represent a universally human, world-embracing axis, and it is unlikely that they might become such in the sequel" (*OG*, 76; translation modified). Nonetheless, Jaspers also claims that "possibilities are open to the [seeming] second axis that were unknown to the first" (*OG*, 76). What these are may become clear as we now turn in some greater detail to this "quite different axis [that] was established by the activities of the Europeans, with their consequences in science and technology, which made their appearance when the West, whose spirit and soul were already in decline, impinged upon an India and China whose spirit and soul had reached their lowest point" (*OG*, 76; translation modified).

Undoubtedly, because of the development of technology, Europe is responsible for the current world-situation, with all its beneficial and disastrous effects, which only came into being as a consequence of the emergence of the European sciences. But because technology also opens "the possibility of universal communications" (*OG*, 74), the "foundation-laying discoveries which finally differentiated human life from the animal kingdom" (*OG*, 97) during the Axial Period could now, in principle, become a world-embracing reality. Indeed, as Jaspers states, "our Age of Technology is not merely relatively universal, like the events in those three mutually independent worlds of the Axial Period, but absolutely universal, because it is planetary" (*OG*, 139–140). And when he adds that "the world has become European through the adoption of European technology and the European demands of nationalism, and it is successfully turning both against Europe," with the result that "Europe, as the old Europe, is no longer the dominant factor in the world" (*OG*, 76–77), he does not simply lament this development. On the contrary, the decline of Europe, the loss of its former place in the world, harbors the promise of a new age of "the planetary unity of the world and of mankind," in short, the possibility of "the factual universal history of the earth, *world history*" (*OG*, 71), and, hence, of a new age. But Jaspers also claims that the factual present, at least, "is no second Axial Period. In the most pronounced contrast to the latter, it is a period of catastrophic descent to poverty of spirit, love and creative energy" (*OG*, 96–97). Indeed, as a result of technology, the present world "is becoming ever more inhuman" (*OG*, 97). Consequently, if we have indeed entered "into a new radical metamorphosis of humanity, this is no repetition of the Axial Period but [on the contrary] a happening that is different to its very roots" (*OG*, 139).

What, then, is it in truth that deprives the present age of technology from being a second Axial Age? I recall that the simultaneous but separate breakthroughs to universal humanity of the Axial Period followed "the period of foundation-laying discoveries which finally differentiated human life from the animal kingdom," that is, it followed "the Promethean Age" only "after a long interval" (*OG*, 97). As we have stressed, the spiritual breakthrough of humanity to universal humanity in the pivotal age takes place in a distinction from the previous high cultures, which Jaspers conceives of in continuity with the Promethean Age. Let us also bear in mind that what he characterized as the second breath of humanity "started with the scientific technological, the new Promethean Age" of the sciences and technology, and is therefore "analogous to the organization and planning of the ancient high cultures" (*OG*, 25; translation modified). To put it differently, the entirely new event that occurs with the development of technology in Europe and its planetary unfolding, rather than a second Axial Age, is another Promethean and high-culture phenomenon. Indeed, the distinct roots of the age of technology to which Jaspers alluded, rather than spiritual, belong to the culture of interaction with, and mastery of, nature. Jaspers remarks that "we may more readily liken ourselves, with our grandiose scientific discoveries and technological inventions, to the epoch of the invention of tools and weapons, of the first use of domestic animals and horses, than with the Age of Confucius, Buddha and Socrates" (*OG*, 140). What follows from this is that the development of European technology made possible by the sciences, rather than originating in a seed present since the

Axial Period in embryonic form in the West, is the result of the continuing Promethean attempt by humanity to master nature, and thus only another high-culture phenomenon. Only the technology's planetary expansion itself, and the developments of technological means for faster and faster communication, can be retraced to "the step into universality" that occurred during the Axial Age. If the age of technology, then, is not a second Axial event, it is because, as another form of culture, the age of technology does not radically transcend nature. On the contrary, the age of technology exasperates human beings' involvement in nature. Even though the meaning of technology is freedom in relation to nature (*OG*, 100), a deviation of this meaning occurs at the moment when tools and activities make themselves independent (*OG*, 102). This is precisely what constitutes "the great historical dividing-line within technology" that ushers in the age of technology (*OG*, 102). Furthermore, by becoming increasingly dominated, at the expense of all other concerns, by the obsession with mastering nature, nature gains an unheard of ascendency over modern man that makes him a slave to nature like never before. Jaspers writes: "Man's attachment to nature is made manifest in a new fashion by modern technology. Nature threatens to overpower man himself, in a manner previously unforeseen, through his tremendously increased mastery of her. Through the nature of the man engaged in technological work, nature really does become the tyrant of humanity. The danger threatens that man will stifle in the second nature, to which he gives birth technologically as his own product, whereas he may appear relatively free vis-à-vis unsubdued nature in his perpetual struggle for existence" (*OG*, 98).

But, as we have also been told, the current age contains possibilities unknown to the first pivotal age.[17] Before we return to them, it must also be pointed out that even though the technologization of the world dehumanizes it through a process by which the destruction of the continuity of tradition deprives the human being of all roots and turns him into "a dweller on the earth with no home" (*OG*, 98), technology alone, according to Jaspers, cannot be held responsible for the current crisis. He writes: "Long before technology had these effects, movements were afoot from which the present spiritual situation springs. The fact that technology became operative and was universally adopted was due to this spiritual world, this way of thought and of life, which it found waiting for it" (*OG*, 135). Let us therefore also remind ourselves that when he addressed the question of whether the developments in Europe in the last several centuries amounted to a second

Axial Age, Jaspers, having showcased the spiritual creation between 1500 and 1800, which even outshined the accomplishments of the sciences and technology, noted that this prodigiously creative flurry of thought and the arts was not an exclusively European phenomenon, and that it took place in spite of the false roads in which Europe found itself engaged, in a resistance against the exacting tradition that bore upon it. Thus, if for Jaspers, "today it seems possible that the whole cultural heritage since the Axial Period will be lost, that history from Homer to Goethe will sink into oblivion" (*OG*, 131), this very spiritual heritage, and particularly its creative revival during the centuries in question, also seems to be the sole hope for realizing the potential for a universal humankind and a world history for which technology, for the first time, provides the material means. Whatever the shortcomings of the European cultural heritage, it is also the promise of "boundless communications," the goal of what Jaspers terms an "infinite task" (*OG*, 264; translation modified).

So, to conclude, I return briefly to the question of whether the unique event that took place in Europe—that is, the development of science and technology—and which established its emergent preeminence in the world, was not the unfolding of something whose chromosomal form was already present in the West during the Axial Period. I already considered whether that form is not the specific form of the world as a limit-world that the break with the previous high cultures brought about during the Axial Period. But if the West occupies within the Axial Period a certain special place, as Jaspers occasionally seems to suggest, it is because during this pivotal age parts of the West already accomplished, in spite of their continuity with the past, the break with the past in more radical ways than the two other areas. Indeed, as Jaspers argues, the West made this more radical break by conceiving itself from the start in relation to the Orient.[18] This Western identity, predicated on a constitutive relation to the other, establishes an ontological privilege of sorts, in that it represents the condition *sine qua non* for the carrying out of what remained only on the level of a possibility in the Axial Age, namely, boundless communication. Indeed, let us bear in mind that the spiritualization that occurred during the Axial Age, and in which three distinct areas of the world raised themselves to humanity, took place without any of these areas being in touch with each other. In other words, the openness to others implied by the spiritualization in question was not consummated and remained only on the level of a possibility. Yet within one of these areas, that is, in the West, the Greeks defined themselves from the beginning in relation to an other—the Persians—and thus prepared, as it were, not only the more radical actualization of what was only realized as a possibility in the Axial Age but also the extension of this principle to plural others in the formation of Europe in the West.[19] Whereas all the participants of the Axial Period raised themselves to humanity, they did so in isolation from one another and remained enclosed within their great walls, as it were. Yet if among all the peoples within the occidental region of the Axial Period the Greeks rose to a certain preeminence, it is because they defined themselves—as the Trojan War, or the confrontation with the Scythians, for example, demonstrates—in relation to a foreign other whom they recognized as an equal—an equal capable of truth. This factual and historical significance of the Greeks' incorporation of an opening to an equal other into the determination of their own identity, for which factual evidence can be found in the narratives, such as those of Homer or Herodotus, subsequently became a structural characteristic of what Europe inherited. In short, if within the configuration of the Axial Period the West enjoys a certain preeminence that only became confirmed later by the fact that the European line of development alone led to the development of the European science and the age of technology, it is primarily because of the role that Greece has played in the formation of the Occident. This is not so much because Greece is the origin of rationality, but because, as we have said, in Greece emerges a concept of identity that is defined by the other. Jaspers writes: "The Greeks founded the West, but in such a manner that it only continues to exist as long as it keeps its eyes steadily on the East, faces up to it, comprehends it and withdraws from it and works over them till they become its own, and engages in a struggle with it in which now the West and now the East gains the upper hand" (*OG*, 67). This opposition between the evening- and the morning-land, is not to be confused with the antithesis between Greeks and barbarians, a difference that one finds in analogous fashion in all the cultures that consider themselves the center of the world, and that fashions the way Chinese, Egyptians, and Indians related to other peoples (*OG*, 67). According to Jaspers, the difference between the East and the West is a difference that "at all times [has] been an element in the make-up of Europe, whereas the Orient merely took it over from Europe and understood it in a European sense" (*OG*, 68). In fact, it is a difference that is constitutive of Europe and implies the recognition that every spiritual phenomenon is divided, and comes to life only when the spiritual heeds the difference that divides it from within, thus establishing it in relation to an other recognized as capable of truth. In Jaspers words: "The spirit only comes to life, is set in motion, becomes fruitful and surges upward, when it becomes cognizant of itself in an antithesis and finds itself in conflict" (*OG*, 68). As the result of a divorce from the Orient—that is, as Jaspers undoubtedly writes with Homer and Aeschylus in mind, "a politically and spiritually . . . equal and admired power" (*OG*, 67)—the West is constituted from the beginning by the difference from a power "from which the West can learn and which exercises a seductive attraction over it" (*OG*, 68), a difference that prevents it from closing on itself.[20] Because of this essential exposure to an other capable of truth, Europe as a spiritual entity is, therefore, also characterized by a fundamental incompleteness and deficiency (*OG*, 68). What is specific to the West is that its identity is constituted under the sign of the other. Jaspers remarks: "China and India always lived in continuity with their own pasts; Greece, on the other hand, lived beyond its own past in continuity with an alien, Oriental past; the Nordic peoples lived in continuity with the culture of the Mediterranean world, which, to begin with, was foreign to them. The West is characterized by the manner in which, at a given moment, it introduced its own originality into a continuity taken over from a foreign source, which it appropriated, worked over and transmuted" (*OG*, 59). This constitutive openness present in the West since the Axial Period is, undoubtedly, the seed that germinated in the shape of modern technology to engender a planetary, but increasingly inhuman, world. However, as Jaspers avers, if there is currently a "tendency, which is becoming increasingly strong to look back toward our origin," it is a sign "that we are tackling the high task of reconstructing [*gestalten*] humanity from its origin, [and] that we sense the fateful question as how we can, in faith, become specifically human beings . . . In this process of self-understanding through the knowledge of whence we come the mirror of the great Axial Period of humanity will perhaps, once more, prove one of the essential assurances" (*OG*, 140).

Notes

1. The conference took place September 1–15, 1946. The speakers were Julien Benda, Georges Bernanos, Karl Jaspers, Stephen Spender, Jean Guéhenno, Francesco Flora, Denis de Rougemont, Jean-R. de Salis, and Georg Lukacs. The conference was followed by five discussions in which, among others, Robert Aron, Lucien Goldman, Maurice Merleau-Ponty, Jean Starobinski, and Jean Wahl intervened. The proceedings of the conference have been

published under the title *L'Esprit européen* (Paris: O. Zeluck, 1947). For a fine account and analysis of the discussion that took place between the participants, and particularly the controversy between Jaspers and Lukacs, see Etienne Tassin, "De l'Europe philosophique à l'Europe politique," in *Existe-t-il une Europe philosophique?*, ed. N. Weill (Rennes: Presses Universitaires de Rennes, 2005), 129–145.

2. Karl Jaspers, "Vom europäischen Geist," in *Rechenschaft und Ausblick. Reden und Aufsätze* (Munich: Piper, 1951), 233. For Jaspers's own comments about the conference, see Hannah Arendt and Karl Jaspers, *Briefwechsel 1926–1969* (Munich: Piper, 2001), 93–94.

3. Jaspers, "Vom europäischen Geist," 234.

4. Jaspers, "Vom europäischen Geist," 237.

5. Hannah Arendt, *Men in Dark Times* (New York: Harcourt Brace, 1983), 88.

6. Jaspers presented the notion of axial time in a short essay titled "Die Achsenzeit der Weltgeschichte" in *Der Monat* 1, no. 6 (1948): 3–9, which was then followed in 1949 by the book-length study *Vom Ursprung und Ziel der Geschichte*. All in-text citations refer to the English translation of this work: Karl Jaspers, *The Origin and Goal of History*, trans. M. Bullock (New Haven, CT: Yale University Press, 1953); hereafter cited in text as *OG*.

7. The works Jaspers refers to are Ernst von Lasaulx, *Neuer Versuch einer alten auf die Wahrheit der Thatsachen gegrundeten Philosophie der Geschichte* (Munich: Cotta'sche Buchhandlung, 1856); Viktor von Strauss, *Lao-Tse's Tao Te King* (Leipzig: von Friedrich Fleischer, 1970); Hermann Alexander Graf Keyserling, *Das Buch vom Ursprung* (Baden-Baden: Hans Bühler Junior, 1947); Alfred Weber, *Kulturgeschichte als Kultursoziologie* (Leiden, 1935); *Das Tragische und die Geschichte* (Hamburg, 1943); *Abschied von der bisherigen Geschichte* (1946).

8. In addition to his reservations about Jaspers's interpretation of technology, this is one of Martin Heidegger's objections. In a letter to Jaspers dated September 21, 1949, after having acknowledged the central importance of conceiving "the simultaneity and synchronicity of Chinese, Indian, and Western centuries as axial time," that is, because "a world axis conceals itself [here], which could become a pivot upon which modern world-technology turns," Heidegger asks about "the measure for interpreting these three simultaneous spaces of time." And he adds: "I cannot hold back the reservation that your interpretation of these spaces, even especially the Greek, perhaps moves within a too-traditional sphere of representation, wherein it indicates more similarity between them than, perhaps, they have." Walter Biemel and Hans Saner, eds, *The Heidegger–Jaspers Correspondence (1920–1963)*, trans. G. E. Aylesworth (Humanities Books, 2003), 176–177.

9. Nor will I take up Jan Assmann's argument that the framework of the Axial Age is, chronologically speaking, too rigid a concept, one that furthermore ignores other civilizational cases and is thus a sort of Procrustean bed of schematic periodization. Indeed, even though for Jaspers the Axial Age is a historical event, it is the historical advent of universal history. From this perspective, specifically, historical caveats do not bear on the concept since the event is thus thought of as something more than a historical event.

10. Perhaps one must also extend Jaspers's acknowledgment that all cultures have produced forms of the universal, but that in the West, "*this universal does not coagulate into a dogmatic fixity* of definitive institutions and notions," to the accomplishments of the Axial Period as well (*OG*, 64).

11. In order to further refine this distinction between culture and what occurred during the Axial period, Kant's distinction between "the ultimate end [*letzten Zweck*]

of nature and "the final end [*Endzweck*]" could serve as a starting point. Indeed, in the Third Critique, Kant defines *culture* as the "ultimate purpose" that nature pursues with respect to the human species. Culture, therefore, remains within the "chain of natural ends [*Naturzwecke*]." Yet, culture as a purpose, or end, of nature is distinct from the final end, or "end in itself [*Endzweck*]," for which culture is only a preparation, and which only the human being, insofar as this aim is "sufficient for itself independently of nature," can give to himself. Immanuel Kant, *Critique of the Power of Judgment*, trans. P. Guyer and E. Matthews (Cambridge: University of Cambridge Press, 2000), 298).

12. Hegel writes, "God is thus recognized as *Spirit*, only when known as the Triune. This new principle is the axis on which the History of the World turns. This is *the goal* and the starting point." Georg Wilhelm Friedrich Hegel, *The Philosophy of History*, trans. J. Sibree (New York: Dover, 1956), 319.

13. This notion of parallelism may also be an indication that one of Jaspers's sources for his conception of the Axial Period may have been Walter Otto's *Vishnu-Narayana. Texte zur indischen Gottesmystik*, trans. R. Otto (Jena: Eugen Diederichs, 1917), 139–160, who, in a concluding chapter titled "Das Gesetz der Parallelen in der Religionsgeschichte," makes a similar point. I am grateful to Giorgi Maisuradze for having provided me with this reference.

14. Jaspers, "Vom europäischen Geist," 239–246.

15. I am obviously referring here to Jaspers's concept of the "ultimate situation" (*Grenzsituation*) as he first developed it in 1919 in *Psychologie der Weltanschauungen* (Berlin: Julius Springer, 1919), 229–279. See also Edwin Latzel, "The Concept of 'Ultimate Situation' in Jaspers' Philosophy," in *The Philosophy of Karl Jaspers*, ed. P. A. Schilpp (New York: Tudor, 1957), especially 182–186.

16. If the Axial Age consisted in the simultaneous realization in three unrelated parts of the world of a spiritualization of humanity, it follows that axiality is determined by the copresence of different temporalities. The limit-world characteristic of Europe would then also be one that is characterized by a nonunitary contemporaneity of diverse temporalities. I thank David Ferris for having pointed this out to me.

17. Technology, for Jaspers, is in no way a monolithic phenomenon. Undoubtedly, it is primarily involved in mastering and exploiting nature at the price of a complete dehumanization of the world and the destruction of the environment, but, at the same time, it also develops the material means for what he terms *boundless communication*, starting with the printing press and, for the time being, ending with the internet, developing modes of transportation that allow crossing continents in a very short time.

18. Needless to say, this constitutive exposure of Europe to the Orient comes also with the inevitable danger of becoming seduced by it to the point of "sinking back into Asia" (*OG*, 70). Jaspers expands on this threat to the fragile identity of what exists only in relation to the other in *OG* 68–70, which would require a lengthy commentary because of the implicit distinction that he makes here between, on the one hand, "the matrix of Asia" (*OG*, 70), and on the other hand, Europe, the West, the Orient, China, and India. I take this as an opportunity for a remark: If it is true that to conceive of the other (such as China and India) as being engaged in a transcendence of cultural immanence similar to the one that occurs in the Axial Period in the West comes with the danger of applying Western concepts to other modes of thinking and being, it is equally true that the inverse attempt to think the other from within itself in unmediated fashion—that is, also on the basis of what sets it radically apart from ourselves—carries the inverse threat of a specifically Western illusion regarding

the other in all its otherness (such as Orientalism). However, without running at the same time *both* risks, no openness to, and encounter of the other is conceivable to begin with.

19. Undoubtedly, this openness to others manifested itself *also* in a negative fashion, that is, through the colonization, oppression, and exploitation of others. However, seemingly against all odds, such negative realization of the principle of humanity also harbors the potential for what Jaspers calls boundless communication.

20. As Simone Weil, to whom Jaspers may well be referring here, has noted, there is an "extraordinary sense of equity that breaths through the *Iliad* . . . One is barely aware that the poet is a Greek and not a Trojan." Furthermore, she holds that "attic tragedy, or at any rate the tragedy of Aeschylus and Sophocles, is the true continuation of the epic." In the case of Aeschylus, one thinks, of course, of the *Persae* (Simone Weil, *The Iliad or The Poem of Force*, trans. M. McCarthy (Wallingford, PA: Pendle Hill, 1973), 32–33). In this context, see also Hannah Arendt, *Between Past and Future. Eight Exercises in Political Thought* (New York: Penguin, 2006), 258.

6

EASTWARD TRAJECTORIES

IN HIS INAUGURAL SPEECH AT THE ACADEMY OF the Sciences in Heidelberg in 1959, where, thanks to his friend Hans-Georg Gadamer he had returned in 1952 after eighteen years of exile in Italy, Japan, and then the United States—a speech that has been republished in a revised form under the title "Curriculum Vitae (1959)" in *My Life in Germany Before and After 1933*—Karl Löwith recalls how in 1919, after some deliberation on whether to study biology or philosophy, he finally decided for the latter and subsequently enrolled in Edmund Husserl's seminars in Freiburg. In the beginning Löwith enjoyed Husserl's strict phenomenological thought, but only until he began to attend the seminars offered by Martin Heidegger, "who [as he states] lured us away from Husserl's naïve faith in a conclusive philosophical method."[1] Apart from his doctoral dissertation on Nietzsche under Heidegger's guidance, Löwith habilitated himself in Marburg in 1928, where he had followed his teacher, with a thesis on "The Individual in the Role of Fellow Human Being" (Das Individuum in der Rolle des Mitmenschen). Although at the time Löwith qualified his own starting point as anthropological, in other words, in clear distinction from the ontologism of Heidegger's analytic of Dasein, the problematic of this work still unfolds within a conception of *world* predicated primarily on the human being and its relations to objects and other human beings. Löwith writes, "the personalized world of I and you (*Mitwelt*), in which each is relatively conditioned by the other . . . this *Mitwelt*, also constituting us as 'individuals,' appeared at that time to be our definitive world [*unsere massgebende Welt*], because it is of direct and everyday concern to us."[2] But shortly after having understood world in this manner, that is, also in implicitly temporal and historical terms—an understanding largely indebted to Heidegger's critical questioning and "Destruktion" in *Being and Time* of the traditional understanding of Being, including, as Löwith adds, "the temporal meaning of Being as it was understood by the Greeks" as that which is always present—Löwith abandoned this conception of world according to which human Dasein is a being that unfolds within a temporal, that is, above all future oriented, in other words, intrinsically historical, horizon, as "an all too human horizon of the world."[3] Building on his earlier concerns for the whole of the natural world—as elaborated by Schopenhauer and Nietzsche, and likewise motivated by his continuing interest in biology, while, undoubtedly, also reminiscent of his studies with Husserl, who referred his students "beyond the transient realities to the timeless 'essence' of phenomena"—Löwith turned away from the human and historical world, a world primarily determined in terms of relations of persons with one another, that until then had been for him the "definitive world," to a conception of the world as, primarily, the world of nature, or the natural world.[4] Yet, by *natural world* Löwith does not mean nature as it is an object of the sciences. The latter do not inquire into the eternal motions of nature, or the universe, as such, but, in Hannah Arendt's words, into its processes, that is, "the history, the story of the coming into being, of nature or life or the universe."[5] Rather, by natural world Löwith understands "the *world as such*, which is the One and Whole of what is that exists by and from itself [*welche das Eine und Ganze des von Natur aus Seienden ist*]." More precisely, in a return to Greek cosmotheology, for him the natural world corresponds to what the ancients referred to as the physical *cosmos*, a whole that is "ever complete," and "entirely independent," that swings in itself, and whose *logos* is the changeless law of the cyclical recurrence of the same.[6] With Heraclitus's Fragment 30 in mind, according to which the "ordered universe (cosmos), which is the same for all, was not created by any one of the gods or of mankind, but . . . was ever and is and shall be ever-living," the natural world, or cosmos, is understood as a whole, which, in distinction from the one that originates in the mythical creation by a determined god or is a product of the human being, is *holon*, in other words, a whole that does not lack anything, that is without beginning or end, and, therefore, is "already qua cosmos *to theion*, that is, divine."[7]

Undoubtedly, in light of the contemporary natural sciences' seemingly endless progress at mastering nature and the earth, the Greek understanding of the physical cosmos as an ordered whole—even though its closed form has been a paralyzing obstacle to the development of the sciences in their modern shape, for which the Greeks laid the ground but did not create themselves—has a particular relevance in that it reminds us of the intrinsic limits that are set to the human effort at mastering that to which human beings themselves belong. Yet the thrust of Löwith's return to the ancients' conception of nature and the universe is not primarily directed against the modern sciences but against the world understood merely in human terms, more precisely, in terms of a temporality and historicity particular to human Dasein. If, as Gadamer has submitted, "no other Greek text seems to illustrate Löwith's intention as well as the pseudo-Aristotelian (Hellenistic-Stoic) work 'On the Cosmos,'" it is because the "'natural concept of world'" that he "uses against both modern historicism and modern science, is clearly of Stoic origin." Indeed, Löwith's reason for focusing on "the eternal cycle of nature, [is] to learn from it the equanimity that alone is appropriate to the minuteness of human life in the universe."[8] But the philosophical significance of this step back from the historical world of men to the natural world, which also dominates Löwith's entire critical debate with Heidegger's early and late thought, whose concept of the historicity of Dasein and of the history of Being, respectively, he characterizes as the epitome of historical and eschatological thinking—in Löwith's words, Heideggerian thought is an "absolutizing of history itself," as a result of which the natural world and the human being's reference to it (*Bezug zum All*) are completely obliterated—comes into view only, I hold, and can only be truly assessed, if it is seen within the phenomenological problematic of what constitutes the "life-world."[9]

Although Georg Simmel coined the term, *life-world* becomes a central philosophical concept only with Husserlian phenomenology and has since then been a persistent concern of all phenomenological thought. For Husserl, who in his early work also refers to it as the "natural world," the life-world is the whole of the natural, that is, of all the originary, intersubjective experiences—a world of pregiven evidences and manifold of validities which, because they are fixed and pregiven, no longer reflect their historical genesis—that constitute the prescientific attitude in and to the world, and which as such is the repressed foundation, as it were, of the sciences.[10] In his later work, particularly *The Crisis of European Sciences and Transcendental Phenomenology*, Husserl's aim is to relate the sciences back to this foundation, that is, to the practical concerns of the life-world, through which alone they could have become meaningful in the first place. From his own very early references to the life-world, it is clear that this theme is also a consistent preoccupation of Heideggerian thought. But since Heidegger's primary concern is the question of Being, the existential and hermeneutic analyses of the life-world, that is, of Dasein's fundamental characterization as Being-in-the-world, are conducted in primarily temporal and historicist terms. By holding, in "Heidegger: Thinker in a Destitute Time," that in order to understand the meaning of Being no analysis of Dasein is necessary, and that the truth of Being is not tied to the essence of the human being, Löwith takes issue not only with Heidegger's thought about the life-world but also with the overestimation of history and the historical world in Western Christian and post-Christian thought, of which, for him, Heidegger's thought represents the very climax. "Heidegger's essential-historical thinking," Löwith contends, is "an extreme consequence of historicism to the extent that, in a historiologically definable way, it thinks in an excessively historical manner," and, therefore, Heidegger, like all previous thinkers, misses the true nature of the life-world.[11] However personal Löwith's criticism of Heidegger may be, his assertion that from Heidegger's elaborations on the destining of Being it would seem that "universal Being as such and as a whole had a predilection for the Occident," and, furthermore, that his understanding of the essence of the human being as a historical essence is only one definite essence, one "among other possible essences that Heidegger ignores," shows that the true target of Löwith's criticism is not Heidegger alone, and not even Heidegger in particular.[12] In fact, as is obvious from Löwith's work on *Meaning in History* (*Weltgeschichte und Heilsgeschehen*), his target is the whole of Christian Europe and post-Christian Europe, which, from Hegel to Heidegger, moves "within the same modern eccentricity of a historicism with regard to the history of spirit and the history of Being," and which as such amounts to an oblivion of the natural world as the true life-world.[13] Löwith's return to the Greeks, that is, to their understanding of the physical cosmos, is a return to the lived world, to the life-world. But when Löwith argues that, notwithstanding Heidegger's emphasis on the Greeks in determining the life-world, the latter's "thinking is not an Eastern meditation nor a Greek beholding of Being as always the same, but instead is a historically conditioned Being-on-the-way that wills in the modern sense," it is also clear that he aims at a definition of the life-world as the natural world that not only reaches back to an understanding of Greek thought—one that is not mediated by Christian and modern conceptions of history—but that also takes non-European, that is, oriental modes of experiencing the natural world into account.[14]

Undoubtedly, as Habermas has observed, Löwith's reference to the living whole of the cosmos carries "a grand conservative sentiment."[15] Indeed, even though Löwith is certainly not the only phenomenologically trained thinker of the period to highlight nature and the importance of experience of nature for the life-world—Eugen Fink would be an example—his explicit aim of demystifying historicism, through a reflection, in Reinhard Koselleck's words, "on history towards a view of the world which precedes all history," inevitably gives his elaborations on the eternal laws of the cosmos an untimely and even anachronistic appearance.[16] In passing let me also point out that the importance that Löwith attributes to nature in trying to resist what he considers an inflated importance of historicism is somewhat questionable, since the opposition of nature and history itself is anything but self-evident. As he himself notes at one point, "the natural antithesis to nature would be not history, but art," that is, the artificial.[17] Hence, unless history is thought as fundamentally artificial—but then, is this not precisely, as Löwith has shown in *Meaning in History*, a conception that from Vico to Marx subtends modern philosophy of history and its notion of progress—is the confrontation of history with the eternal and cyclical laws of nature in order to unseat its priority in the European universe,not also an intrinsically "unnatural" enterprise? But let me return to the question of Löwith's recourse to a natural concept of world in what amounts to a clear provocation of our historically oriented way of understanding the world.[18] In spite of a number of ambiguities, this attempt at retrieving a natural view of the world, I hold, does not amount to a simple return to the ancient theory about the cosmos and nature. Although the Greek physical cosmos with its eternal laws is the starting point of Löwith's reflections on a natural concept of world, his understanding of this concept cannot simply be reduced to ancient cosmotheology. In his late work, *Gott, Mensch und Welt in der Metaphysik von Descartes bis zu Nietzsche*, he submits that "biblical anthropo-theology, i.e., the partnership of God and man, has become as foreign to us as the more humane cosmo-theology of the Greeks."[19] But as he also notes, "something so old and yet always so new as eternity cannot easily be revived again, even with the most modern techniques."[20] Some commentators have pointed out that Löwith has left his conception of a natural world quite vague. But, if this is the case, then it is because rather than being simply an anachronistic retrieval of a fully elaborated theory, Löwith's reaching back to the natural concept of the world is a function of his attempt to develop in the face of historical consciousness a conception of the life-world in tune with the beginnings of philosophy in Greece and whose grand object was nature. More precisely, if philosophy as it emerged in Greece has been tied to the thinking of the natural world, then what is at stake for our thinker is nothing less than a retrieval of philosophy itself for our times. The reconstruction of a natural concept of world, by means of which modern historical consciousness is to be lead back to "the true beginning of philosophy, the problem of nature," not only must take place by way of a detour through history, as Manfred Riedel (a Löwith student himself) has argued, it does not entail (which is certainly more problematic) "a departure from history, but the recovery of a dimension of knowledge, for which historical consciousness has no standard."[21] But even more important evidence that Löwith does not consider ancient Greek cosmotheology a fully sufficient response against the modern historicist conception of the world is to be found in the fact already pointed out that a full elaboration of the natural concept of world must also take non-European, that is, oriental forms of experiencing the world of nature into account.

At this point let me circle back to Löwith's biography and to the trajectory of his exile that brought him from Heidelberg to Rome, from Rome to Sendai, from Sendai to Hartford and New York, and that comes to a conclusion in Heidelberg—that is, an eastward trajectory, that forced him to circumnavigate the entire globe before returning to his point of departure. In his essay on Löwith, Habermas observes that while reading the latter's "artful autobiography" in his inaugural address before the Heidelberg Academy of Sciences, he became "fascinated by the quiet logic of this philosophical career. How was it possible that a destiny so outwardly driven about by political catastrophes—the fate of one who emigrated via Rome to Tokyo, from the East to the West, and from the United States to Germany—could have made inwardly possible not only the identity of the person, not only the continuity of doing philosophy at all; that in such a shell early seeds eventually bore the fruit of developed thought in an almost cyclically maturing evolution?"[22] In what follows I will seek to respond to some of Habermas's questions regarding Löwith's almost cyclical maturing evolution by tying the latter's reflections on the life-world to one of, if not the most experientially decisive stops on his departure from Germany, namely, the five years that he spent at the Tohoku University in Sendai where, thanks to a recommendation by Kuki Shuzo, he was offered a position in 1936 when, under the pressure of national socialist foreign propaganda, his position in Rome became insecure. In "Curriculum Vitae," Löwith remarks that he "did not remain untouched by the experience of the no longer Far East, but [that, on the contrary, he] obtained an unforgettable impression of the country and its people, its subtle civilization and the great Buddhist art."[23] The same cannot be said, I think, of his subsequent sojourn in the United States, where Paul Tillich and Rheinhold Niebuhr helped him obtain a position in 1941 at the theological seminary at Hartford, Massachusetts, before he was appointed to the New School in 1949, even though during his stay at the Protestant seminary the contracted obligation to teach the early fathers nurtured in him the plan to write his famous study on the *Meaning in History*. Certainly, Löwith's experience of Japan did not prevent him from severely criticizing, as we will see, certain aspects of Japanese mentality. Moreover, toward the end of his stay he had become intellectually isolated to such a degree that he looked forward to moving to the United States, even though, as Gadamer remarks, the country that received him so hospitably was also "the one that could the least in a natural fashion meet his own way of being [*das seinem Wesen der Sache nach am wenigsten auf natürliche Weise entgegenkommen konnte*]."[24] In many ways one could say that his long sojourn in the US was only a stay in transit. Several entries in his posthumously published *Von Rom nach Sendai, von Japan nach Amerika: Reisetagebuch 1936 und 1941* about the trip from San Francisco—"S. Francisco is still half European [*noch halb Europa*]"—to Chicago characterize his experience of America in such a manner. He writes: "On the way: summer resorts, they all look like gas stations," or, "The places, none of which are towns, but rather gas stations," that is, places that one only passes through.[25] In "Curriculum Vitae," he also observes that, while "it was quite impossible to avoid some kind of 'adjustment to the American way of life' if one wanted to be accepted"—as a German Jew, for example, although converted to Protestantism, he was required to teach Protestant theology in America—"in Japan [by contrast] nobody expect[ed] a foreigner to adapt and, therefore, to become Easternized."[26] Since the Japanese wanted "to study the European cast of mind from the European," in contrast to America, which thinks of itself as having surpassed the old Europe, Löwith could even teach in his own native language at Sendai.[27] But in addition to the fact that, as Gadamer noted, Japan provided Löwith with "a frame that was especially adequate to the composed fatalism of his nature, but also to his high artistic sensibility and his need for a dignified distance with respect to human beings and the world," Japan became important for him in a crucial way for still another reason.²⁸ Indeed, his privileged situation at the Imperial University of Sendai gave him the freedom not only to experience Japan in all its difference from Europe but also, as he remarks in "Unzulängliche Bemerkungen zum Unterschied von Orient und Okzident" (1960), as, above all, an other that gave him the chance to redelimit, or redefine, himself in relation to this other, in a way not unlike the one by which "the Greeks became aware of themselves as Greeks as they became conscious of their difference with respect to [*von und zu*] the 'barbarians.'" What is at stake in his experience of Japan, which provides him with the opportunity to "distinguish himself from himself [*Selbstunterscheidung*], or of a 'critique' of himself," that is, of himself as a European, is nothing less than a rediscovery of what allowed the Greeks to build their identity on a relation to others and, in the same breath, of what, in principle, constitutes the essence of Europe insofar as its origin lies in Greece.²⁹ Shortly after his arrival in the United States, Löwith writes that "some years in the Far East are almost indispensable for a critical, i.e., discriminating understanding of ourselves."³⁰ In any case, once his experience in Japan had made it possible for him to rethink "old Europe," America, which boasted of having left old Europe behind, could only become a place in transit before Löwith's final return to the old country.

After having invoked the two thousand years of European history that he had constantly before his eyes in Rome, Löwith writes in the first entry in his diary about his departure from Rome for Japan: "But now everything is supposed to become different—in the 'Far East,' whose remoteness will perhaps bring 'Europe' closer again to oneself [dessen Ferne einem 'Europa' vielleicht erst wieder nahebringt]."³¹ From the beginning, Löwith's journey eastward is linked to a hope that the remoteness and foreignness of the East will make him rediscover what is closest to him. On the boat he learns that upon arrival in Sendai he is to immediately give an inaugural address at the university, and Löwith files a telegram in return with the title of his lecture: "Die Idee von Europa in der deutschen Philosophie der Geschichte." The additional remark that "Hegel's Philosophy of History in the luggage compartment is what will save him," shows that while the idea of Europe that he will seek to retrieve in his stay in the Far East may certainly have to be uncoupled from the philosophy of history as it culminated in Hegel's thought, Löwith's openness to the East in view of recapturing the idea of Europe remains nonetheless modeled, at least up to a point, after the Hegelian dialectic of self and other.³² Incidentally, featured among the other books that Löwith took with him in 1936 to go to Japan was Franz Rosenzweig's *Letters*. In his essay from 1942–43, "M. Heidegger and F. Rosenzweig: A Postscript to *Being and Time*," Löwith remarks after having read these letters in 1939, "The impression Rosenzweig's personality made upon me was so strong that I immediately procured also his principal work in philosophy, *The Star of Redemption*, and his collected essays, *The Shorter Writings*. In part, my interest was aroused by the striking similarity between Rosenzweig's philosophical starting point and that of my own teacher, Heidegger."[33] But the essay is also intended to show that the similarity of both Heidegger's and Rosenzweig's starting point—what Hermann Cohen had labeled "the new thinking of our times," a thinking that starts out with the facticity of one's own Dasein in a clear and systematic opposition to German Idealist thought—did not prevent both thinkers from developing their thoughts in thoroughly opposite directions. If I briefly linger on the difference between both thinkers that points to another aspect of Löwith's interest in Rosenzweig, it is because the problematic in question is not unrelated to what I will construe in the following as his experience of nature in pagan Japan. He writes that whereas "Heidegger destroyed the Greek and Christian tradition that had been accepted up to the time of Hegel and for which true Being is always existent and everlasting" for the benefit of finite time, "Rosenzweig was able to affirm the Star of David as the eternal truth within the limits of time, from what was a more fortunate position due *his* factical inheritance, his Jewry and his conscious return to it."[34] Against Heidegger's "concept of 'worldliness' and 'world-time' which are implicitly nourished by the Christian notion of '*saeculum*' that Heidegger's philosophy attempts to secularize, but in vain," and which is rooted in the latter's double inability "to restore the natural philosophy of the ancients [and] to reject the Christian distinction between the born and the re-born man, authentic and inauthentic Dasein," the religious Jewish thinker paradoxically offers Löwith a way to revalue the tenets of the pagan world.[35] Indeed, even though in the first volume of *The Star of Redemption* it is argued that "the truth of the pagan world is . . . an enduring truth," it is, however, "unrevealing," and "is 'everlasting' only as an 'element,'" and that, furthermore, "the place of the ancient cosmical order is taken over by the new order of creation in which man and the world belong together only as a creation of God," Rosenzweig succeeds in restoring the idea of the formative unity of the cosmos that "has been destroyed since the appearance of Christianity and Judaism in world history."[36] In short, what Rosenzweig offers Löwith against the radical historicism of Heidegger is a way to do justice to the principles of the eternal order constitutive of the Greek pagan view of the world, which became of crucial importance for his experience of Japan, and, subsequently, his understanding of the essence of Europe, even though for Rosenzweig these principles in the end became sublated in the higher order of Jewish religious thought.[37]

Even though Löwith and his wife "soon felt at home" in Sendai, unaware at first of their "isolation . . . and the physical strain of this transplantation," Löwith's fascination with things Japanese was not of the order of the "ill-fated love" for the East as professed by, for example, Lafcadio Hearn.[38] Also, when he refers to the East, or Orient, as opposed to the West, or of Asia in relation to the concept of Europe, which "develops not from out of itself but rather from out of its essential contrast to Asia," Löwith fully acknowledges that Japan is not *the* Orient, or *the* East.[39] In the essay "Unzulängliche Bermerkungen zum Unterschied von Orient und Okzident," he writes that "it is impossible to speak about *the* East and *the* West since the differences between India, China, and Japan are more radical than those that exist between Spain, France, and England, and than those of the entirety of all European countries when compared with America."[40] But if, in the essay in question, Löwith singles out the Orient as the European encounters it in modern Japan, it is for the simple reason that thanks to his forced emigration and five years of teaching at a Japanese university, he has a firsthand knowledge of Japan. Since the aim of his reflections on the otherness of the East, as he encountered it in Japan, is to retrieve a notion of Europe distinct from the "new Europe" that he had to leave behind, it should also be noted that, according to Löwith, we lack "all the presuppositions to conceptualize in a philosophical way" the "obvious differences" that one experiences in Japan, "which, for the foreigner, is at first a topsy-turvy world [*verkehrte Welt*] that puts what is proper to oneself and habitual for a long time, on its head." This difficulty of conceptualizing what is other about Japan manifests itself precisely in the only way we have at first to assess the difference in question, namely to consider Japanese customs, actions, and reactions as "just antipodal to ours."[41] But the difficulty reaches deeper since "the will to grasp conceptually is as such something specifically Western, and even of Hegelian origin," as Löwith holds. "It is the 'work' of the 'concept.'"[42] Japanese thinking itself is not primarily conceptual. If Zen is "the intellectual root of the Japanese way of thinking," and each transitory event is understood sub specie aeternitas, that is, as an "*absolute* reality," then all "images, words, concepts are never more than pointers" to what is grasped "by momentary intuition, in a sudden enlightenment, without reason or analysis."[43] Hence all efforts to account for the difference between Europe and Japan encounter severe problems. This predicament is further complicated by the fact that, as Löwith suggests in the "Afterword to the Japanese Reader" of the Japanese translation of his essay "European Nihilism: Reflections on the European War," the Japanese's self-infatuation, that is, their self-love and unwillingness to engage in self-criticism, which alone allows one to see what is proper to oneself and distinct from others, in turn inhibits them from conceptualizing their own culture. He writes that compared to the Chinese ideal of a correspondence of their culture to the order of the universe, the Platonic Eros, the Christian supramundane faith, or the European will, and especially the will to know, Japanese culture "has no definable principle at all, and lives from an undetermined fundamental attunement [*Grundstimmung*] that can only be expressed through paradoxes."[44] However, this inability that the foreigner experiences in seeking to conceptualize the differences between the Orient as he or she encounters it in Japan concerns primarily "the obvious differences" on which Löwith expands in truly remarkable and beautiful descriptions. One such example, among many, is his observation that "understanding language in Japan does not appear to take place directly through the hearing of the articulated word, but through the presentification of the Chinese-Japanese characters of writing." Indeed, as Löwith remarks, it is not unusual that "in conversation the Japanese make an imprecise or unequivocal word clear to their listeners not by rendering it more precise, but by drawing in painterly fashion the respective ideogram with their fingers in their air or on a table surface."[45] By contrast, the difficulty of conceptualizing in a philosophical way what is distinct about Japan does not bear, it would seem, on that which makes Löwith feel at home in Japan, that is, that aspect of the Orient in Japan that, though less obvious, serves to bring Europe close to him again.

The stop at Hong Kong during which, on his way to Sendai, Löwith visits a Shinto shrine needs to be briefly mentioned here because what he witnesses on this occasion foreshadows what becomes the core of his experience of the Japanese Orient. In his diary he confides his surprise of getting, for the first time, an idea of what a "pagan" temple, in general, and a holy grove that stands in harmony with the powers of nature are like. He writes: "In view of these very popular and still used temples one gets a much more clear representation of what a pagan center of cult worship is than from the pale remainders of the Greek temples in Sicily and Athens." Rather than a religion and a faith in the Christian sense, Shintoism, he adds, must, on the contrary, "most likely be understood from the Greek and Roman cults."[46] And indeed, the unforgettable impression that Japan makes on Löwith is to a large part due to the similarities that he discovers between classical Greece and the Orient as he experiences it in Japan. Whereas Europe, even when anti-Christian, is Christian to the point that its Greek origin is covered over, "paganism [in Japan] is still a living power, as fresh and genuine as before Christ," and "the family shrine in every household is a perpetual reminder of the religious customs and cults of the Greeks and the Romans."[47] This similarity between Japanese and Greek paganism concerns, above all, the similar ways in which both the Orient and Greece relate to the natural world, and the way they experience history. One passage, among many others, in which Löwith describes the Greeks' stance on these issues must suffice here: "The Greeks were deeply impressed by the visible order and the beauty of the universe, and the natural law of becoming and disintegrating determined also their vision of the historical world. In the eyes of the Greeks that which is always the same and everlasting, as it appears year after year in the 'revolution' of the heavenly bodies, manifested a deeper truth and aroused a higher interest than any radical historical change."[48] Something similar is felt in Japan, Löwith contends, and as a consequence, the experience of the Japanese's relation to nature provides him, for the first time, with an opportunity to understand what the Greeks meant by *physis* and *cosmos*, and thus also to gauge, as we will see, another sense in which Greece is the origin of Europe. Indeed, after acknowledging in "Curriculum Vitae" that "what appeals to the European person [in Japan] is not the advancing modernization of the old Japan, of course, but rather the continuation of the Oriental tradition and the native Shintoistic paganism." He adds, "In the face of the popular consecration of all natural and everyday things—the sun and the moon, growth and decay, the seasons, the trees, the mountains, rivers and stones, fertility and nourishment, rice planting and housebuilding, the ancestors and the Imperial House—I have for the first time understood something about the religious paganism and political religion of the Greeks and Romans."[49] This point is taken a step further in the opening lines of "Unzulängliche Bemerkungen," where it is noted that Old Chinese thought, for which "the divine is the way [*der Gang*] (Tao) of the heavens (T'ien), in distinction from the earth, and according to which the heavens and the earth (T'ien-ti) are seen as the origin of all creatures, and the earth as the habitat of earthly men," is similar to Greek thought, which conceives of "the right and just order of the human world in accordance with the unswerving order of the world of the heavens," in short, the physical cosmos.[50] Furthermore, if for the Japanese, human and historical catastrophes are experienced in the same way as natural cataclysms, this is a sign that "Oriental thinking does not know the contrast between nature and history."[51] Neither has the natural world been historically appropriated in the Orient, nor has history itself gained here an independence from nature, one that testifies to the hubristic overestimation of what is human. Thereby Japan resembles classical Greece as well, which "never fancied that history has a purposeful and meaningful orientation toward a future fulfillment," in contrast to what Jews and Christians, including post-Christians, believe.[52] As Löwith submits: "Classical antiquity and the Orient have never asked for the meaning of world history."[53]

In exile from Europe and on a journey eastward, in Japan, that is, in a culture that remains thoroughly foreign in spite of all its appropriation of European modernity, Löwith experiences a relation to nature and history that allows him to retrieve a sense of the Greek understanding of the cosmos that is no longer adumbrated by Christianity.[54] Only in exile, in a thoroughly foreign land, is he capable of recovering a meaning of Greece, and hence of Europe, that had not dawned on him in Europe, and which, because of the predominance of the sciences and of historicism (philosophy of history), could not be experienced there at all.[55] But if, as Löwith remarks in a footnote in "Unzulängliche Betrachtungen," "the Greek cosmopolitics and its closeness to the Oriental has barely been acknowledged, it is [also] because Greek philosophy has always only been considered as the origin of European philosophy and not also as a transformation of Oriental tradition."[56] In other words, even though exposure to the Japanese Orient made it possible for Löwith to grasp a dimension of Greek thought of which he had not been aware before, this also means that in spite of all the similarities between the East and the West, significant differences exist between both precisely because of the transformation that the Oriental tradition itself undergoes in Greek philosophical thought. In spite of all the resemblances between them, the Greek conception of the cosmos and its paganism are not exactly the same as the relation to nature and the pagan cults that Löwith witnesses in the Orient. The difference consists in the fact that Greek cosmotheology is something that has been appropriated by the

Greeks from the East and has, in the process of this appropriation, been transformed.

What Löwith brings home from the Orient's relation to nature and history in Japan is only what the Greeks inherited from the Orient, and which they subsequently transformed into something specifically Greek. In "Afterword to the Japanese Reader," in the context of a discussion of Japanese self-love, the Greeks' very ability to simultaneously be open to what is foreign and be capable of transforming it, is shown to be the hallmark of ancient Greece. In other words, what Löwith discovers in Japan is not so much the pagan view of nature and the world that the Orient shares with Greece, than the Greeks' ability to relate to, and appropriate in a transformative manner, what is other and foreign. Such an ability to relate to what is foreign is what is specific about Greece and represents the true heritage that it bequeathed to Europe, and with which "the new Europe," from which Löwith had to flee, has to be confronted.

The following observations on the Japanese's failure to live up to what they took over from European civilization may sound a bit condescending and politically incorrect today, but it should be kept in mind that from the Meiji period on, Japan has been involved in the attempt, ordered by an imperial decree, to Europeanize itself, and as a result a critique of such Europeanization in the name of what is specifically European is even called for by this Japanese effort itself. But in spite of this failure, the Japanese's deliberate willingness to Westernize, that is, to open themselves to foreign influence, is, for Löwith, clearly something that Japan shares again with Greece. And this gives Japan a distinct mark in Löwith's eyes, even though its failure to truly appropriate what is Western, and thus foreign, will lead him onto the path of valorizing the Greek way of relating to what is other, particularly the Orient, over the Oriental mode of encountering otherness. Anyhow, distinct from the Greeks' reception of the Oriental tradition, the Japanese, although they have taken over a great deal of Western civilization—at least its "material civilization," as Löwith contends, as opposed to China, which has been open to the "religious, scholarly, and moral foundation" of European culture—they have appropriated European civilization in only such a way that it did not involve any self-alienation, or distancing oneself from oneself.[57] Unaware of the fact that within the Kyoto School, as Bret W. Davis has shown, at least Kitaro Nishida had also advanced "an internal principle of self-negation [as] a condition for becoming open to other cultures and thus a participant in world history," which, no doubt, is "a partial analogue" to self-alienation, Löwith denies this ability of distancing oneself from oneself to the Japanese mentality.[58] Self-alienation, for Löwith, is a positive condition for an encounter of the other and the foreign because it opens up the critical relation to oneself, without which no encounter worth its name is conceivable. Furthermore, because of the lack of self-alienation in the Japanese's reception of Europe and the West, that which is taken over is not taken over *as* something other, or foreign—a reception that would have also required a transformation—the implication being that no genuine exposure to, and no genuine challenge by, the otherness of the European civilization took place in Japan. Indeed, without such exposure to the other *as* other, and its subsequent transformation, no reception worth its name is possible. Only on the condition that the other be encountered *as* other can the difference between him and oneself come into view, and only on the basis of this can a comparison be made and hence a critical self-distinction become possible. Löwith writes: "European spirit and the history without which it would not be what it is, were not taken over because they cannot be taken over, unless by means of an appropriation that intensively transforms them."[59] In short, even though a thinker such as Nishida had shown that without an analogue of self-alienation no encounter with another is possible, Löwith's additional emphasis on the subsequent appropriation of the foreign seems to confirm his assessment of the Japanese's self-centeredness. Davis writes, "whereas Nishida had emphasized self-negation and becoming 'free from oneself' as an opening to dialogue with others and to the indigestible alterity of the other in the depths of the non-substantial self, for Hegel and Löwith such 'self-alienation' is ultimately a step on the way to 'transforming the foreign into something of one's own' so that one can come back to an expanded 'freedom for oneself.'"[60] Indeed, such appropriation of the foreign is for Löwith the very criterion for an exposure to the other, or foreign, to have taken place. Appropriation is an index of how, rather than having been left indifferent by the other, or foreign, the encounter has profoundly affected oneself; for even when made into one's own, the appropriated foreign marks within oneself an infraction of otherness in oneself. What Löwith diagnoses in 1940, that is, in the wake of a resurgence of nationalism in Japan, as a "*renunciation of Europe*" in order "to be oneself again, i.e. purely Japanese," is based, first and foremost, on a "reflection on one's own essence and one's own task [that is, on] an observance of European counsel."[61] But, according to Löwith, even this desire to be oneself taken over from Europe is inhibited from the start by the Japanese "naïve trust in their own superiority," that is, their self-love hampers the development of a genuine identity.[62] By excluding the possibility of self-criticism, self-love prevents the formation of genuine selfhood, which can only come into being through a distancing of oneself from oneself, becoming other to oneself, before appropriating what is other and transforming it in such a way as to shape an identity of one's own, an identity that is distinct, in difference, from the other as an other insofar as it relates to the other *as* other. Let me then focus a bit more intensively on what, by contrast to the Japanese, the Greeks accomplished.

According to Löwith, who closely follows the Hegelian model of the processual relation of self and other (though it is taken out of context, and hence not simply Hegelian), according to which a self is with itself only by being free in the other, "the Greeks took a world whose roots were foreign, and made it into their home. Of course they received the substantial beginnings of their religion, education, and social cohesion more or less from Asia, Syria, and Egypt; but they wiped out, transformed, processed, and changed what was foreign in this origin, they made something different out of it, to such an extent that what they, like us [Europeans] value, acknowledge, and love in it is precisely what is essentially their own."[63] What sets the Greeks apart from the high cultures of the ancient Orient where "there was knowledge long before the Greeks" arrived, is that in receiving and transforming what they encountered from the Orient, they demonstrated the ability of "free emergence from out of oneself, and the consequent power of appropriation which proceeds from a free attitude toward oneself and the world," in other words, from a critical attitude to oneself.[64] As the following statement shows, this freedom of self-alienation, of distancing oneself from oneself—at once the possibility of self-critique and of the encounter of the other *as* other—and the subsequent recognition of oneself in the other, that is, the ability of "coming from the other back to oneself," appropriating what is other in the other, so as to be, as Hegel puts it, with oneself in being-other, this is the specificity of Greece, and implicitly also the foundation of Europe. Löwith avers: "Only the Greeks, as the first-born Europeans, have panoramic eyes, as Burckhardt calls it, i.e., the objective, concrete view of the world and oneself that can make comparisons and distinctions and that recognizes oneself in the Others."[65]

In exile in Sendai, the discovery of ancient Japan with its sensitivity to nature and disinterest in history as a manmade order with its own autonomous laws, is at first a rediscovery of a similar concern in ancient

Greece. This rediscovery leads in turn to a conceptualization of the way Greece relates to otherness and the foreign, which is not only entirely different from the Japanese way of appropriating what is foreign but which also leads Löwith to reconceive Europe in terms of this very specific Greek heritage. This new way of thinking about the Greek essence of Europe ultimately programs his continuing eastward trajectory until he finally reaches the West again.[66] Toward the end of his "Afterword to the Japanese Reader," Löwith tells his reader that the "new Europe," which has become an annihilating civilization, spreading its violent progress over the entire earth, "is not the Europe of which I wrote, in which I take part as a German, and which I consider is valuable to disseminate through writing and teaching."[67] The Europe of which he has been speaking is one that has been forgotten in the Christianization of Europe and the subsequent secularization of the history of salvation into a faith in progress, and the concomitant lack of a consideration of nature in all its naturalness that makes its subservience to exploitation for human purposes possible.[68] By contrast, the Europe that Löwith has been thinking and writing about is a Europe that circles back to the firstborn Europeans that are the Greeks.

As we have suggested, on his eastward journey Löwith discovers in Japan a mode of contemplation of nature and a disinterest in history that not only seems to resemble similar attitudes in ancient Greece but that also, by allowing him to understand for the first time something essential about Greece as the beginning of Europe, will finally orient his further circumnavigation of the globe until, finally, it brings him back to Heidelberg. This leads me to the question about the difference between the ancient spirit of Japan and that of Greece as regards nature and history. Undoubtedly, the Japanese relation to nature and history only reminds Löwith of the Greeks' conception of the cosmos and makes it possible for him to understand in greater depth the extent to which this conception is the very birth of a certain Europe. But what is it precisely that distinguishes the Greek orderly cosmos with its harmony and stability from ancient Japanese thought regarding the cyclical nature of the natural world? Let us remind ourselves of Löwith's contention that the Greeks received the elements of their cosmology as something other from the Orient and that they transformed it in such a way as to be with themselves in this foreign heritage, by being themselves in being-other. This transformation and appropriation of what is other, which presupposes a critical self-alienation, this freedom is what makes all the difference and makes Greece into the beginning of Europe.

At this juncture a closer look at the striking difference between Japan and the West already alluded to is warranted, namely, the Japanese's nonconceptual way of thinking as opposed to the specifically Western will to grasp everything conceptually. This difference, which I would tend to categorize as one among what Löwith had termed "obvious differences," is one that makes it especially difficult for a foreigner to philosophically fathom the Japanese mentality for which "images, words, concepts, and doctrines are never more than pointers."[69] The same is valid of Japanese "philosophy": it does not "rely on forms at all," and is, in fact, as Löwith, while citing D. T. Suzuki and Kitaro Nishida, stresses, a "philosophy without concepts."[70] In other words, Japanese philosophy does not seek to delimit things and realities within the clear outlines in which they shine forth, and thus skirts clear and distinct definition. Löwith avers, "The characteristic symbol of true enlightenment in Japanese philosophy and poetry is not the blinding and burning light of the sun but the calm and impersonal beam of the moon, which shines without affecting us."[71] The difference with Greek thought, which is a philosophy of light within which the clear-cut shapes or forms of things show themselves, could not be more marked: in the light of the moon nothing acquires a sharp and definite shape, and everything changes at every moment although it is, at the same time, experienced as yet always the same. It is, therefore, also not insignificant to note that according to Löwith "the Japanese have today [1943] only one original thinker, Nishida, who is comparable to any of the living philosophers of the West in depth of thought and subtlety. Yet he is by no means Western," since "even this man's work is no more than an adaptation of Western methodology, the use of it for a logical clarification of the fundamental Japanese intuitions about the world."[72] Now let us bear in mind that what interested Löwith about Japanese thought and poetry is the importance that the experience of nature represents for them, and compared to which all change pales in importance with respect to what remains everlasting and the same. The Japanese's prime concern with nature in both their philosophy and art reminds Löwith of early Greek philosophical thought, which was also primarily a philosophy of nature. Yet as we have seen, contrary to the Oriental "philosophical" take on nature, Greek philosophy proceeds conceptually. Hence, what Löwith discovers, or rediscovers, by way of his experience of the Japanese relation to nature and its dismissal of history, is thus nothing less than philosophy itself insofar as philosophy, for him, is primarily philosophy of nature, and so, in a rigorous sense, only if it also proceeds conceptually.

At the end of "Curriculum Vitae," Löwith notes that the first question, the one with which Greek philosophy began, is the question about "the *world as such*, within which we find the human being and its history." Of the whole of nature, that is, the cosmos, Heraclitus says in "Peri kosmou," or "Of the World," that "it is always 'the same' . . . 'for everything and everyone' (Fragment 30), not created by a special God or by any human being."[73] Philosophy begins with the inquiry into this natural world, a world that is the life-world of man and within which we find the human being and its history, and philosophy is philosophy in a strict sense only as the contemplation of the everlasting order of this world. With reference to Marx, Löwith writes: "He who wants to 'change' the world—who wants it to be different from what it is—has not yet started to philosophize, and mistakes the world for world *history*, and that for a human creation."[74] By contrast, according to ancient, that is, Greek wisdom, "the end of man [is] to contemplate the natural universe of heaven and earth, which is free of purpose."[75] It is interesting to see that when Löwith reflects on what has happened to our perception of nature, particularly in our scientifically organized world, he stresses that "naturalness is no longer the standard of nature."[76] In "Curriculum Vitae," it is stated that "the naturalness of nature, physis, has been lost through modern physics."[77] In other words, the ancient contemplation of nature is characterized by a relation to nature in which nature is experienced *as* nature. Let us also remind ourselves that the cosmos, with its logos, that is, the ordered natural world as the whole of what is, is something that "is ever complete and entirely independent, and [as such] also the precondition for all dependent existences" such as human beings.[78] Moving and existing of its own accord, the natural world is wholly other than the fleeting whole of the human world. Greek contemplation of the natural world as such, aware of it *as* the cosmos, *as* physis, is not only philosophical but also is conceptual, and this conceptual take on nature, which is also an appropriation of it in all its otherness, is what distinguishes the Greek relation to the natural world, to "the world as such, which is the One and whole of what is that exists by and from itself [*welche das Eine und Ganze des von Natur aus Seienden ist*]," from the Japanese "conception" of the life-world.[79] The philosophical attitude as a relation to the order of nature in which this order is understood *as* cosmos, *as* an orderly whole, is predicated on a critical self-distancing of the human being that allows for a contemplation of this order in all its otherness, as other than the passing concerns of humans within the historical world, but that also makes it possible for human beings to be, as Hegel put it, with themselves precisely in being-other. As Löwith remarks in "Curriculum Vitae," in returning to Heidelberg from Japan where he realized for the first time what Greece is all about and in what sense it is the beginning of Europe, "the 'life history' of my thinking thus seems to be coming to a logically consistent conclusion and, by detour, back to the true philosophical beginnings."[80]

Notes

1. Karl Löwith, *My Life in Germany Before and After 1933: A Report*, trans. E. King (Urbana: University of Illinois Press, 1994), 158.
2. Löwith, *My Life in Germany*, 159.
3. Löwith, *My Life in Germany*, 158–159.
4. Löwith, *My Life in Germany*, 27.
5. Hannah Arendt, *The Human Condition* (Chicago: University of Chicago Press, 1958), 296.
6. Löwith, *My Life in Germany*, 166 (translation modified). As Löwith points out, it is Nietzsche who was the first to seek such a return to the Greek understanding of the whole of what is, but Nietzsche, he also argues, remains stuck in historicism.
7. Kathleen Freeman, *Ancilla to the Pre-Socratic Philosophers* (Cambridge, MA: Harvard University Press, 1983), 26; Karl Löwith, "Das Verhältnis von Gott, Mensch und Welt in der Metaphysik von Descartes und Kant," in *Sitzungsberichte der Heidelberger Akademie der Wissenschaften* (Heidelberg: Carl Winter, 1964), 6.
8. Hans-Georg Gadamer, "Hermeneutics and Historicism," in *Truth and Method*, 2nd ed, trans. J. Weinsheimer and D. G. Marshall (New York: Continuum, 1995), 532.
9. Karl Löwith, *Nature, History, and Existentialism and Other Essays in the Philosophy of History*, ed. A. Levison (Evanston, IL: Northwestern University Press, 1966), 18.
10. In contrast to the modern, that is, Copernican understanding of the world, the earth in the originary experience of the life-world is not round and does not move. As the ground for everything that moves, the earth, according to this immediate and intuitive (*anschaulich*) representation, is flat. See Edmund Husserl, "Grundlegende Untersuchungen zum phänomenoligschen Ursprung der Räumlichkeit der Natur," in *Philosophical Essays: In Memory of Edmund Husserl*, ed. M. Farber (New York: Greenwood, 1968), 307–325). Even though there is a definite tension between the scientific view of the earth and the view of the life-world, Husserl also admits elsewhere that the sciences transform the way the life-world is experienced. In any event, Löwith's rediscovery of the life-world on his eastward trajectory presupposes the very roundness of the earth.
11. Karl Löwith, "Heidegger: Thinker in a Destitute Time," in *Martin Heidegger and European Nihilism*, ed. R. Wolin, trans. G. Steiner (New York: Columbia University Press, 1995), 57, 93. In the face of this criticism, even Habermas, who certainly cannot be accused of having much sympathy for Heidegger, felt compelled to defend him against Löwith's unfair treatment of his former teacher.
12. Löwith, "Heidegger: Thinker in a Destitute Time," 72.
13. Löwith, "Heidegger: Thinker in a Destitute Time," 71.

14. Löwith, "Heidegger: Thinker in a Destitute Time," 70. Heidegger's call on the Greeks to think the life-world as an intersubjective world of Dasein is most explicit in his early lectures on Aristotle's rhetoric (1924) in Marburg, which Löwith must have attended.

15. Jürgen Habermas, *Philosophical-Political Profiles*, trans. F. G. Lawrence (Cambridge, MA: MIT Press), 82.

16. Reinhardt Kosellek, "Foreword," *My Life in Germany*, by Karl Löwith, xiii

17. Löwith, *Nature, History, and Existentialism*, 17.

18. Although initially Löwith's interest in the natural world is rooted in his discovery, or rediscovery, of the Greeks, his reflections on the one physical world are crowned, as it were, in his later works by his discovery (or rediscovery?) of Spinoza, who, as he observes, "is unique in his kind because he took a position outside the anthropo-theological tradition of the Bible, and therewith recovered a natural understanding of man and world." Karl Löwith, *Gott, Mensch und Welt in der Metaphysik von Descartes bis zu Nietzsche* (Göttingen: Vandenhoeck & Ruprecht, 1967), 206. However, it is also clear from this work that Spinoza's radical criticism of the notion of purpose—and with it of the biblical conception of creation, according to which the world has only been created for the benefit of man and is thus "nothing in itself, and even less the One, the Whole, and the Perfect" (222), which Spinoza's metaphysics unconditionally affirmed—comes only to fruition in Nietzsche. In fact, Nietzsche is overall the most likely source of inspiration to which Löwith's concern with the natural world must be retraced. For an overarching look at the importance of Nietzsche in Löwith's thought, see Wiebrecht Ries, *Karl Löwith* (Stuttgart: J. B. Metzlersche, 1992), 11–12.

19. Löwith, *Gott, Mensch und Welt*, 250

20. Löwith, *Gott, Mensch und Welt*, 78.

21. Manfred Riedel, "Karl Löwiths philosophischer Weg," in *Heidelberger Jahrbucher* 14 (1970): 132.

22. Habermas, *Philosophical-Political Profiles*, 95.

23. Löwith, *My Life in Germany*, 162

24. Hans-Georg Gadamer, "Karl Löwith zum 70. Geburstag," in *Natur und Geschichte. Karl Löwith zum 70. Geburstag*, eds. H. Braun and M. Riedel, Stuttgart: Kohlhammer 1967, 456. See also, Adolf Muschg, "Meine Japanreise mit Löwith," in Karl Löwith, *Von Rom nach Sendai, Von Japan nach Amerika: Reisetagebuch 1936 und 1941*, eds. K. Stichweh and U. Von Bülow, Marbach: Deutsche Schillergesellschaft, 2001, 111–155.

25. Löwith, *Von Rom nach Sendai*, 105–106.

26. Löwith, *My Life in Germany*, 163.

27. Löwith, *My Life in Germany*, 163.

28. Gadamer, "Karl Löwith zum 70. Geburstag," 456.

29. Karl Löwith, "Unzulängliche Bemerkungen zum Unterschied von Orient und Okzident," in *Die Gegenwart der Griechen im neueren Denken. Festschrift fur Hans-Georg Gadamer*, eds. D. Henrich, W. Schulz, K. H. Volkmann-Schluck (Tübingen: J.C.B. Mohr, 1960), 142.

30. Karl Löwith, "Japan's Westernization and Moral Foundation," in *Sämtliche Schriften* (Stuttgart: J. B. Metzler, 1983), 2:541.

31. Löwith, *Von Rom nach Sendai*, 8. A bit later in the diary he adds that "he goes with Ada to a foreign country in order to become, amidst a truly foreign race, a 'German' again, while oneself is slandered and defamed by the 'compatriots (Volksgenossen)' of one's own country" (13).

32. Löwith, *Von Rom nach Sendai*, 53.
33. Löwith, *Nature, History, and Existentialism*, 52.
34. Löwith, *Nature, History, and Existentialism*, 76.
35. Löwith, *Nature, History, and Existentialism*, 63.
36. Löwith, *Nature, History, and Existentialism*, 63–64.
37. This leads me to venturing the following question: Could it be that "the natural world" in Löwith is a secularized conception of what Rosenzweig construed as the ontological uniqueness of the meta-historical temporality of the Jewish people, one that takes them squarely out of the flux of history? In Peter Eli Gordon's words, according to Rosenzweig, the Jewish people, by observing a temporal law that "allows them to pull back from any attachment to their surroundings," enjoy, in distinction from all other people who, in order to be eventually redeemed, must progress through history, "redemption as a present experience." Peter Eli Gordon, "Rosenzweig Redux: The Reception of German-Jewish Thought," *Jewish Social Studies* 8, no. 1 (2001): 1–57.
38. Löwith, "*My Life in Germany*," 117; Löwith, *Martin Heidegger and European Nihilism*, 175.
39. Löwith, "European Nihilism: Reflections on the Spiritual and Historical Background of the European War," in *Martin Heidegger and European Nihilism*, ed. R. Wolin, trans. G. Steiner (New York: Columbia University Press, 1995), 173.
40. Löwith, "Unzulängliche Bemerkungen," 148.
41. Löwith, "Japan's Westernization and Moral Foundation," 541.
42. Löwith, "Unzulängliche Bemerkungen," 148–149.
43. Karl Löwith, "The Japanese Mind: A Picture of the Mentality That We Must Understand if We Are to Conquer," in *Sämtliche Schriften* (Stuttgart: J. B. Metzler, 1983), 2:562, 564–565.
44. Löwith, "Unzulängliche Bemerkungen," 152.
45. Löwith, "Unzulängliche Bemerkungen," 148.
46. Löwith, *Von Rom nach Sendai*, 75–76.
47. Löwith, "Japan's Westernization and Moral Foundation," 545.
48. Löwith, *Nature, History, and Existentialism*, 23.
49. The passage continues as follows: "What is commonly shared is the awe and worship of omnipresent, superhuman powers, called '*Kami*' in Japanese, the Roman '*supiri*,' which literally mean the same thing—simply the 'superiors' who are above us human beings." Löwith, *My Life in Germany*, 163.
50. Löwith, "Unzulängliche Bemerkungen," 141.
51. Löwith, *Nature, History, and Existentialism*, 22.
52. Löwith, *Nature, History, and Existentialism*, 23.
53. Löwith, *Nature, History, and Existentialism*, 22.
54. It is also the experience of a parallelism (perhaps even including simultaneity, considering the ancient nature of Shintoism), not unlike the Axial Age in Jaspers, which Löwith refers to in "Unzulängliche Betrachtungen," 166.
55. Löwith, *Nature, History, and Existentialism*, 20.
56. Löwith, "Unzulängliche Bemerkungen," 141.
57. Löwith, *Martin Heidegger and European Nihilism*, 230.
58. Bret W. Davis, "Dialogue and Appropriation: The Kyoto School as Cross-Cultural Philosophy," in *Japanese and Continental Philosophy: Conversations with the Kyoto School*, eds. B. W. Davis et al. (Bloomington: Indiana University Press, 2010), 42.

59. Löwith, *Martin Heidegger and European Nihilism*, 231. Löwith repeatedly contends that the Japanese live in two different worlds, in houses with two unrelated floors, as it were, and notes that the Japanese who have been in Europe have one "European room" in their home.
60. Davis, "Dialogue and Appropriation," 42–43.
61. Löwith, *Martin Heidegger and European Nihilism*, 228,
62. Löwith, *Martin Heidegger and European Nihilism*, 231.
63. Löwith, *Martin Heidegger and European Nihilism*, 231.
64. Löwith, *Martin Heidegger and European Nihilism*, 231–232.
65. Löwith, *Martin Heidegger and European Nihilism*, 232.
66. By going from West to East, Löwith's journey goes against the course of world history, which according to Hegel "goes from East to West." "Asia is the beginning of world history, [and] Europe is simply its end." What the implications of this reversal of direction are for understanding history would need to be worked out. Georg Wilhelm Friedrich Hegel, "Introduction," *The Philosophy of History*, trans. L. Rauch (Indianapolis: Hackett, 1988), 92.
67. Löwith, *Martin Heidegger and European Nihilism*, 234.
68. See my "Remainders of Faith: On Karl Löwith's Conception of Secularization," in *Divinatio. Studia Culturologica Series*, 2008, 28:27–50.
69. Löwith, "The Japanese Mind," 565.
70. Löwith, "The Japanese Mind," 560, 564.
71. Löwith, "The Japanese Mind," 561.
72. Löwith, "The Japanese Mind," 560. In distinction from Löwith, who credits Nishida for having appropriated Western thought in view of a clarification of Japanese thought for the West, Bret W. Davis holds that, on the contrary, "Nishida . . . sought to reappropriate sources in the Japanese tradition that would open it up to mutually enhancing dialogue, and not antagonistic competition, with the West." It is true that apart from Kitaro Nishida, whom he knew personally but whom he seems to have read really only after his departure from Japan, as Davis has also argued, Löwith "neglected to take account of the Kyoto School's significant attempts to navigate a passage through the pendulum swing within modern Japan between deferential Eurocentrism and a reactionary Japanism." Davis writes: "The philosophers associated with the Kyoto School were not only keenly aware of the issues pointed out in Löwith's critique; they had in fact set out to address them long before Löwith arrived in Japan to teach them the ways of Western appropriation." Davis, "Dialogue and Appropriation," 41, 33, 39.
73. Löwith, *My Life in Germany*, 167.
74. Löwith, *My Life in Germany*, 160.
75. Löwith, *Nature, History, and Existentialism*, 24.
76. Löwith, *Nature, History, and Existentialism*, 20.
77. Löwith, *My Life in Germany*, 164.
78. Löwith, *My Life in Germany*, 166.
79. Löwith, *My Life in Germany*, 166. Translation modified.
80. Löwith, *My Life in Germany*, 167.

7

FEELING ANEW FOR THE IDEA OF EUROPE

In *The Crisis of European Sciences and Transcendental Phenomenology*, Edmund Husserl argues that for Europe to have a distinct identity, a being that is truly its own, it has to reactivate its teleological beginning in Greece, that is, in the "absolute idea" that marks the birth of the European spirit.¹ What causes this inborn idea in European humanity to be absolute is that it is concerned, not with a geographical, national, ethnic, or religious entity but with humanity's struggle to understand itself. Yet, we may ask, by what nature of certainty can Husserl establish this idea? What kind of judgment leads him to the assertion that this idea alone can guarantee European identity, if not even confirm identity in general? Is it a judgment based on theoretical determination? Since, as Jacques Derrida put it in *The Other Heading*, Europe's "self-identification as repetition of itself," is based on "repetitive memory," and "anamnestic capitalization,"² the idea of Europe must have all the characteristics of ideality, if it is not even the idea of ideality itself. Undoubtedly, this idea at the heart of Europe is about universal and apodictic rational insight, and, on the basis of the ideal nature of its implications, it can also identically be reactualized. Yet the fact that, indeed, this idea is the spiritual *telos* of Europe, that it is its "eternal pole," is not something of which the Europeans can have determined cognitive certitude.³ As Husserl remarks in the "Vienna Lecture," we Europeans only "feel (and in spite of all obscurity this feeling is probably legitimate) that an entelechy is inborn in our European civilization which holds sway throughout all the changing shapes of Europe and accords to them the sense of a development toward an ideal shape of life and being as an eternal pole."⁴ In other words, the certainty we have of this idea in relation to Europe is of the order of a feeling and a "presentiment."⁵

It is noteworthy, therefore, that in several of the attempts made over the last decades, especially in France or Italy, to salvage the philosophical idea of Europe, for all its ideological and historical datedness—an effort that is also clearly intent on disputing the New Right's formulations of European identity—the idea in question is also no longer seen as something that European humanity possesses as an always reactivatable, and unshakeable, knowledge about itself. But before even hinting at what this novel conception of Europe might be, and especially at what its status is, if, indeed, it is not an assured cognitive truth, I should emphasize from the outset that these attempts at securing a future for the idea of Europe did not arise because of some nostalgia for a lost greatness. Neither did they seek to rescue the old idea of Europe, by opposing to its discredited expansionist and universalist conception a "new" model of European identity, based on cultural self-sufficiency and a nervous nationalism, as has been the case with the New Right. Rather, the attempt to rescue the philosophical concept of Europe derives first from the insight that this endeavor is a more politically efficient way of combating the old idea of Europe, as well as of resisting its new nationalist version in the New Right, than would be an outright rejection of the idea of Europe itself. Moreover, is Europe not responsible for the idea of Europe and for all that has been done and thought in its name? Can Europe simply walk away from this responsibility, in search of another identity, just as if it did not matter that it had thought of itself as an idea? However, to acknowledge this responsibility entails the abandonment of any attempt to save what of the old Europe is bound to come to an end, since the desire to protect it from the decadence and decline of its former values not merely forfeits the possibilities of Europe—its future—but by this desire, Europe, as Massimo Cacciari has noted, "betrays itself, its own *etymon*."[6] Hence, if the mentioned attempts to rescue the idea of Europe persist in not outright discarding this notion, it is due to a feeling that, qua philosophical idea, the idea of Europe might still harbor critical possibilities that until now have not been actualized. Europe, it is felt, is not comparable to a content whose form could be thrown away like an empty shell, once extracted and realized. Unwilling to set aside a concept before all its resources have been tapped, the thinkers involved in reassessing the philosophical concept of Europe have argued that this concept is not necessarily outdated, that, indeed, it still harbors critical potential; and in particular, a potential for Europe itself whose past has been intimately linked to this idea that it had of itself.

In the context of this reassessment, the theoretical, and hence knowable idea of Europe is replaced by a feeling for Europe, by a felt European identity. Among those who have taken it upon themselves to explore a possible critical potential for the idea in question, Derrida admits that he has been speaking "with names (event, decision, responsibility, ethics, politics—Europe) of 'things' that can only exceed (and *must* exceed) the order of theoretical determination, of knowledge, certainty, judgment, and of statements in the form of 'this is that,' in other words of the *present* or of *presentation*" (*OH*, 81). For Derrida, "Europe" is thus not, first and foremost, a theoretical issue. The opening sentences of the book describe the imminent and unique crisis of Europe today as one in which one no longer knows what the name Europe refers to and what the identity of Europe is. But this failure to know what the idea of Europe is about, and the actual impossibility of discursively establishing its meaning, is not seen as something fatal. It might well be an opportunity, if not even a chance. As Derrida suggests, "the very old subject of European identity" with its "venerable air of an old, exhausted theme," might still "retain a virgin body," a body that in spite of all theorizing about it, has been left uncharted (*OH*, 5). It should not, therefore, come as a surprise if Derrida, having established himself as an old European, although not quite by birth, opens his discussion of the idea of Europe, and of European identity, by confiding a feeling to his reader. This feeling is made instantly and explicitly into the first axiom of his text. By definition, an axiom is a fundamental statement requiring no proof, since it is considered either to be self-evident or to implicitly contain the definition of its own terms; thus the axiom serves as the premise for a series of statements. Here, however, it is a feeling, rather than a proposition, that is postulated and made into an axiom; a feeling, of course, that is not a private feeling but one that is, or might be, shared by "we Europeans." Used in apposition to the noun *Europeans*, the pronoun plural "we" highlights the fact that the feeling in question is not a subjective feeling but one through which Europeans qua Europeans take responsibility for Europe in a communal fashion. It is the paradoxical, if not aporetic, feeling that "we are younger than ever, we Europeans, since a certain Europe does not yet exist," but, at the same time, "already old and tired," and "already exhausted." Derrida's second axiom is an axiom in the stricter sense, since it formulates an intelligible necessity, rather than a feeling. According to this second postulate, "what is proper to culture is not to be identical to itself." This axiom does not stipulate that a culture would have no positive identity whatsoever or that to have one would be a mystification. On the contrary, it establishes that a culture has identity only on condition of its being nonidentical to itself, of its being in "difference *with itself* [*avec soi*]." This constituting difference of a culture *with itself* is double in kind. Identity presupposes, first of all, an external difference. This is a difference with itself that derives from identity's continual reference to the identity of other cultures over and against whom any self-identity is established. These other cultural identities, as identities of the other, can simply be different from the one of European culture, but they can also be identities that stand in a relation of opposition to European identity. Yet since *avec soi*, in addition to meaning "with itself," also means "at home (with itself)," or *chez soi*, Derrida makes use of this "strange and slightly violent syntax," to maintain that for cultural identity to be possible, it must be further divided by an internal difference, a self-difference that "would gather and divide just as irreducibly the center or hearth [*foyer*] of the 'at home (with itself)'" (OH, 9–10). This internal difference is the difference of any identity not from the state of nonidentity from which it had to be wrenched but with a "state" anterior to the difference of identity and nonidentity. The difference in question opens all identity to its divergence and is the necessary condition under which a center or hearth can be gathered and made to relate to itself. Up to this point in his text, Derrida has spoken of cultural identity. But with his statement that "there is no self-relation, no relation to oneself, no identification with oneself, without culture, but a culture of oneself *as* a culture *of* the other, a culture of the double genitive and of the *difference to oneself* [*à soi*]" (OH, 10), Derrida extends the axiomatic law in question to identity in general, to what is properly one's innermost own. The second axiomatic law thus states that the inmost own, which is, in this case, the cultural identity of Europe, is *per essentiam, sine essentia.*

As Derrida recalls in *The Other Heading*, Europe has always understood itself as a head and heading, both geographically and spiritually. But if the second axiom establishes a law for all identity formation, then Europe's self-identification as a head and heading presupposes the double difference with and to oneself. More precisely, what follows from this law is that if Europe wishes to understand itself as a head and a heading, it is incumbent upon it, first of all, to recall, to remember, and *reactivate* the other already constituted identities thanks to which it is, in distinguishing itself from them, what it most properly and truly is. If all identity necessarily presupposes a relation to a constitutive external difference, then in order to be itself, Europe cannot ignore what Derrida calls "the other heading," or, given that all cultures presuppose "an identifiable heading, a *telos*" (*OH*, 17–18) toward which they move, Europe cannot ignore "the heading of the other" (*OH*, 15). Without relating to the trace of the other heading within the heading that is most properly its own, Europe as a head and heading would in all rigor cease to be an identity. It would achieve absoluteness. In Jean-Luc Nancy's terms, it would become fully immanent to itself, and death would thus become its truth.[7] Commenting on the title *The Other Heading*, Derrida remarks that in addition to suggesting a change in direction and destination, the expression *the other heading* "can mean to recall that there is an other heading, the heading being not only ours, but the other, not only that which we identify, calculate, and decide upon, but the *heading of the other*, before which we must respond, and which we must *remember, of which* we must *remind ourselves*, the heading of the other being perhaps the first condition of an identity or identification that is not an egocentrism destructive of one self and the other." However, identity also requires the internal difference that, while continuing to divide identity, also makes it possible for identity to gather itself into its own. This difference within which identity collects itself is a difference with something that is altogether of a different order than identity, and hence something other than nonidentity. The internal difference that divides all identity is a difference with identity in general, with that which is conceived in terms of the identifiable, and which, consequently, also precedes the thought, or concept of the nonidentical. Derrida, therefore, continues: "But beyond *our heading*, it is necessary to recall ourselves not only to the *other heading*, and especially to the *heading of the other*, but also perhaps to the *other of the heading*, that is to say, to a relation of identity with the other that no longer obeys the form, the sign, or the logic of the heading, nor even of the *anti-heading*—of beheading, of decapitation" (*OH*, 15). For Europe to be what it most essentially is—a head and heading—it must recall that without which it could not constitute itself at all, and that for this very reason affects it most fundamentally—the other heading—and recalls itself to it. But it must further recall, and recall itself to that which, while not being its opposite—headlessness, and a drifting without direction—is no longer of the order of the head and of a heading but is the very thing from, and thanks to, which the binary oppositions of heading and the other heading, of self and other, of identity and nonidentity, can distinguish their meaning. With this openness of the question of European identity (and ultimately of any identity) to a "constituting" difference of identity of the order of the other *of* identity, hence also of nonidentity, Derrida forces open the interlocked and predictable programs of Eurocentrism and anti-Eurocentrism, to acknowledge something that is no longer of the order of the concept of Europe, or of its opposite, but is, in some way, presupposed by this concept. What, then, is this "other *of* the heading," one might ask? In distinction from the differences that constitute identity externally, and that can be qualified in terms of the nonidentical, and in further distinction from any previously constituted identities—"the other headings"—whether or not they stand in a relation of opposition to it, the other *of* the heading is structurally impossible to identify. It is neither identical to itself nor nonidentical. The question, What is the other *of* the heading? must remain a question; it "should remain, even beyond all answers," Derrida remarks (OH, 16–17). Indeed, the other *of* the heading, or more generally the other *of* identity, is but the place or trace in the heading, or in the identical, of that which cannot be calculated according to the logic of identity and nonidentity, but to which this logic, in order *to be what it is*, must necessarily refer (in a mode of referring that is not simply one of negation) as its "undeterminable" other.

The exposition of the second axiom, according to which "what is proper to culture is not to be identical to itself," has thus laid bare an intricate system of reference that is constitutive of identity in general. This system of structural exigencies, without which no identity can get off the ground and remain in its distinctness, considerably complicates the traditional conceptions, including Husserl's, of what composes Europe's specificity. Much more than just the origin, as Husserl still thought, needs to be reactivated in order for Europe to gain an innermost own. If Europe is to have an identity, "it must be equal *to itself and to the other*" (OH, 45), in other words, it must meet the "impossible" requirement to respond at the same time to the two contradictory demands in question. At this point, let me recall the first axiom, according to which Derrida felt that the idea of Europe, although old and tired, could still hold some potential. Indeed, as the second axiom spells out, when that which is most proper to Europe opens onto other already constituted headings, but especially onto the other *of* the heading, that is, onto what is unpredictable, unanticipatable, and uncalculatable (and hence thwarts all programs), in short, onto the future, then the concept of Europe, it is felt, encounters, perhaps, a chance.

The identity of Europe, defined as a head and a heading, is not without the double difference, the external, but also the internal difference that presupposes a "relation" to the other *of* the heading. Thus the question of the identity of Europe is a very old question, not merely because it has been posed since antiquity, but, more fundamentally, because as an identity Europe is dependent on something older than itself, older than an "itself," and in relation to which its difference has had to be negotiated from the very beginning. But Derrida claims that although "this question is also very old, as old as the history of Europe . . . the experience of the *other heading* or of the other *of* the heading presents itself [today] in an absolutely new way." What Derrida intimates here is that the necessary structural, that is, intelligible conditions under which European identity is constituted, are today experienced, and felt, in a radically singular way. With this proposal, the first axiom is further specified. Derrida asks: "And what if Europe were this: the opening onto a history for which the changing of the heading, the relation to the other heading or to the other of the heading, is experienced [*ressenti*] as always possible? An opening and a non-exclusion for which Europe would in some way be responsible? For which Europe *would be*, in a constitutive way, this very responsibility? As if the very concept of responsibility were responsible, right up to its emancipation, for a European birth certificate?" (*OH*, 17). Undoubtedly, Europe has in the past repeatedly posed to itself the question of its own identity, its conceptual nature, its inherent telos, its difference and relation to the other heading, and even to the other of the heading. But compared to past discussions and reflections on this question, the new, and absolutely new experience of European identity consists not only in the fact that it is a *felt* (*ressenti*) identity but also in the fact that this feeling is about the *always possible* change of that identity. More exactly, since the experience in question concerns the constituting traits, the structural conditions of possibility of European identity itself, it is the feeling that precisely those traits that secure its identity in the first place, are also responsible for the possibility of this identity's change. Indeed, given that these conditions of possibility are such that they include a reference to the other of Europe—the other headings and the headings of the other—as well as to an other that is no longer categorizable in terms of self-identity and this identity's others, the inscription of such otherness in identity necessarily opens it to a possible alteration. What is felt "today," thus, in a feeling of the moment—the always possible "changing of the heading, the relation to the other heading or to the other of the heading," in short, that identity can only be achieved on the condition that it is always—necessarily and structurally—exposed to possible change—is, at the same time, a transcendental experience (of sorts) of the conditions of all identity and its limits.⁸ Differently put, this feeling that registers an essential debt to the other heading, and the other of the heading, a debt so essential that the possibility of change is intrinsically tied into the positivity of identity, hence, that an element of unpredictability is inevitably part of identity, is the "new" felt identity of what it means to be European. Unlike the responsibility of European humanity to its inborn telos, and to the idea of a universal rational essence of mankind, the new experience of identity to which Derrida refers is marked by an essential insecurity. As a felt idea, the idea to which European identity is tied, it also lacks the security that a cognitive approach to it still offers. Furthermore, the responsibility that comes with the transcendental experience in question is not a responsibility for anything inborn but, rather, for openness and nonexclusion, not only to the other, to other concepts or horizons, but also to the other of the concept and the horizon, without which no self-identity is thinkable.⁹

As I have intimated, Derrida's recasting of the notion of European identity as a feeling of an identity that in an essential manner implies an openness, and a debt toward the other heading and the other *of* the heading, is a further development of the Husserlian conception that what is most properly Europe's innermost own is something felt by Europeans. It is a feeling of identity that assumes responsibility for everything identity implies. Commenting on this new experience of the constituting difference of European identity as an affirmative experience of the always possible change (precisely insofar as identity is owed to the other, and, if I may say so, to the other *of* the other) of these seminal differences without which there can be no identity whatsoever, Derrida writes that this experience "presents itself in an absolutely new way, not new 'as always' [*comme toujours*], but newly new" (*OH*, 17). As an absolutely new experience, it is a truly singular experience, and not a variation on the old ways in which Europe has questioned the conditions of its identity. But if this experience is so new, why still call it by the old name "Europe"? What necessity compels retaining this designation to identify something never identified under the name of Europe, something entirely new? Does not Derrida make it amply clear that "that which seeks or promises itself *today*, in Europe," is not given, "no more than its name, Europe being here only a *paleonymic* appellation" (*OH*, 30–31)? Is it because the name "Europe" has essentially something to do with identity itself? Is it because what is in question here is the possibility of an effective intervention, and reshaping, of what hitherto has been meant by identity? If the new experience, and the responsibility in question, are still named

Europe, is it not, first, because of Europe's legacy as far as the thought of universality is concerned? Is it not because of what "we, Europeans," as Derrida writes, "recall (to ourselves) or what we promise (ourselves)" (*OH*, 82)? Precisely because Europe has been the name for the concept or idea of universality—of an innermost own rationality of mankind—it is incumbent upon Europe to assume the responsibility to and for the felt openness and nonexclusion that all claims to identity, willingly or not, imply. But there is yet another reason why this responsibility should still be called by the old name Europe, a name synonymous with universality. Indeed, to use the name Europe as a denomination for the responsibility in question, is to engage the Europeans, first and foremost, in that responsibility. Calling it by that name is a performative, a first singularization, of this responsibility, one that is binding and which calls on Europeans to respond to its call insofar as they are Europeans, that is, the inheritors of a mode of thinking that sought universality from the start. But to designate this universal responsibility by that name is also to emphasize that it articulates a feeling that no longer pretends to speak in the name of the other and on his or her behalf. However, if it is true that this responsibility concerns the Europeans first and foremost, it does not follow at all that the identity that it confers would merely consist in Europe's turning in on itself. No withdrawal into any particularity takes place here. Rather, the felt responsibility, that is, its extreme singularization (because felt) of a universal respect for the other, radically commits the European. Finally, even if the feeling of such a universal respect excludes making demands on the other, this does not in any way diminish the universal sweep of the Europeans' singular responsibility. An experience as the one described, not only applies to Europe. But the responsibility that it articulates does not tolerate summoning the other to act accordingly. It allows even less to impose this responsibility on the other.

Before further exploring the necessities that tie Europe to this responsibility, in other words, before explicitly taking on the question of universality and singularity in *The Other Heading*, I return to the experience in which the identity of Europe is established by way of the feeling of the always possible changes of the constituting traits of identity itself, and which I have qualified as transcendental. How can Derrida lift a feeling, a mere feeling, one would like to add, to such heights and make it do what seems to properly belong only to the competence of reason? Undoubtedly, in the history of philosophy, certain *pathe* have been shored up and freed from their intrinsic irrationality, and thereby granted a philosophical status beyond the merely private one that is normally associated with them. One thinks, for instance, of admiration in Descartes, respect in Kant, love in the early Hegel. One is especially reminded of the kind of feeling that, according to Plato and Aristotle, is at the origin of philosophy itself—the feeling of wonder. If, hereafter, I shall seek to clarify Derrida's referral to a transcendental feeling of sorts via a somewhat long digression through a text by Heidegger, it is because that text not only seeks access to the essence of philosophy from the singular feeling of the *thaumazein* but also because it determines philosophy as an essentially Greek approach, in short, as synonymous with Greece, and to some extent with Europe as well. Understood this way, Europe exists first, although only implicitly so in Heidegger's text, as, and in accord with, a certain state of mind.[10]

In *What is Philosophy?*, Heidegger argues that although "sentiments, even the finest, have no place in philosophy," a feeling, or more precisely, a mood or state of mind (*Stimmung*) characterizes philosophy and philosophizing at its most fundamental level. This fundamental disposition or affection by which philosophy moves and concerns us (*uns be-rührt, uns angeht*) is neither of the order of "that which is usually called feelings and emotions, in short, the irrational," nor of rational thinking, but is prior to this distinction, and is a transcendental disposition of sorts as well.[11] By confronting Heidegger's elaborations on the state of mind that is coeval with philosophy and also with the West or Europe,[12] with Derrida's understanding of the new feeling concerning European identity, I hope to show, first and foremost, that in *The Other Heading*, Derrida stages a critical debate with Heidegger's notion of Stimmung, and the latter's claim that such a disposition is what properly constitutes the specificity of philosophy, and hence also of Europe or the West.

Heidegger reasons at the beginning of his text that any response to the question, What is philosophy? not only requires an attunement to what specifically resonates in that word but also to what is implied by a question such as this, a question that asks "what is." Without such an attunement, the answer not only remains exterior to what is in question and to the questioning mode but also remains exterior to the questioner, rather than concerning him or her expressly and in depth. The answer, therefore, demands not only that one "hear the word 'philosophy' coming from its source . . . the word ['philosophy'], as a Greek word," but also that the question that inquires into the whatness of something be heard as an "originally Greek question" (*WP*, 29, 39). I will take up, one after the other, Heidegger's expositions on the original meaning of the word *philosophia* and on the intrinsically Greek nature of the question itself.

According to Heidegger, "the word *philosophia* tells us that philosophy is something which, first of all, determines the existence of the Greek world [*Griechentum*]. Not only that—*philosophia* also determines the innermost basic feature [*innersten Grundzug*] of our Western-European history" (*WP*, 29). Essentially, philosophy is Greek because "in origin the nature of philosophy is of such a kind that it first appropriated [*in Anspruch genommen hat*] the Greek world, and only it, in order to unfold" (*WP*, 31). It is Greek not primarily because its factual emergence dates back to sixth-century Greece, but because the Greeks were the first to answer its claims and to make its idea the basis for the singular existence of the Greek world. Indeed, it is the response of Greece as a whole to the idea of philosophy that endows Greece with its singular firstness and makes philosophy a Greek thing. Philosophy is Greek to such an extent that even the fact that it has been guided and ruled since the Middle Ages by Christian conceptions does not make it Christian in any way. No religious faith, nor authority of any other kind, can change philosophy's originary Greekness. A non-Western philosophy is a contradiction in terms, philosophy and the West being exchangeable notions, Heidegger holds. He writes: "The statement that philosophy is in its nature Greek says nothing more than that the West and Europe, and only these, are, in the innermost course of their history, originally 'philosophical'" (*WP*, 31). Greece itself was the first to embody this ideal, and Europe is "philosophical" at least inasmuch as the innermost trait of its intellectual history is concerned. Heidegger's only supporting argument, echoing Husserl's elaborations in *The Crisis* that the development of the sciences is proof of Europe's "philosophical" nature and destiny, provides a first clue as to what the word *philosophy* implies. Indeed, if the modern sciences' ability "to put a specific imprint on the history of mankind upon the whole earth" and to inaugurate "ages" of the world (*Weltalter*), is interpreted as proof of their stemming "from the innermost Western-European course of history, that is, the philosophical" (*WP*, 33), then the philosophical becomes intimately linked to a concern with humanity and the world as a whole. Philosophy, then, is the theoretical and practical assumption of a responsibility for the concerns of mankind as such, and for what is of the order of the whole earth, the whole world. Consequently, philosophy's original Greekness consists in nothing less than the fact that this singular nation conceived of itself and acted in accord with universal principles, principles that transcended Greece as a particular nation and people. Only in this sense, Heidegger concludes, can the philosophical—the word *philosophia*—be said to "appear on the birth certificate of our own history" (*WP*, 35).

Undoubtedly, questioning is not the sole privilege of Greece and the Western world. But what then is the supposedly specifically Greek mode of questioning? *Ti estin*, what is it, inquires not only into the *whatness* of a singular thing, it also gives "an interpretation . . . of what the 'what' means, in what sense the *ti* is to be understood" (*WP*, 39), Heidegger explains. As is obvious from the hyphen that in the German title of Heidegger's piece—"Was ist das—die Philosophie?"—both separates the question "what is" from that which is being questioned, "philosophy," and also simultaneously gathers these two parts together, the question "what is" inquires into something distinct from the singular subject of the question, something that is of the order of the universal rather than of the singular. The Greek question, a question that (by way of its form) already contains its answer, postulates an engagement of the universal in the singular something. It interprets the singular, its whatness, from a dimension that is, in principle, recognizable by all at all times, even though it may have received very different determinations throughout the history of philosophy. The specificity of the Greek questioning mode thus resides in its asking after the meaning of the whatness of something singular, and that in distinction from this singular thing, is universally shareable. Further, the form itself of the question *ti esti* makes it a question pertinent to everyone as well. By virtue simply of its form, it can claim universality. Hence, to ask the question, What is it—philosophy? is to ask a Greek question both in form and content. "We ourselves belong to this origin even when we do not mention the word 'philosophy.' We are peculiarly [*eigens*] summoned back into this source and are re-claimed for and by it as soon as we not only utter the words of the question, 'What is philosophy?' but reflect upon its meaning," Heidegger remarks (*WP*, 39). In short, for Heidegger as for Husserl, this responsibility for and to universality, not merely as a theme but as a form as well, in other words, universal answerability, is the proper heritage of the Greek tradition, the "innermost basic feature" of what Europeans can claim most properly as their own. To be European is to be Greek, and to be Greek means to be concerned not with oneself but with what is to be universally predicated of all; more precisely, to be Greek means to be concerned with things as they present themselves, with their whatness *in propria persona*, before the arrival of any concealing interpretation, resulting from factors such as customs and beliefs, traditions and traditionalisms. Furthermore, to be Greek is not only to be concerned with what is relevant to humanity at large; it is also to be concerned with it in a form capable of universal validation.

Before evoking what resonates in the word *philosophia* when heard with a Greek ear, Heidegger makes, and I quote his own words, "a statement of principles": to "listen . . . to the words of the Greek language . . . [is to] move into a distinct and distinguished domain . . . [because] the Greek language is no mere language like the European languages known to us. The Greek language, and it all alone, is *logos*" (WP, 45). Greek is distinct from all known European languages in that it is hardly a language to begin with, if language is thought to be constituted by signs and to be idiomatic in nature. By contrast, in the Greek language, language *is* in an immediate fashion what it names (*nennen*); its words *are* the *whatness* of things. Heidegger holds: "What is said in it *is* at the same time in an excellent way what it is called. If we hear a Greek word with a Greek ear we follow its *legein*, its direct presentation [*Darlegen*]. What it presents is what lies immediately before us. Through the audible Greek word we are directly in the presence of the thing itself, not first in the presence of a mere word sign" (WP, 45). With the Greek language one is thus in the direct presence of the whatness of a thing or concept. It is a language transparent to a point that its words, by directly presenting the very essence of something, are indistinguishable from what they name. Not only does this language postulate that all particular things have their universal concepts but also as the language *of* conception and conceptualization, rather than of some particular idiom, it is a universal language, universality as language itself. In sum, the Greek language is a language that breaks with Greek as an idiom, that executes the essence of language, in order to say and exhibit things as they are originally in themselves, that is, before their universally shareable whatness becomes clouded by the sedimentations and interested coverings-up of particular idioms, including that of Greek itself.

Philosophia as a Greek word is, then, the direct presentation of what it names! Authorized by the Heraclitean use of the word *philosophos*, Heidegger defines the originary Greek meaning of philosophia as speaking in accord, in harmony, with the *logos* that gathers everything that is into its Being. And he adds that philosophia arises at the moment when "the fact that being is gathered together in Being, that in the appearance of Being being appears," becomes "the most astonishing thing for the Greeks" (WP, 49). This immediate accord alone, this harmony, or correspondence with the logos—an accord coextensive to the feeling of astonishment—describes the properly Greek meaning of philosophia. Philosophia, it follows, is a double accord, not just of thought and Being, but of thinking and feeling; more precisely, of a thinking anterior to "philosophy" and the isolated *pathos* of astonishment. Indeed, Heidegger claims that thinking becomes "philosophy" as soon as this original harmony is lost—as soon as thinking, no longer in accord with Being, becomes *episteme theoretike*, that is, the search for what, in Aristotle's words, is forever and forever missed, namely, the search for what is Being—and this claim only underscores the prerational, pretheoretical, and precognitive nature of a thinking that is originally inseparable from a certain kind of feeling, a feeling ennobled by the "fact" (a "fact" of universal bearing) that provokes it.

Significantly enough, for Heidegger, the thinking/feeling of philosophia is not yet a thinking that questions. Thinking enters the questioning mode characteristic of philosophy only at the moment when the initial accord no longer prevails, when thinking becomes a "yearning search for the *sophon*, for the 'One (is) all'"; or more precisely, when "the being in Being . . . becomes the question, 'What is being, in so far as it is?'" (*WP*, 53). The philosophical questioning mode "what is" (*ti estin*) betrays already a loss of access to Being itself, and is thus derivative from the lost accord that had been achieved in philosophia. Thus, it is not so much the question *ti estin*, as it is the thinking/feeling of philosophia in harmony with the *logos* and with a "fact" of universal sweep, which is specifically Greek. This thinking/feeling alone, indeed, deserves to be truly called Greek. But at the same time, every mode of thought, whether it is a declaration of the loss of philosophia, an attempt at rescuing it, an all-out attack on it, or even a deliberate ignoring of it, depends for its intelligibility on this original harmony of a thinking that is not yet thinking (in that it is not yet distinct from feeling), and a feeling that is not yet feeling (that is, in distinction from thinking), which is in harmony with Being, and which thus remains inherently Greek—that is to say, European, or Western. This is all the more the case for a discourse in the philosophical questioning mode, one that asks "what is," and singularly, What is philosophy? An answer to this question, if there is to be one, can, therefore, "only be a philosophizing answer which, as a response, philosophizes itself" (*WP*, 65). Such an answer requires that the philosopher be attentive to what has been lost and to what it is, which, by its loss, provokes the question in the first place. A philosophical answer is, therefore, not a reply to a question in the form "what is." It presupposes, instead, a displacement of the questioning and answering mode. A philosophical question, in Heidegger's terms, must correspond (*ent-sprechen*) to what is in question, or more precisely, to what in the question addresses the philosopher. He writes: "If this correspondance is successful for us, then, in the true sense of the word, we respond to the question, 'What is philosophy?'" Response demands here a prior listening to that which has already avowed itself to us, and of which the question into the whatness is only, as it were, a negative, in order for the response to become a correspondence. "In such a correspondence we listen from the very outset to that which philosophy has already said to us, *philosophy*, that is, *philosophia* understood in the Greek sense" (*WP*, 69 and 71). What then is the nature of this correspondence?

Resuming his discussion of the role of "fine sentiments" in philosophy, Heidegger writes:

> *Philosophia* is the expressly accomplished correspondence which speaks in so far as it considers the appeal of the Being of being. The correspondence listens to the voice of the appeal [*Stimme des Zuspruchs*]. What appeals to us as the voice of Being evokes [*be-stimmt*] our correspondence. "Correspondence" then means: being de-termined [*be-stimmt*], *être disposé* by that which comes from the Being of being. *Disposé* here means literally set-apart, cleared, and thereby placed in relationship with what is. Being as such determines speaking in such a way that language [*Sagen*] is attuned [*sich abstimmt*] (accorder) to the Being of being. Correspondence is necessary and is always attuned [*gestimmtes*], and not just accidentally and occasionally. It is an attunement [*Gestimmtheit*]. And only on the basis of the attunement (*disposition*) does the language [*Sagen*] of a correspondence obtain its precision, its tuning [*Be-stimmtheit*]. (*WP*, 75–77)

If in the correspondence of philosophia express attention is given to the voice of the appeal or avowal of Being, correspondence is determined by that voice, affected by it, as it were, and granted a voice itself. In correspondence, the voice of Being, by avowing itself, not only opens up the space for a possible addressee and respondent but also attunes the addressee's speaking, by tuning it to Being's own voice. A correspondence thus achieves an accord, an accord that is, first and foremost, a *Gestimmtheit*, a mood, sentiment, disposition, or state of mind. Heidegger concludes:

> As something tuned and attuned [*ge-stimmtes und be-stimmtes*], correspondence really exists in a tuning [*Stimmung*]. Through it our attitude is adjusted sometimes in this, sometimes in that way. The tuning understood in this sense is not music of accidentally emerging feelings which only accompany the correspondence. If we characterize philosophy as tuned correspondence, then we by no means want to surrender thinking to the accidental changes and

vaccilations of sentiments. It is rather solely a question of pointing out that every precision of language [*Sagens*] is grounded in a disposition of correspondence, of correspondence, I say, heading the appeal. (*WP*, 77–79)

The disposition in question is an essential (*wesenhaft*) disposition. It is neither of the order of sentiments, in the sense of irrational counterparts of thinking, nor of the order of intellectual adequation to things; rather, already presupposed by such orders, this disposition precedes the classical distinction between feelings and rational thought. In all rigor, attunement (Stimmung) is not a feeling. It precedes feeling, just as much as the accord that it brings about between saying and the voice of Being precedes rational thinking, and thus precedes any propositional definiteness and determinateness.

To characterize philosophy by this essential disposition of correspondence is, for Heidegger, an insight that refers back to the early understanding of philosophy in Greek thought, as belonging "in the dimension of man which we call tuning (in the sense of tuning and attunement)" (*WP*, 79). Indeed, Heidegger holds that according to Plato and Aristotle, the fundamental pathos of wonder, or astonishment, is not only the starting point of philosophy but is also the mood that "carries and pervades philosophy" at all times (*WP*, 81). Every single moment of philosophizing reactivates this special "feeling" in which "we step back, as it were, from being, from the fact that it is as it is and not otherwise," to face, in a fascination of sorts, Being, the Being of being itself. Yet what one is drawn to in the retreat from beings, is something that extends beyond all particular beings, is Being itself—in traditional philosophical language, a universal shared by everything that is. Being, as Heidegger puts it in *Being and Time*, is "*the* transcendens *pure and simple*."[13] The feeling that retreats and is drawn to this "universal" is, as it were, universal, as well. Tuned and attuned to Being as the transcendens pure and simple, it is by right a feeling ennobled by this transcendens, a feeling unlike all other feelings.

From what I have just said, I retain that philosophia is, first and foremost, a corresponding attunement to Being itself. As an attunement to Being, philosophia is thus something essentially Greek, or rather is that which alone merits to be called Greek. Greekness is understood here no longer as the essence of Greece in an empirico-historical, or sociocultural sense. Greekness is but the enobling ability of a peoples (the Greek, for example) of breaking with, and departing from, itself as a particular peoples in time and space. Europe, or the West, insofar as its innermost basic features are

Greek, is thus to be understood according to that same qualification. At its most elementary, Greece, or Europe, is, for Heidegger, and in distinction from Husserl's understanding of Europe as rooted in a rational idea, nothing but a universally shareable feeling—even though Heidegger does not speak of universality, the term having too traditional and humanist connotations—about the enigma of Being.[14] This tunement and attunement to Being, named Europe, or the West, sets Europe not only necessarily apart from other cultures that have not raised themselves, by concerning themselves with *the* transcendens pure and simple, above their particularity, but also from itself as well. Yet, even though this attunement to Being, and its openness, makes Europe different from itself and should, in principle, prevent it from closing itself on itself, this difference with and to itself inevitably tempts Europe to cultivate this difference for its own sake. For Derrida, this temptation is not absent from the writings of Heidegger, as his reference in *The Other Heading* to "the vigilant sentinels of being" shows. These sentinels, in the name of Being, guard the border that the difference between self and other creates within Europe or the West, so that the latter's identity should not be exposed to other conceptions of universality, or to the other of universality (*OH*, 26). Attunement to Being, that is, to the difference which, according to Heidegger, makes all the difference, can also become a powerful incentive to remain at home, entrenched in cozy and smug self-sufficiency. How then are we to distinguish Derrida's reference to a feeling that is constitutive of the identity of Europe, from Heidegger's elaborations on a fundamental attunement? Is not Derrida's call to reactivate the debt to the other, and also to the other *of* the heading, an attempt to open the fundamental disposition or attunement, an attempt to complicate the always alluring tendency to turn the difference with and from self, caused by the concern with Being, into a self-achievement? Could the reactivation of this debt have been conceived of specifically in order to address the possibility that the difference with itself, which is at the heart of Europe's idea of universality, can also always become a means for self-closure; a possibility that seems to have escaped the vigilance of the vigilant sentinel of Being? In this case, however, the feeling that pervades *The Other Heading* is entirely different from any previous notion of feeling. It is less fundamental than Heidegger's fundamental attunement but is, at the same time, indebted to, and doing justice to, other headings; which is still to say nothing of that which eludes the logic of identification altogether, the other *of* the heading.

In order to begin answering these questions, it is not without significance to remark on the thoroughly different tone of Heidegger's and Derrida's discussion of feeling. Compared to Heidegger's solemn, if not pompous, seriousness, Derrida's approach to the subject maintains a certain ironic distance and, as is evident from the first axiom of the book, plays on a self-irony regarding his own undoubtedly earnest identification with what is European. It is an irony motivated by a particular tension, namely, that as a European one can subscribe to what "Europe" has stood for, and still promises, only by also looking elsewhere. But this difference in tone is indicative of a much deeper difference in concern. Undoubtedly, the feeling Derrida calls Europe is a feeling that is also universalist in its sweep. But unlike Stimmung, which is the fundamental attunement to Being, Derrida's Europe is a feeling that acknowledges that, however insuperable the thought of Being may be, Being as a "universal" is indebted to, and limited by, other universals (and possibly by the opposite of the universal), and even by something other than the universal and the nonuniversal. It articulates a feeling concerning both the limits, and also the always possible alteration, of what precisely it is that remains necessary in order to secure something universal, and to identify this universal as such. There is no question here of substituting one universal principle for another, or for the opposite of universality, but rather of recognizing (by way of feeling) that any universal principle is what it is in demarcation from other, possibly opposite principles, including the opposite of a principle, and from something that eludes the fundamental difference between the universal and the particular. In short, the sentiment evoked in *The Other Heading* takes on the Heideggerian conception of Stimmung, to demonstrate that however legitimate the appeal to Being is in determining the essence of philosophia, and simultaneously of Europe, this very appeal presupposes both a relation and an indebtedness to the other, neither of which may be overlooked or discounted. This felt debt changes the Stimmung from top to bottom. The recognized debt to the other includes the debt to what has been called the other *of* the universal, without thereby rephrasing that other as a particular; and what is felt to have universal pertinence under the name of "Europe" commits the European, first of all, to that debt.

One problem has been left in abeyance, and it concerns Europe's claim to being a head and a heading in the first place. In his discussion of the ongoing debate among the European nations about a possible site for a capital of European culture, Derrida notes that what is at stake is "not only the predominance of a national language, tongue, or idiom, but the predominance of a *concept* of the tongue or of language, a certain idea of the idiom that is being put to work" (*OH*, 46–47). Undoubtedly, this discussion betrays the fierce struggle between the European nations for control over European culture and for national hegemony in the domain of European culture. But, as Derrida writes, "national hegemony is not claimed—today no more than ever—in the name of an empirical superiority, which is to say, a simple particularity." Indeed, national hegemony "claims to justify itself in the name of a privilege in responsibility and in the memory of the universal and, thus, of the transnational—indeed of the trans-European—and, finally, of the transcendental or ontological" (*OH*, 47).[15] The point made here is that Europe's claim to be a head and heading is not merely an expression of what it undoubtedly has been, namely, a region characterized by its factual technological superiority and its cultural arrogance, but is also a further expression of its inherent drive for hegemony. All claims in this regard take for granted a superiority of Europe; and they are justified, as Derrida points out, not on empirical but on universal grounds. Yet why would this be so? Could it have to do with the fact that all hegemony claims, whether made by Europe or by anyone else, presuppose a prior self-identification; and could it be that any identity claim is a claim to some superiority?

Derrida puts forth the argument that universality, and the difference it makes—particularly in the case of Europe—is a value that cannot be surrendered without condoning the worst violence; therefore, he claims, one must subscribe to the logic of capitalization and maximization by which universality is brought about. At the same time, one must not fail to look for something other, which means not only "for what is already found outside Europe . . . [but also] to the to-come of the *event*, to that which *comes*, which comes perhaps and perhaps comes from a completely other shore" (*OH*, 69). After making these points, Derrida returns to the question of the relation of universality and singularity. Universality as a *value* implies singularity, Derrida maintains; it is, necessarily, the universal of singulars and must therefore embody itself in exemplary fashion within the singular. Conversely, Derrida explains that any "self-affirmation of an identity always claims to be responding to the call or assignation of the universal. There are no exceptions to this law. No cultural identity presents itself as the opaque body of an untranslatable idiom, but always, on the contrary, as the irreplaceable *inscription* of the universal in the singular, the *unique testimony* to the human essence and to what is proper to man" (*OH*, 73).

What this means is that, in every instance of self-identification, wherever a singularity seeks to identify itself, it must make the claim that its singularity represents in exemplary fashion the universal values of humanity. In the case of Europe, the conception that it has had of itself as a head and a heading is a response to this inevitable requirement for a consolidated identity to begin with. In addition, wherever and whenever self-identification takes place, which is to say, not only in the case of Europe but also in every case, then the claim for a special responsibility to the universal is made. "Each time, it has to do with the discourse of *responsibility*: I have, the unique 'I' has, the responsibility of testifying for universality. Each time, the exemplarity of the example is unique" (*OH*, 73). To illustrate the generality of this formal law, according to which no self-identification is possible without taking charge of the universal, and putting oneself in charge of it, Derrida refers to a "personal impression" of Paul Valéry, according to whom the French *believe* and *feel* that they are "*men of universality.*" Notwithstanding the subjectivity of the impression, and the subjectivity of the phenomena itself, the belief and feeling in question are, according to Valéry, "constitutive of the essential or constitutive traits of French consciousness in its 'particularity.'" The French, as it were, feel themselves into what they are, by believing, as Valéry phrases it, that they "specialize in the sense of the universal" (*OH*, 74). Identity, the identity of a singularity—in this case, Frenchness—is thus constituted by the feeling on the part of the French that they exemplarily represent humanity, or the universal. But Derrida holds that the paradox "is not reserved for the French. Not even, no doubt, for Europeans" (*OH*, 75). Because of the formal law linking all self-identification of a singularity to universality, this feeling of specialization within the universal may well be—"paradox of the paradox" (*OH*, 75)—a universal feeling. If this is so, then the implications of this paradox must be drawn out with care.

From this final paradox, it follows that all claims ("all the propositions and injunctions") by any self-identifying singularity, which are, as we have seen, claims to universality, are inherently divided and deidentified. Indeed, if all singularities such as nations can, and even *must*, claim this status as "men of universality," then any identity, any heading, any superiority "is related to itself not only in gathering itself in the difference *with itself* and with the other heading, with the other shore of the heading, but in opening itself without being able any longer to gather itself" (*OH*, 75). Any exemplary embodiment of universality, any exemplary responsibility to and for what is common to all humanity, presupposes an openness to the other, and the other *of* the other; to the point where all successful gathering into a closed and undivided self-identity becomes impossible. Far from implying that all gathering is therefore an illusion or mystification, this opening is precisely the condition of possibility of gathering. Only *from* the other's identity and claim to a privileged representing of universality, as well *from* the other *of* identity and universality, do the exemplary embodiment and the responsibility to and for universality become meaningful in the first place. To conclude, it is, therefore,

> *necessary* to take note of this [namely, that everything in the position of a head or heading, a limit or concept, is indebted to the other head and heading, and to what is other to this order of things or concepts], which means *to affirm in recalling*, and not simply to record or store up in the archives a necessity that is already at work anyway. It has begun to open itself onto the *other shore of another heading*... Yet it has at the same time, *and through this even*, begun to make out, to see coming, to hear or understand as well, the other *of* the heading in general. More radically still, with more gravity still—though this is the gravity of a light and imperceptible chance that is nothing other than the very experience... of the other—it has begun to open itself, or rather to let itself open, or, better yet, to be affected with opening without opening *itself* onto an other, onto an other that the heading can no longer even relate to itself as *its* other, *the other with itself*. (OH, 75–76)

I recall that for Derrida, "Europe" is, today, the experience, or sentiment of this necessity that all identity and all universality claims require nonexclusion and an opening to the other, the non-Western, but also to what is still strictly to come, hence not calculable, hence other than the opposition of the Western and the non-Western. It is the limit-experience of the constitutive deidentifying traits, without which there can be no identity, concept, limit, or horizon. Defined in these terms, Europe is the idea of responsibility itself. Indeed, as the recalling-experience of the traces of the other in identity—of their reactivation—Europe could be understood as an identity responding to, affirming, and reaffirming the other from which it draws the possibility of (being) itself. Europe, in what constitutes it most properly, could thus be construed not only as a thankful acknowledging experience of the debt to the other but also as the demand for universal responsibility to and for the other. This experience of Europe, its singular feeling that any identity must, at heart, be that of a responsibility to and for the other—a feeling of universal scope—still merits being called Europe, because the name Europe has always meant a head and a heading. It is what could still make Europe potentially different, and put it ahead of itself, in the position to no longer be itself. It might make Europe different from itself if it were understood to name and embody the universal demand that justice be done to the other. As a demand for openness, universally, this feeling is not only a demand that Europe not close itself and not make itself homey in its difference with itself and others. It is the demand made on the Europeans above all, that is, on those who have seen themselves ahead, to seek their identity in opening and nonexclusion, and in abiding universally by the limits to which all responsibility, even a responsibility to and for responsibility itself, remains indebted.

Notes

1. Edmund Husserl, *The Crisis of European Sciences and Transcendental Phenomenology*, trans. D. Carr (Evanston, IL: Northwestern University Press, 1970), 16.

2. Jacques Derrida, *The Other Heading: Reflections on Today's Europe*, trans. P.-A. Brault and M. Naas (Bloomington: Indiana University Press, 1992), 12, 19. Hereafter abbreviated in the text as *OH*.

3. Husserl, *Crisis of European Sciences*, 275.

4. Husserl, *Crisis of European Sciences*, 275. See also Derrida's discussion of these lines in Jacques Derrida, *The Problem of Genesis in Husserl's Philosophy*, trans. M. Hobson (Chicago: University of Chicago Press, 2003), 157–159.

5. Husserl, *Crisis of European Sciences*, 275.

6. Massimo Cacciari, *Gewalt und Harmonie: Geo-Philosophie Europas*, trans. G. Memmert (Munich: Carl Hanser, 1995), 170.

7. Jean-Luc Nancy, *The Inoperative Community*, trans. P. Connor et al. (Minneapolis: University of Minnesota Press, 1991), 12.

8. At the risk of the always possible reinscription into a classical problematic of precisely that which Derrida's text seeks to displace, I shall call this *singular feeling*, because it is also one about conditions of possibility, a transcendental feeling, as it were. I make this claim in order to demarcate this feeling from what one ordinarily understands by that term and to emphasize its singularity. Needless to say, Derrida's texts question the possibility of the distinction between the empirical and the transcendental, but such detranscendentalization does not, for that matter, seek a return to the ontic, the empirical, the historic, or relative. What is at stake for Derrida is not the necessity of the distinction but rather the possibility of its absoluteness. The point Derrida makes is that a transcendental experience occurs in a singular experience, and in the case of the conditions of European identity, moreover, in a mode that is not cognitive but rather of the order of sentiment.

9. See, for instance, *OH*, 78–79, where Derrida speaks of the duty of "tolerating and respecting all that is not placed under the authority of reason," and the necessity to respect even "whatever refuses a certain responsibility."

10. For a discussion of the pathos of wonder as the fundamental attunement at the origin of European identity, see Klaus Held, "The Origin of Europe with the Greek Discovery of the World," *Epoché* 7, no. 1 (Fall 2002): 88.

11. Martin Heidegger, *What is Philosophy?*, trans. W. Kluback and J. T. Wilde (Estover, UK: Vision Press, 1989), 27. Hereafter abbreviated in the text as *WP*.

12. "The often heard expression 'Western-European philosophy' is, in truth, a tautology," Heidegger claims (*WP*, 29–30).

13. Martin Heidegger, *Being and Time*, trans. J. Macquarrie and E. Robinson (London: SCM, 1962), 63.

14. Undoubtedly, Heidegger's reservations regarding the concept of universality go much deeper. Unlike the rational idea of Husserl, an idea that can, and must, claim universality, the thought, or feeling of being, though not antiuniversal, implies a displacement of that concept and conceptuality.

15. The same is valid for singling out and imposing one language as the language of European culture. On philosophical and conceptual grounds, rather than on the basis of any empirical or even pragmatic superiority, one might justify placing one language ahead of all the others as the representative of a more promising idea of language. In other words, a language's superiority can be justified only on the grounds of its greater ability to reach beyond the national, the idiomatic; that is, on the grounds that its conceptual range extends beyond the particularity of its idiom, to include the implicit responsibility for and to what is universal that comes with that greater range. It is a superiority that presents itself, in short, that makes claims for itself and answers to the claims it makes.

8

AN IDEA IN THE KANTIAN SENSE?

Undoubtedly, when speaking about "Europe" it is far from clear whether this name designates a concept, a notion, or an idea. Yet, if Europe is a task, in fact, an infinite task, as has been suggested throughout the reflections on Europe within phenomenological thought from Husserl to Derrida, then its determination as a task entails that Europe is, first and foremost, an idea rather than a concept. As a concept, that is, as a cognitive representation, Europe would necessarily have to be something unified, something that holds a multiplicity of geographical entities and histories together in one whole, through one essence, which would be difficult, if not impossible, to assert both geographically and historically. Indeed, a concept of Europe would require the conclusive determinateness, or definite outlining, of its object within its particular limits. If Europe is not a reality that a concept could make known to us, then, to speak about Europe as an idea suggests, at first, that it is just that: merely, solely an idea, in short, a nebulous or ambiguous representation to which nothing really corresponds from an empirical perspective. But if an idea does not present its object by way of complete determination of the elementary components of its essence but only highlights certain moments of it, is it not because the idea, as opposed to the concept, suggests that the object is incomplete, that there is something missing? Although its object is thus lacking in determinateness, the idea itself, therefore, is something definitely unified, complete, and determined. As *eidos* or *idea*, the idea confronts all things that derive from and participate in it with the form of the thing itself, the *ontos on*, that is, an ideality more perfect than the one that things themselves can accomplish. And even when the idea becomes a representation, a mental copy of what *is* in post-Cartesianism, this representation continues to offer to the subject a presence of what is, whose ideality objects can only imitate in imperfect ways.

Now, when we speak of Europe as an idea, without, however, implying that it is therefore something nebulous or vague, what in fact do we mean? Must we not even admit that we have become so accustomed to referring to Europe in this way that we don't realize any more what it really means to speak of ideas, to connect Europe to an idea of Europe, and to measure Europe against an idea of itself? As a unity of sense, in distinction from the unity of the object that the concept provides, the idea points to something in its object that is deficient, that still demands work. Conversely, if the object indulges in self-sufficiency and the illusion of complete determination, the idea has the subversive effect of breaking open such self-closure. Thus, François Jullien points out that the vocation of the idea of universality tied into the idea of Europe consists in protesting against what is and in "reopening a breach in all enclosing and satisfied totality, so as to re-launch within it an aspiration" toward something beyond.[1] But the idea is perhaps linked to the question of Europe in an even more radical way. Indeed, take the famous comparison that Nietzsche draws between Europe and the rest of the continent in *Beyond Good and Evil*. As a "little peninsula" protruding from ancient Asia, "which wants to signify as against Asia the 'progress of man,'" the thrust of this characterization suggests that Europe is heading off the continent, detaching itself from its own geographical moorings in the landmass to which it remains barely attached by an isthmus, and stretching out toward something beyond its limits as a spatial and historical entity and identity.[2] Nietzsche here suggests that Europe is constituted by an ideational movement in which it uproots itself from the landmass of the continent and even strives to detach itself from itself, reaching for a beyond of itself in the form of an idea such as (but, as the inverted commas indicate, this is just a dated example) "the 'progress of man,'" without ever being exhausted by any determined idea. Europe is, in essence, nothing but this movement of making itself into an idea, without coming to a rest in one final representation of it. When we speak of an idea of Europe to begin with, without yet specifying its content, it is this movement of a relation to itself in which Europe transcends itself that is emphasized. To be of the order of an idea means that Europe detaches itself from its own immediacy, relates to itself in a self-critical manner, and faces itself as an other in relation to itself. Furthermore, to be an idea implies that this process of self-transcendence is infinite and that it is made up of infinite tasks.

Thus defined as an idea, one, moreover, of infinite tasks, is to conceive of Europe—to employ an expression coined, as far as I know, by Husserl—as an "idea in the Kantian sense."[3] Obviously, qualifying "idea" in this way suggests that idea is to be taken in a specific sense here, presumably in distinction from Plato's understanding of the term but also more broadly, from the general or common sense of the term. Before we can judge what is at stake in speaking of Europe as an idea in a Kantian sense, and what the difference may be in arguing eventually that the idea of Europe must not, or even should not, be characterized in this manner, it is, of course, obvious that we should ask, first, what is an idea according to Kant and, in particular, an "idea in the Kantian sense"? Instead of the lengthy, and rather technical discussion of Kant's conception of idea in the original full-length version of this paper, I must for reasons of time, limit myself to answering this question in the most economical way. Let me, therefore, first offer something resembling a schematic dictionary entry: an idea in the Kantian sense is not only a representation to which no congruent sensory or empirical object corresponds but which, nonetheless, is necessary to the function of reason. Ideas are, by definition, ideas of reason. In reason's theoretical employment, the ideas of reason have a merely regulative function with respect to the manifold of the understanding and serve to bring systematic unity into this manifold. In the case of practical reason, ideas, although they cannot theoretically be validated, function as postulates whose recognition secures the possibility of the moral law that the human being has a duty to observe.

Kant develops his doctrine of the ideas, first and foremost, in the context of his elaborations on theoretical reason in the First Critique, more precisely, in the first book of "The Transcendental Dialectic," and in "The Appendix to the Transcendental Dialectic." For what follows, it is not insignificant to keep this primarily theoretical interest of Kant's theory of the ideas in mind, namely, the fact that the ideas are first of all defined with respect to the role they are to play within the domain of cognition. Kant introduces the notion of the ideas in a remarkable debate with the Platonic notion of eidos. It is a remarkable debate, indeed, to the extent that although Kant's prime concern is to show that ideas have a necessary role to play in theoretical cognition, the deciding examples from Plato to which he resorts to develop his own conception of idea are nonetheless almost all taken from the practical realm (the question of virtue, and above all Plato's republic). And yet, Kant's doctrine of the ideas is not only geared toward establishing, first of all, the ideas' significance with respect to theoretical cognition, but his definition of them also takes place in analogy to what obtains for the a priori concepts of the understanding. (In the same way as the pure concepts are derived from the judgments of the understanding, the ideas are shown to be latent in the syllogisms of reason.) But, let me first emphasize that ideas are not just any kind of representations. Above all, they do not concern objects; they do not contribute anything to their understanding. Whereas the understanding creates concepts for particular objects, thus making their cognition possible, reason creates ideas only in order to bring systematic coherence into the manifold of objective cognition. In other words, rather than having a cognitively constitutive character, the ideas in theoretical reason concern only the whole of what understanding can know, the whole of empirical cognition, or, simply put, understanding itself. They are "concepts" of a maximum of systematic coherence with which reason confronts the understanding and the manifold of its cognitions, and for which they serve as signposts, say, to orient cognition toward bringing about the comprehensive systematic unity of this manifold. It is in this sense that, in distinction from the pure concepts of the understanding, ideas are characterized as "merely" regulative. Qua ideas of reason, ideas are transcendental, but they are transcendental not in the sense that they provide the constitutive pure concepts for the understanding of objects but in the sense that they furnish the unconditional, that is, the totality of all conditions, for all conditional experience, so as to meet reason's demand that knowledge have the unity of reason.

As ideas of reason, ideas are necessary representations of a maximum of perfection, a maximum of systematic unity in knowledge. But as such maxima to which no sensory, or empirical object, can ever be fully adequate, ideas can only theoretically (and practically) be approximated, that is, can only be accomplished in a tangential fashion. It is also in this sense that Kant can speak of the ideas as tasks to be completed. Although it is in the interest of reason that such tasks be carried out, they are never finished, yet not simply because like the Platonic ideas, their intrinsic determinative completion could not possibly be objectified in a sensory, that is, finite fashion. Indeed, a further characteristic of the idea in the Kantian sense is that in distinction from the Platonic *eide*, ideas for Kant are not exhaustively determinable. Speaking of the limits set to the full realization of ideas in the practical realm, Kant says, with respect to the idea of freedom, for instance, that no one should try to determine this limit "just because it is freedom that can go beyond every proposed boundary" (*CPR*, 397).[4] The same is valid of the idea of God or the unity of the soul. Finally, ideas are not only representations of maxima of reason with which reason confronts the understanding in the face of the manifold of its cognitions. As representations that help the understanding to orient itself in reason's effort to bring systematic unity into the manifold of knowledge, the ideas also provide the understanding with rules of how to accomplish, by way of approximation, the unity in question. In fact, without the guiding ideas, the unity of reason remains abstract, or rather undetermined, in the same way as the actions of the understanding remain undetermined without their schematization (579). In what amounts to, perhaps, the most fundamental definition of the idea, Kant characterizes it as an analogue of a schema. He writes, "The idea of reason is an analogue of a schema of sensibility, but with this difference, that the application of concepts of the understanding to the schema of reason is not likewise a cognition of the object itself (as in the application of the categories to their sensible schemata), but only a rule or principle of the systematic unity of all use of the understanding" (602–603). It is precisely because of their nature of a schema of sorts, that the ideas in the Kantian sense are no longer "merely empty thought-entities," but, on the contrary, effective rules of thought for bringing forth the unity of cognition demanded by reason (605).

As Kant holds in the "Appendix," the systematic unity that is to be accomplished with regard to the cognition of objects rather than being "taken . . . from the constitution of the object," is taken "from the interest of reason in regard to a certain possible perfection of the cognition of this object" (603). Grounded on this "single unified interest" of reason, the idea as an analogue of a schema is, thus, a subjective principle, also called a "*maxim* of reason" (603). As also becomes clear from the chapter concluding the "Transcendental Dialectic," the way the "schema, ordered in accordance with the conditions of the greatest unity of reason," is to achieve the greatest systematic unity within our empirical cognitions is by deriving "the object of experience, as it were, from the imagined [*eingebildeten*] object of this idea as its ground or cause" (605–606). Thanks to the imagination, which provides the idea with an object (for example, that of a supreme intelligence), the idea is schematized and thus rendered capable of being related to objects given in experience. Whereas in the case "*an object absolutely* [*Gegenstand schlechthin*]" is given to me, concepts serve to secure the determination of this object; in the case an object is given to me "*in the idea*

[*Gegenstand in der Idee*]," this object is only a schema that serves the understanding to represent other objects by way of their relation to this idea with respect to their systematic unity (605). In accordance with the subjective nature of this principle, under whose guidance the objects of experience are to be interconnected as much as possible, this derivation of the objects of experience can thus only be indirect. The one unified interest of reason manifests itself by proceeding *as if* the manifold of cognitions derived from an ultimate intelligence, or were grounded in one single substance, or an "original image of all reason" (607). The unity that is thus achieved by way of a regulative idea is, as Kant remarks, "only a *projected* unity, which one must regard not as given in itself, but only as a problem; this unity, however, helps to find a principle for the manifold and particular uses of the understanding, thereby guiding it even in those cases that are not given and making it coherently connected" (593). With this, the regulative nature of ideas in the theoretical realm is finally circumscribed. Construed as an analogue of a schema, it becomes clear one more time to what extent the notion of idea is conceived here exclusively in a theoretical vein.

In view of what I have developed so far with respect to the notion of an idea in the Kantian sense—that is, an idea of unity and a maximum of perfection that can be approximated only progressively but still has to play a capital, although only regulative role in the domain of knowledge in spite of its indeterminacy—I ask whether "Europe" can be characterized in this way as it has been from Husserl onwards. Indeed, Derrida, whose conception of Europe will concern me hereafter, forcefully suggests that Europe is not an idea to begin with and explicitly takes issue with its determination as an idea in the Kantian sense.

In *Europe, or the Infinite Task*, I have shown that Derrida's conception of Europe in terms of an identity that differs from itself and that is characterized by unlimited hospitality, unconditional responsibility toward the other, or the to-come, aims at a declosure of the horizon of the world as an opening that has already determined in advance who and what the other is prior to his or her arrival, a horizon, in short, that from the beginning is already closed.[5] Such declosure and bursting open of the horizon is the condition for any world worthy of its name, a universal world, that is, a world in which any other as other would be welcome, would have a chance to come into being. In *Of Hospitality*, Derrida writes that "'Europe' perhaps designates the time and space propitious to this unique event: it was in Europe that the *law* of universal hospitality received its most radical and probably most formalized definition."⁶ However, for the present purpose, rather than considering Derrida's elaborate reflections on hospitality in the aforementioned book, I will concentrate on his response to a question concerning hospitality addressed to him by Giovanna Borradori in her interview, "A Dialogue with Jacques Derrida." After Derrida's evocation of the aporetic nature of the injunctions that form the core of hospitality, which demands unconditional realization although it also seems that it can only be realized in conditional ways, Borradori remarks that what Derrida has exposed of hospitality "sounds like a regulative idea," adding, "though I know you do not like this expression. . . ."⁷ Undoubtedly, starting with *Speech and Phenomena*, Derrida has regularly addressed the notion of the idea in the Kantian sense in a critical fashion, but it is in his response to Borradori that, to my knowledge, he provides not only his most direct and extensive but also his most nuanced account of the notion in question.⁸ Of course, we are not dealing here with a written text by Derrida but with spontaneous improvisations on the theme of the idea in a Kantian sense, and thus some interpretive caution is warranted. In any event, on this occasion he notes that, rather than "straightforward objections," his quibbles over the notion of the idea in the Kantian sense are merely of the order of reservations. In other words, while withholding his full assent, the notion of an idea in the Kantian sense is at the same time thought of as an ultimate reserve, or resource. Derrida avers, "For lack of anything better, if we can say this about a regulative idea, the regulative idea remains perhaps an ultimate reservation. Though such a last recourse risks becoming an alibi, it retains a certain dignity; I cannot swear that I will not one day give in to it."⁹

In the dialogue Derrida offers just three reservations, although there is also an intimation that he has several more in mind when at the end he submits that "these [three] are a few of the reasons why, without ever giving up on reason and a certain 'interest of reason,' I hesitate to use the expression 'regulative idea.'"¹⁰ Now, as the last of the three reservations reveals, his hesitations, rather than concerning a loose concept of this idea, are ultimately directed against the strictly Kantian notion of the regulative idea as, indeed, it is elaborated in the context of the "Appendix to the Transcendental Dialectics." Furthermore, even though the first two reservations are about only a loose understanding of the regulative idea, Derrida's criticism of it already takes place, however implicitly, in light of the meaning that the idea in a Kantian sense has in "its strictly Kantian context."¹¹ As is clear from the interview, Derrida's talk of a loose way of speaking of the Kantian notion of idea, as opposed to a strict one, refers to all those occasions in which this notion is evoked without taking the slightest account of its systematic place in Kant's thought as a whole. Finally, by targeting the loose talk about the idea in the Kantian sense in the first two reservations, it is suggested that any critical approach to the idea in question must take into account the technical details in which Kant works out this notion, as well as its place within the architectonics of Kantian thought. In his first reservation, Derrida holds that in its loose sense "the regulative idea remains in the order of the *possible*, an ideal possible, to be sure, one that is infinitely deferred, but one that participates in what at the end of an infinite history would still fall into the realm of the possible, the realm of what is virtual or potential, of what is within the power of someone, some 'I can,' to reach, in theory, in a form that is not wholly freed from all teleological ends."[12] Apart from understanding the human being as constituted by a set of faculties, abilities, or potentialities, such loose talk about the regulative idea, which, according to Derrida, currently prevails in philosophical discourse, is symptomatic of a very classical concept of reason that, to quote *Rogues*, refers to "what presents itself or announces its presentation according to the *eidos*, the *idea*, the ideal, the regulative Idea or, something else that here amounts to the same, the telos."[13] In this case the regulative idea is a very well-determined conception of possibilities (including potentialities or virtualities) that are, or can be, fully known in advance of their actualization, even though their complete execution may be infinitely deferred. Yet, in spite of the fact that such an idea is always only approximated imperfectly and may in the end remain inaccessible in its full extent, it is nevertheless conceived as being in the power of a subject for whom it serves as a determined telos for all its thoughts and deeds. If a full realization of it proves impossible in the end, it is merely for reasons of the subject's finitude. In many ways, what Derrida says here about a loose conception of the regulative idea resonates with precisely what Kant himself says about it. Additional proof of this is offered by the fact that, on the many other occasions that Derrida has taken issue with the idea in a Kantian sense, he has criticized it on precisely these grounds that here are associated with its conception within a very classical conception of reason. In other words, the loose talk about the ideas in the Kantian sense is part and parcel of Kant's own discourse on them, but within the "strictly Kantian context" there is also another, stricter conception of them.

To such an understanding of the regulative idea as remaining in the order of the possible, that is, of what can be known and calculated in advance and can become the content of a program to be deployed, Derrida opposes in the dialogue "the im-possible . . . what must remain (in a nonnegative fashion) foreign to the order of my possibilities, to the order of the 'I can,' to the theoretical, descriptive, constative, and performative orders."[14] Before I pursue this line of thought, however, let me recall that in my commentary on the regulative idea in Kant, I already highlighted, however briefly, a reason that prevents accessibility to the unconditionality in question, one that is distinct from the subject's sensible nature and finitude that, according to the classical interpretation of the regulative idea, inhibits all full realization of it. Indeed, are what Derrida calls structural reasons, on the basis of which he questions the traditional philosophical interpretation of Kant's regulative idea, not already broached by Kant himself? Kant writes, "For whatever might be the highest degree of perfection at which humanity must stop, and however great a gulf must remain between the idea and its execution, no one can or should try to determine this, just because it is freedom that can go beyond every proposed boundary" (397). If the regulative idea is the maximum of a perfection for which there is no adequate equivalent in experience, it is not primarily because of the limits of the human being as a sensible being but because of the nature of freedom, which goes beyond every boundary and thus cannot be fixed in a determined end. The inevitable approximation that comes with such a conception of the idea is thus due to the fact that it lacks a definitely circumscribable content. As noted by Paul Natorp, a neo-Kantian philosopher who has extensively discussed the idea in the Kantian sense in terms of an infinite task, since "the task is, as is clear, an infinite one, there is strictly speaking no approximation to a fixed end, but only a progression into the infinite in which the aim poses itself always in a new, and grander fashion."[15] According to Natorp, then, the regulative idea is not so much an idea that is brought progressively closer in the infinite effort to realize it than "a clearly prescribed direction toward it," through which one comes closer and closer but that simultaneously shows the end in a progressively "new, and grander fashion."[16] Despite the ambiguities of this formulation, if Kant's statements on perfection and freedom are taken into account, these lines suggest that the idea is never the same but infinitely open to freedom's own transgression of all boundaries in which it could be enclosed as within a horizon and that, consequently, the direction to it, the act of approximating it or the regulative use of it in an infinite task that may require reconceiving the notion of infinity itself, makes up the core of the idea in question. Undoubtedly, freedom is a reason for the ultimate inaccessibility of the idea, but whether it is a structural reason in the sense that Derrida understands it will have to be left unanswered here.

For Derrida, as opposed to the regulative idea understood as the idea of something that is within the range of my possibilities even though I am not fully able to realize it, and something thus infinitely deferred, the im-possible is of the order of a demand or law that, rather than originating within me, comes from the other, for example, the other human being, but also the other within me, and confronts me with something that from my perspective and abilities is flatly im-possible. Take, for example, the demand of hospitality to the other, which comes from the other precisely insofar as he, she, or it is *other* and demands that he, she, or it be received without having to compromise his, her, or its own otherness. But this demand of unconditional hospitality, whose *law* transgresses all the conditional laws of hospitality, also has the effect of, ultimately, making hospitality impossible. Furthermore, the *laws* of hospitality, which unconditional hospitality requires in order to become effective, stipulate limits that defy the unconditional law of hospitality, making hospitality, in turn, impossible. In each case, the im-possible is demanded of me with respect to the other. The demands that come with both the law and the laws are not only aporetic; they are demands regardless of my possibilities, in short, demands if ever there were such things. Now, as Derrida goes on to say,

> this im-possible is not privative. It is not the inaccessible, and it is not what I can indefinitely defer: it is announced to me, sweeps down upon me, precedes me, and seizes me *here now*, in a nonvirtualizable way, in actuality and not potentiality. It comes upon me from on high, in the form of an injunction that does not simply wait on the horizon, that never leaves me in peace and will not let me put it off until later. Such an urgency cannot be *idealized*, no more than the other as other can. This im-possible is thus not a regulative *idea* or *ideal*. It is what is most undeniably *real*. Like the other. Like the irreducible and nonappropriable difference of the other.[17]

If the im-possible, with which the heteronomous law—heteronomous since it comes from the other—confronts me, is not privative, it is because in the way that it challenges me the question of whether I am capable or incapable of responding to it does not pose itself. If, furthermore, it is not inaccessible, it is because the nature of such a demand allows for no gradual approximation and challenges me in the implacable fullness of its aporetic exigency. Such a demand, then, cannot be idealized, cannot be construed as an idea or ideal, because it is a demand from the other that solicits me without mediation, right here and now, and that defies me to respond on the spot.[18] Rather than a confrontation with an idea of the unconditional, it is one with a most real instance of an injunction to act in a way for which I am never prepared, and to act now, at this very moment, immediately. If, indeed, the notion of the regulative idea is understood as providing the rules, or guidelines, for orientation in the practical realm and for doing something by which, precisely because it is within my possibilities, I must abide, even though I cannot ever hope to make my actions fully adequate to its norms, Derrida's thematization of the responsibility that is demanded of me by the other as other is one that no idea in a Kantian sense can capture. It is not of the order of an idea to begin with. It does not compel me to act out of duty but, rather, right now, without any order or rule.[19] But, as should also be clear, to say that "Europe" is not an idea (regulative or not) is in no way to minimize the "idea" of Europe. On the contrary, that name now calls for the realization of something that is, perhaps, more demanding than what an idea can represent, a realization even more urgent, even more pressing than that of the idea of an ordered world or of humanity as such. Without the command of a categorical duty, the very existence of something like a world nonetheless depends on it.

According to Derrida's second reservation regarding the notion of the regulative idea as it is understood within the parameters of the classical notion of reason, "The responsibility of what remains to be decided or done (in actuality) cannot consist in following, applying, or realizing a norm or rule. When there is a determinable rule, I know what must be done, and as soon as such knowledge dictates the law, action follows knowledge as a calculable consequence: one *knows* what path to take, one no longer hesitates; the decision then no longer decides anything but simply gets deployed with the automatism attributed to machines. There is no longer any place for justice or responsibility (whether juridical, political, or ethical)."[20] Whereas the first reservation took as its focus the fact that the idea calls upon a subject's possibilities to approximate the maximum that it represents, the second reservation puts the regulative aspect of the idea in the Kantian sense in question insofar as the rules by which it regulates all my actions are by definition cognitive. Yet, if in the face of any need to act I know in advance which rules to follow, then no decision, no ethical putting oneself on the line, is required anymore. I already know what I have to do, and I act according to this knowledge. "Regulative," understood as providing knowable directions and orientations for actions, thus makes of the idea a norm, a prescriptive set of rules to follow that no longer makes any demand on the subject to decide. Furthermore, in an encounter with the other there is no time to apply rules; the response must be invented without ado, immediately—otherwise it is not a response in any strict sense. This does not mean, of course, that decision would exclude analysis and knowledge (or memory) but only that analysis and knowledge cannot lay claim to generality but must in each decision be unique, singular, that is, conform to the situation in which the im-possible decision occurs.

This brings me, then, to the final reservation. Derrida avers that "if we come back this time to the strict meaning Kant gave to the *regulative* use of ideas (as opposed to their *constitutive* use), we would, in order to say anything on this subject and, especially, in order to appropriate such terms, have to subscribe to the entire Kantian architectonic and critique."[21] The point of reservation consists in saying that to appropriate the notion of the regulative in a strict sense would require subscribing to the whole framework of Kant's philosophy. Perhaps, then, this is also the moment to recall that Kant's theory regarding the regulative ideas is developed primarily within the context of his theoretical philosophy, where its aim is to provide the understanding with a systematic unity that would secure it against the suspicion of contingency. Undoubtedly, in elaborating on the role that the regulative idea must play within the domain of cognition, Kant acknowledges that ideas also have a practical employment. In *Critique of Pure Reason* he even goes so far as to intimate an ascendency of the practical over the theoretical employment of the ideas in question. But it remains the case that the whole theory of the regulative idea, in all its technicality, is developed from the beginning in terms of its role in the cognitive realm. The very distinction between the regulative use and the constitutive use of ideas, to which Derrida alludes and according to which their constitutive use would amount to a usurpation of a use that only the categories or pure concepts of the understanding can legitimately claim, shows to what extent Kant's elaboration on the regulative idea is a function of the problematic of experience and cognition. This is also the case concerning his definition of the idea as analogue of a schema that represents the condition under which it can guide the understanding in realizing the systematic unity that reason demands from it. To appropriate the idea in question without reservation would thus require one not only to adopt the whole Kantian project but also to subscribe to the theoretical over-determination of the notion of the regulative idea even there where its use may be practical.

While acknowledging that within the context of a dialogue he cannot with any seriousness proceed to develop all the implications that come with the notion of the regulative idea in a strict Kantian sense, implications to which one would have to subscribe if one were to adopt it, he notes that, in order to expand on these implications, one "would have to begin by asking about what Kant calls 'those differences in the interest of reason,' the *imaginary* (the *focus imaginarius*, that point toward which all the lines directing the rules of understanding—which is not reason—tend and converge, the point they thus indefinitely *approximate*), the necessary *illusion*, which need not necessarily deceive us, the figure of an approach or approximation [*zu nähern*] that tends indefinitely toward rules of universality, and especially the indispensable use of the *as if* [*als ob*]."[22] Indeed, all these topics dominate the immediate context, in the "Appendix to the Transcendental Dialectic," in which Kant elaborates on the regulative function of the transcendental idea. The way in which these themes are interlinked and their implications have been broached, however cursorily, in the preceding short account of Kant's conception of the ideas. It seems to me that in listing all these themes that are interconnected with the regulative nature of the idea in question, Derrida, at first, puts a special stress on the concept of approximation. (And for good reason, especially since this is what is usually associated with the notion of an idea in the Kantian sense.) Approximation, coming or bringing into nearness (*annähern*), presupposes that the object of this objective is there in advance and in full presence. But the theme of the "as if" is highlighted as well, and, even though Derrida notes in a footnote that he is "sometimes tempted to make 'as if' [he] had no objections to Kant's 'as ifs,'" the conception is nonetheless sorted out as one that needs circumspection.[23] As already suggested by the reference to the imagination, but also and above all by the massive citations in a footnote from the "Appendix" regarding the use of the "as if" in the determination of the regulative idea, the interconnection of the latter with the problematic of the "as if" makes its use for thinking through the demands that come with the encounter of the other highly problematic.[24] According to the "Appendix," it is in the interest of reason to proceed as if all experience yielded a systematic unity, and phenomena are to be connected as if they were the expression of a supreme purpose. This kind of necessary fictionality involved in what the regulative idea effectuates, or rather that gives the rule for it to be regulative, not only remains fully under the sway of its opposite, namely, cognitive certainty, but also lacks a certain seriousness, I dare say. Ultimately, in the response to the other there is no room for fiction. As a final reason for why the idea in the Kantian sense requires caution "when speaking of the to come or of the democracy to come," both imminently interlinked in Derrida with the idea of Europe, he reminds his interlocutor "that the very idea of *world* remains a *regulative idea* for Kant, the second one, between two others that are themselves, so to speak, two forms of sovereignty: the 'myself' [*Ich selbst*], as soul or as thinking nature, and God."[25] "World," as Kant understands it here, is one of the forms of totality that the regulative idea seeks to foster with respect to the whole of the cognizable, whose purposive unity of all things requires, in turn, in the mode of the "as if," the thought that every ordinance in the world has its source in the intention of a highest reason.

To speak of Europe as a task, thus, cannot mean to conceive of it as a regulative idea, insofar as such an idea is one of a purposeful unity that regulates all our actions so as to make them progressively approximate this goal without, however, ever coming near its completion and perfection. Now, if this is the case, does one not have to wonder whether Europe even can be an idea in the first place? Understood from the aporetic tensions implicit in unconditional hospitality, Europe can in no way be conceived as an idea, that is, as an exigency of unity or a whole. If Europe is neither a concept nor an idea, with what, then, are we left? In one of Derrida's last texts, "Double Mémoire," presented in 2004 at the Festival d'Avignon just a couple of months before his death—a text in the form of a telegram addressed to "Old Europe"—Derrida apostrophizes "Europe," using the familiar "tu" (you) in speaking to her. The text opens, indeed, with the words: "'Vieille Europe, Je ne t'ai jamais tutoyée'" (Old Europe, I have never been on familiar terms with you).[26] But whom, or what, is Derrida addressing when he invokes Europe on a first-person basis? The addressee is neither Europe as a geopolitical entity, nor Europe as an idea. Indeed, if Europe is a proper name, as such a name it cannot be an idea. "Europe" as the addressee to whom Derrida says "tu" is, first of all, Europe as a name, a singular token for an equally singular referent, namely, the "luminous memory" of what in the name of Europe has been promised as philosophy, democracy, or the Enlightenment, but also for Europe's nocturnal memory. Europe, here, is invoked in propria persona, as it were, as present in everything that her singular name promises in defiance of the crimes that have been perpetuated in her name throughout history and that constitute the other, "nocturnal" side of her memory. Europe is that double memory to which, as Europeans, we have a responsibility, the luminous side of which Derrida addresses as "Old New Europe" in the express hope that, on the basis of this double memory, Europe commit herself to a way that she alone can go because of the luminous side of her memory, namely, a way that brings about a resolutely *altermondialiste* Europe and, ultimately, a world.[27]

Thus understood as the memory of a set of exigencies, in particular, the exigency of an unconditional openness to alterity in defiance of the other, darker side of its past, the ideational status of Europe as an infinite task needs to be reconsidered. In order to accomplish this, it is important to recall the nature of the injunctions that are linked up with the luminous side of European memory: unconditional hospitality to the to-come, the other, the singular, the event, and so forth, but also, and not least of all, the conditional laws of hospitality that both make the unconditional law effective and at the same time secure the host's right against the arrival of the worst. What philosophy, democracy, and the Enlightenment promise—a resolutely *altermondialiste* world, a world worthy of its name—is thus based on aporetic injunctions. It is precisely this aporetic nature of the demands that make up the luminous memory of Europe that require rethinking the latter's ideational status. The concepts of the idea, or of the regulative idea, are not capable of adequately accounting for the aporetic nature of the demands in question or the invention each time anew of a response to them.

Made up of a set of unconditional injunctions without which that which the name of Europe promises could not come into being, Europe is not a theoretical model to be practically realized. Nor is it, furthermore, an idea in the Kantian sense, a maximum of reason to be incrementally realized without ever bringing it to full completion. In distinction from an idea of Europe or from Europe as a regulative idea, which provide the guidelines and telos for a praxis aiming at its full realization or, respectively, guidelines for action so as to approach that goal in an infinite process, Europe understood as rooted in the demand of an unconditional openness and responsibility toward the other is not a theoretical representation in advance of the effort to practically implement it. As the promise associated with the luminous memory of Europe, Europe is not a predetermined goal that could be actualized over time with the help of a plan and a sequence of operations that constitute the means for accomplishing it. A law other than that which presides over the practical realization of a theoretical conception commands the notion of Europe.[28] Based on unconditional aporetic injunctions that have to be met at the same time, without compromise, Europe is an "idea" that requires execution here and now, without delay, in the entirety of the injunctions in question and at every single moment. In every instance, the contradictory injunctions of, say, hospitality without reservation *and* that of the conditional, that is, historical and cultural laws that also restrict hospitality in view of self-preservation, must be met not by way of discovering in a vision (*skopos*) the golden middle between the extremes but by facing them in their full exigency without giving in one way or the other. Whenever and wherever a decision takes place, whether it is an individual or institutional act, that is, when and where the aporetic demands of Europe are met head-on, Europe takes place. Rather than a step forward to its realization in a process of progressive approximation, every such decision, however small, is the realization of Europe in its entirety, each time anew, each time newly reinvented. If Europe is a task, moreover, an infinite one, it is because in its very finitude each decision regarding its demands is infinite in itself. Each decision is infinitely finite precisely because no idea or ideal can serve as a measure for such an act. Furthermore, it is infinite because Europe will not be an *altermondialiste* world without the full confrontation of the contradictory promises at all moments and at all times. Finally, if Europe is an infinite task, it is also because, rather than a goal infinitely to be approximated, each decision in the ethical relation to the other reinvents Europe in a new way.

Notes

1. François Jullien, *De l'Universel, de l'uniforme, du commun et du dialogue entre les cultures* (Paris: Fayard 2008), 271.

2. Friedrich Nietzsche, *Beyond Good and Evil: Prelude to a Philosophy of the Future*, trans. W. Kaufman (New York: Vintage, 1989), 65.

3. Edmund Husserl, *Ideas: General Introduction to Pure Phenomenology*, trans. W. R. Boyce Gibson (New York: MacMillan, 1931), 397–398.

4. Immanuel Kant, *Critique of Pure Reason*, trans. P. Guyer and A. W. Wood (Cambridge, MA: Cambridge University Press, 1998), 397. Hereafter abbreviated in the text as *CPR*.

5. See my *Europe, or the Infinite Task: A Study of a Philosophical Concept* (Stanford, CA: Stanford University Press, 2009), 265–338.

6. Jacques Derrida and Anne Dufourmantelle, *Of Hospitality*, trans. R. Bowlby (Stanford, CA: Stanford University Press, 2000), 141.

7. Giovanna Borradori, *Philosophy in a Time of Terror: Dialogues with Jürgen Habermas and Jacques Derrida* (Chicago: University of Chicago Press, 2003), 133.
8. Jacques Derrida, *Speech and Phenomena*, trans. D. Allison (Evanston, IL: Northwestern University Press, 1973), 101–102.
9. Borradori, *Philosophy*, 133–134.
10. Borradori, *Philosophy*, 135.
11. Borradori, *Philosophy*, 134.
12. Borradori, *Philosophy*, 134.
13. Jacques Derrida, *Rogues: Two Essays on Reason*, trans. P.-A. Brault and M. Naas (Stanford, CA: Stanford University Press, 2005), 135.
14. Borradori, *Philosophy*, 134.
15. Paul Natorp, "Philosophie und Psychologie," *Logos* 2/4 (1913): 183.
16. Natorp, "Philosophie und Psychologie," 183.
17. Borradori, *Philosophy*, 134.
18. Such immediacy does not, of course, imply that one just act out of the blue and that no rules whatsoever weigh in on one's decision, but only that they are not in the last resort what informs the act.
19. It is a law by which I am not expected to abide because of an ought. It is not an imperative that I have to follow because of some obligation or duty. See Derrida and Dufourmantelle, *Of Hospitality*, 83.
20. Borradori, *Philosophy*, 134–135.
21. Borradori, *Philosophy*, 135.
22. Borradori, *Philosophy*, 135.
23. Borradori, *Philosophy*, 193.
24. At this juncture it would be necessary to turn to the many contexts and occasions in which Derrida has taken up the problematic of the "as if."
25. Borradori, *Philosophy*, 135.
26. Jacques Derrida, "Double Mémoire," in *Le Théâtre des idées. 50 penseurs pour comprendre le XXIe siècle*, ed. N. Truong (Paris: Flammarion 2008), 15.
27. See Jacques Derrida, "Force of Law: The 'Mystical Foundation of Authority,'" trans. M. Quaintance, in *Acts of Religion*, ed. G. Anidjar (New York: Routledge, 2002), 247–248.
28. This other law for the actualization of Europe is not of the order of an alternative to the Western logic of modelization as is, according to François Jullien, the Chinese way of exploiting the potential of a situation by relying on the propensity of things to successfully obtain a hoped-for result. See François Jullien, *A Treatise of Efficacy: Between Western and Chinese Thinking*, trans. J. Lloyd (Honolulu: University of Hawai'i Press, 2004).

9

RESPONSIBILITY, A STRANGE CONCEPT

ALTHOUGH IT IS AT THE CENTER OF PHENOMENOLOGICAL and postphenomenological reflections on ethics today, the concept of responsibility only emerged rather recently. In fact, it was not until the end of the eighteenth century—more precisely in the context of the French Revolution—that the substantive "responsibility" first appeared in French, initially as a political term. Responsibility at that time referred to the obligation of the government—particularly of its ministers—to answer for and to take responsibility for their actions. The term acquired yet another sense in the Napoleonic Code—this time a juridical one—where it meant not only being the one who causes damages but also, and especially, being obligated to respond to questions before a court, to justify one's acts, and to repair the damages that one had caused.[1] However, it was not until the nineteenth century that "responsibility" became a philosophical concept. The names of Kierkegaard and Nietzsche mark the most important stages in the transformation of a term whose origins are political and juridical, into a philosophical and ethical one. It is not, however, until we come to the breakthrough of phenomenological thought that the notion of responsibility becomes *the* central concept of ethics. This "pure ethics" was sketched out in Husserl's work of the twenties, notably in the articles he wrote for the Japanese journal *Kaizo*; it elaborates an ethics based on the exigency of an absolute self-responsibility (*absolute Selbstverantwortung*). In evoking the replacement of traditional ethics, or an "ethics of presence"—that is to say, an ethics of virtues ensuring a way of life that would be the best one possible in the present, but that would not project itself into the future—by an ethics of responsibility that would have the future of humanity as its object, Hans Jonas explains this substitution according to a radical change in human activity: to wit, the unrivaled increase of the power of man over nature and life such that humankind becomes responsible both for and before nature.[2] But it is not enough to simply narrate this transformation: we must also ask ourselves what it was that predestined phenomenological philosophy to bring about this transformation. Likewise, we must clarify for ourselves the reasons why, from Husserl to Derrida, this ethics of responsibility develops by interlacing itself with a reflection on the origin and the future of Europe. Indeed, should we not ask ourselves whether or not this approach to the concept of responsibility put forward by phenomenology—in Husserl, in Heidegger, and many others—can still be called an ethics? Can the increasing dominance of the theme of responsibility in recent reflections on ethics be explained by the simple substitution of one theme for another? Or, would ethics itself be in doubt at the moment in history where the concept of responsibility came to replace the idea of the virtues? These questions, especially the most nuanced among them, will not all be answered here. However, they will be at the heart of what I will try to develop.

It would obviously be tempting to reconstruct the movement that takes us from the responsibility of an absolute self to the notion of a "responsibility without limits" in Derrida, by way of originary *Schuldigsein*—and all the more so since this notion is more or less explicitly elaborated in his debates with Husserl and Heidegger. However, to limit myself, I will have to focus my reflections on the relation that a thought of "responsibility without limits" would maintain with the problematic of Europe in Derrida's work. We should bear in mind that, in the course of his meditations on law and justice in "Force of Law," Derrida emphasizes that such a responsibility, which is both excessive and incalculable, is first of all a responsibility "before memory."[3] As in Husserl, for whom one is an "*heir* of the past" only insofar as "the inner vocation" of the philosopher "bears within itself at the same time the responsibility for the true being of mankind," in Derrida, responsibility is intimately linked to heritage, both cultural and philosophical.[4] Responsibility, then, takes shape as a response to a heritage that predates the free subject. And the first obligation before memory consists in receiving this heritage and in responding to its call in affirming it as inheritance. In *For What Tomorrow: A Dialogue,* while underlining the risk he takes in advancing "a few generalities on the notion of heritage," Derrida remarks that "the concept of responsibility has no sense at all outside of an experience of inheritance."[5] Now, this experience concerns first and foremost concepts corresponding to demands, injunctions, prescriptions, and imperatives. "Before memory" does not only simply refer to "a philologico-etymological task or a historian's task," but also to "responsibility in the face of a heritage that is at the same time the heritage of an imperative or of a sheaf of injunctions."[6] If responsibility responds before memory, with memory understood here as an ensemble of transmitted exigencies, then the obligation to this heritage must evidently measure up to these injunctions. As Derrida remarks, "even before saying that one is responsible for a particular inheritance, it is necessary to know that responsibility in general (responding for, responding to, responding in one's own name) is assigned to us, and that it is assigned to us through and through as an inheritance."[7] In other words, the demand to be responsible is a part of an inherited legacy and, consequently, to be responsible means not only to respond to all of the demands that concern us but also, in particular, to respond to the demand to be responsible, and to respond to this duty in a responsible fashion. What Derrida says on the subject of justice in "Force of Law" applies equally well to the concept of responsibility; "the first way to do it justice is to hear, read, and interpret it, to try to understand where it comes from, what it wants of us, knowing that it does so through singular idioms" like European languages, such that it is then a matter of "delimit[ing] [them] in relation to others."[8]

Let us note right away that, if "this responsibility toward memory is a responsibility before the very concept of responsibility that regulates the justice and appropriateness [*justesse*] of our behavior, of our theoretical, practical, ethico-political decisions" then it is no longer possible to speak rigorously of an ethics of responsibility.[9] If it is true that ethics concerns the relation to the other, the relation to being in common with the other, as well as the relation to the absolute other, then responsibility toward the legacy of injunctions and prescriptions preempts ethics proper, locating its origins instead in an experience of inheritance. Understood as a duty to respond, in one's name, to heritage, responsibility is indeed anterior not only to ethical action as practical decision-making but also to the domain of the theoretical insofar as the theoretical implies decision-making; as such, the theoretical is a domain that has to be both respected and transgressed in any decision that could be called responsible. Responsibility precedes the opposition between the theoretical and the ethical, that is, it precedes the differential relation from which ethics has taken its sense from Aristotle onward. For Derrida, ethics cannot be based on the hitherto constitutive values of "the person, the subject, consciousness, the self, the other as 'self,' as a conscious other, as a soul." This would define ethics in a way that has never satisfied Derrida. Rather, responsibility could refer to what, in *Alterités*, he refers to as an "ultra-ethics" (*ultra-éthique*), one which would bear on "duty itself, but . . . a duty that orders [us] to pose questions on the subject of the origin and the limits of ethics."[10] We should add that this reaffirmation of tradition as heritage of the concept of responsibility implicates all of the concepts tied to responsibility. Thus, responsibility before heritage entails not only the duty toward the concept of responsibility but also toward related concepts such as will, freedom, the self, and the person; it is a duty that consists precisely in the interrogation of these concepts.

To say that all responsibility presupposes the experience of inheritance does not amount to simply saying that the free subject stands before the obligation to receive the tradition and repeat this heritage faithfully. As Husserl had already emphasized, our relationship to heritage is a critical relationship. Derrida follows Husserl in claiming that in order for the subject to respond to the call of what has come before him as one assumed to be free, he must choose, prefer, sacrifice, exclude, and even abandon parts of the tradition. However, in doing so, Derrida also displaces the Husserlian concept of critique, since terms such as "choose," "prefer," "sacrifice," and "exclude," to which he resorts in order to qualify the responsible relationship to the tradition, are not equivalent to what Husserl calls "critique." In some way it is in one's own name that it becomes a matter of betraying one's heritage. To summarize, European memory requires a double affirmation from us; insofar as we selectively sift through what we have inherited, and therefore reinterpret what we have inherited, we respond to, for, and in the name of heritage in a responsible manner. The experience of inheritance—without which one could not have responsibility—is thus an aporetic experience. As such, it is one of conflicting demands. It is the demand to welcome the tradition while choosing, repeating, and betraying it. Such being responsible for what comes before us can only be responsible in selecting from what is bequeathed to us in order to reinvent what has been transmitted. Furthermore, since the concept of responsibility is connected to the notion of decision, fidelity to heritage implies cutting off and a selective resolution about what has been assigned to us. In other words, since it is born of an experience of what one has not chosen but of what one has received, responsibility toward heritage and, in particular, toward the (ethical) concept of responsibility itself, includes "a dissident and inventive rupture with respect to tradition, authority, orthodoxy, rule, or doctrine."[11] Being responsible in our own name for the heritage is demanded by the necessity of intervening in what one has received, thereby reopening this very heritage in a new and singular fashion. If it is a matter of responding for this heritage—and of responding for it "in one's name as in the name of the other"—then this is because the other whom we are speaking of here is first of all that which is other to the European heritage. But it is also that which, from the vantage point of this heritage, is not foreseeable: an other to come.[12]

Let us return to the question of the aporia. Derrida remarks that "responsibility, if there [is] any, will only ever have begun with the experience and experiment of the aporia."[13] There would be no responsibility were we to renounce one of the contradictory imperatives. Responsibility thus requires that there not be any rule or solution that would decide the conflict in advance. Making use of such a rule would be, Derrida writes, "the surest, the most reassuring definition *of responsibility as irresponsibility*."[14] There can be no responsibility without enduring the aporia in question. To quote Derrida, "When the path is clear and given, when a certain knowledge opens up the way in advance, the decision is already made, it might as well be said that there is none to make: irresponsibly, and in good conscience, one simply applies or implements a program."[15] More precisely, it is "impossible to conceive of a responsibility that consists in being responsible *for* two laws, or that consists in responding *to* two contradictory injunctions."[16] However, without this experience of impossibility, there could not be responsibility. Taking the rule of the impossible into account in this way means rethinking responsibility, thinking it otherwise. When Derrida writes in *The Other Heading*, "The condition of possibility of this thing called responsibility is a certain *experience and experiment of the possibility of the impossible: the testing of the aporia* from which one may invent the only *possible invention, the impossible invention*," it is to highlight the singularity of every responsible response.[17] A response will only bring an alliance of contradictory injunctions into being if no one but the author behind it will have produced it. But this is also to say that there is responsibility only on the condition that we let the impossible come. The endurance of the aporia—fidelity to European memory and its simultaneous betrayal in the name of the other, and of the other of the other—inscribes an opening to the future in the structure of responsibility, an opening that is likewise an opening to the incalculable and the unpredictable. To respond to the call of this heritage entails the obligation to always receive that which, from the other, could transform this heritage. If it is true that there can be no responsibility without an experience of heritage, then this same experience is also that of the possibility of an unforeseeable transformation of the heritage itself.

Since the (first) formulation of the concept of absolute self-responsibility (that is, the imperative of giving an account of oneself and of justifying each utterance said according to a universally acceptable method) in the articles written for the review *Kaizo* right up to *Crisis*, the question of responsibility in Husserl's writings turns out to be inseparable from a reflection on the origins and the future of Europe. To my knowledge, this link has never been called into question in the very interior of phenomenology itself. Seeking to develop a genealogy of responsibility, Jan Patočka, for example, conceives of this genealogy as "a genealogy of European responsibility or of responsibility as Europe, of *Europe-responsibility*."[18] Conversely, in *The Other Heading*, the question of the cultural identity of Europe is posed first in terms of responsibility when Derrida asks how such an identity can "respond and in a responsible way—responsible for itself, for the other, and before the other," in this case, to "the double question of *le capital*, of capital, and of *la capitale*, of the capital."[19] And after having defined this European cultural identity as an opening not only to identities other than those of Europe but also to what differs from these other, already constituted identities, and thus to what is other otherwise, Derrida poses the following question: "And what if Europe were this: the opening onto a history for which the changing of the heading, the relation to the other heading or to the other of the heading, is experienced as always possible? An opening and a non-exclusion for which Europe would in some way be responsible? For which Europe *would be*, in a constitutive way, this very responsibility? As if the very concept of responsibility were responsible, right up to its emancipation, for a European birth certificate?"[20] Clearly, the identification of European cultural identity with the concept of responsibility is here established by way of questioning—a question that is, moreover, modulated by the conditional. But Derrida does so only in order to submit the terms of this identity to the law that, according to *The Other Heading*, regulates every identification. Additionally, when it comes to European identity—this means that, however necessary it might be to anticipate a heading under which Europe could be gathered, this heading must not be "given"—"that is, it must not be identifiable in advance and once and for all."[21] The establishment of a fixed European essence would prevent Europe from identifying itself as the opening to the other and to the other of the other. For the moment, I will do nothing more than call attention to the comparative and conditional proposition according to which the concept of responsibility itself—that is, according to its phenomenal essence—testifies "right up to its emancipation, to a European birth certificate."[22] This echoes some of Husserl's propositions from *Crisis* in addition to pronouncements he made in Vienna in 1935. Moreover, if the concept of responsibility presupposes the experience of inheritance, then this heritage is precisely that of the European discourse on Europe, and Husserlian discourse is exemplary in this regard. In *The Other Heading*, Derrida writes:

> Now, we must ourselves be responsible for this discourse of the modern tradition. We bear the responsibility for this heritage, right along with the capitalizing memory that we have of it. We did not choose this responsibility; it imposes itself upon us, and in an even more imperative way, in that it is, as other, and from the other, the language of our language. How then does one assume this responsibility, this capital duty [*devoir*]? How does one respond? And above all, how does one assume a responsibility that announces itself as contradictory. . . ? It is necessary to make ourselves the guardians of an idea of Europe, of a difference of Europe, *but* of a Europe that consists precisely in not closing itself off in its own identity and in advancing itself in an exemplary way toward what it is not, toward the other heading or the heading of the other, indeed—and this is perhaps something else altogether—toward the other *of* the heading, which would be the beyond of this modern tradition, another border structure, another shore.[23]

The discourse on what constitutes Europe, or what points toward and promises in the name of Europe, is the heritage before which, and in response to which, responsibility itself arises. It is born from the call of this heritage that comes before us, a call that is other to us, which pulls us away from our roots, which liberates us from all linguistic limitations, and that finally opens us up to the other. Being called to this responsibility by European memory, we are obligated by it precisely to the extent that it is foreign to us. And it is foreign precisely because it calls us to liberate ourselves from those limitations that are ours. Paradoxically then, responsibility constitutes our identity in its difference from itself, an identity that from the outset is based on the other. As the "language of our language," the responsibility toward European memory subtends all of our relations, both to ourselves and to the other, as a language that is our own precisely insofar as it is capable of opening itself up to the other. Derrida determines the first duty then as one that "respond[s] to the call of European memory," in "re-identify[ing] Europe." Thus, "this *duty* is without common measure with all that is generally understood by the name duty, though it could be shown that all other duties perhaps presuppose it in silence."[24] Consequently, responsibility would arise neither from a link to the supreme Good, nor from a relationship to the human other and/or the divine. It would, therefore, neither be an ethics nor a religious law, but would instead be called by the memory of what was promised in the name of "Europe" at the origin of Europe in Greece; that is, it would itself be called by the project to find a proper identity in the will to free oneself from all identifying limitations. This universalizing demand is the project of philosophy. And, insofar as this responsibility toward and before this universalizing demand would be the duty toward an injunction to depart from oneself, to have one's identity outside of oneself, and to be oneself only from the vantage point of the other, it subtends the entirety of the so-called ethical dimension. Indeed, it is only on the basis of a prior commitment toward this heritage, from a responsibility toward the concept of responsibility and thus to all that is implied by such a concept, that the sense of properly ethical responsibilities are established, whatever such responsibilities are to God, the gods, or to the dead, humans, animals, and the inanimate world. Even before any of these responsibilities could be determined, "we have," as Derrida writes, "begun to respond. We are already caught up, we are caught out, in a certain responsibility, and the most ineluctable responsibility—as if it were possible to think a responsibility without freedom. We are invested with an undeniable responsibility at the moment we begin to signify something." The "heteronomic and dissymmetrical curving," or the "law of originary sociability," according to *Politics of Friendship*, precedes all experiences of friendship and of justice.[25] Likewise, the free or responsible subject is, from the start, taken in by the call of European memory. This call engages him before every deliberated commitment, precisely insofar as this relation to memory is a dissymmetrical relation to the other.

Insofar as we are the heirs of European culture, the responsibility in which we are invested, and which obligates us before all responsibilities and deliberate decisions, is a responsibility that comes before, I dare say, all constituted *Mitsein*—that is to say, that comes before any being-organized with other individuals in a concrete, real community; it also comes before all of the responsibilities that are born out of this social being. (It could perhaps be the case that this responsibility even comes before the existential structure of being-with.) It does not come from us as autonomous subjects, nor does it come from the other as an other human, as a neighbor, brother, friend, enemy, and so forth. The responsibility in question takes both the autonomous and the socialized self by surprise. To use a word from *Sein und Zeit*, responsibility is delivered over or entrusted [*überantwortet*] to the self. The self is entrusted to this responsibility that is given to it, set free, and handed over, and to which, inversely, the self is indebted. Heidegger evokes the term *Überantwortung* in his analysis of the call of conscience—an analysis that must both be brought together with, and demarcated from, what Derrida has to say on the subject of memory—to designate the fact that Dasein, as being-thrown, is not only a *factum* of being but that, as being-thrown, Dasein has always already been delivered over to existence. Heidegger writes, "*As this being* to which it has thus been delivered over [*überantwortet*], it *is, in its existing*, the basis of its potentiality for being."[26] Dasein, which is not itself at the origin of itself, and which is never at any masterly foundation of its most proper being, receives the duty to be this foundation in projecting itself in the possibilities in which the singular Dasein finds itself thrown. Indeed, it is in existing that Dasein has its being in being this foundation. If space permitted, I would have to attempt to show that the *Überantwortung* is the existential matrix of the so-called responsibility (*Verantwortung*) of Dasein toward itself—that is, the responsibility toward the strangeness, the *Unheimlichkeit* of its being-thrown. Thus, as the responsibility that Dasein has to be this responsibility in turn founds all of the existentiell possibilities of responsibility: "having debts" (*Schulden haben*), "being responsible for" (*Schuldsein an*), and "making oneself responsible" (*sich schuldig machen*).[27] As with *Überantwortung*, where the duty to be its own thrown source is assigned to Dasein, the duty to be this absence of foundation—while at the same time being in the world and with others, the responsibility that is bequeathed to us as heirs—does not come to us from ourselves as autonomous subjects but comes down to us from the past in the form of a cultural legacy, of imperatives regarding the self and its relations to itself and to others. It is in this sense that I understand "the law of originary sociability" that Derrida speaks of in *Politics of Friendship*. It is a law that, as a relation to the other, obligates us before any (determinate or deliberate) relation with the other. This law is the law of a *Mitsein* that, before any determinate or determinable relation to the other, subordinates such relations to the promise of the possibility of a relation to an other—the democracy to come, for example—since European memory is nothing less than the opening onto this other.

Since its elevation to the level of a philosophical concept, responsibility has been brought into relation with the traditional concepts of justification (*Rechtfertigung*) and the duty to account for (*logon didonai, rationem reddere*). Yet even here, its identity has largely been determined by reference to the notion and the experience of the response. As Derrida tells us, responsibility consists in "a certain experience and experiment of the response that here bears the whole enigma." And, continuing, he asks, "What is 'to respond?' To respond to? To be responsible for? To respond for? To respond, be responsible, before?"[28] *Politics of Friendship* drafts a response to this question. It outlines a "brief grammar of the response" in attempting to decipher how three modalities of response—responding for, responding to, and respond before—are mutually entailed and intertwined. Although this is sketched out on the basis of French, as Derrida points out, the concepts that constitute this grammar are not at all limited by this language: "This is not to say that they hold together *in general* beyond all languages (syntax and lexis) but that, in this context, they appear translatable within a group of European languages which authorize us here to question something like *our* culture and our concept of responsibility. Suffice it to say that this grammar, however schematic, will be little more than a grammar."[29] It is not only the case that the concept of responsibility only has meaning in the European context, it is also the case that the experience of response that informs this concept is structured according to concepts that are common to all European languages. Derrida notes that "*in this case at least*"—in the case of what "respond" means—the concepts that make up the experience of the response are no longer a matter of a specific grammar. The concepts, as well as the modalities of their arrangement, are shared by European languages. Though they do not correspond to universal concepts, these concepts are still much more than simple grammatical concepts. This, then, is the brief grammar in question: "One *answers for*, for self or for something (for someone, for an action, a thought, a discourse), *before*—before an other, a community of others, an institution, a court, a law. And always one *answers for* (for self or for its intention, its action or discourse), *before*, by first responding *to*: this last modality thus appearing more originary, more fundamental and hence unconditional."[30] At first glance, the response that is determined in this way would seem to cohere enough to form a unitary phenomenon. However, according to the commentary that follows the exposition of this grammar of the response in *Politics of Friendship*, the self that responds for itself only possesses the unity of the proper name, that is, the unity of a name that comes to the self from another and that is in itself for the other. What prevents the phenomenon of the response from gathering into itself is principally the fact that every response is a response to the other. The response presupposes the preliminary hearing of a call that—even if it comes from us, as is the case with the Heideggerian *Gewissen*—is always other and falls on us from elsewhere, as it were. Every response to this call implies a commitment on its behalf, an affirmation of that to which one is called, and an affirmation of what the response is answerable for. If the dimension of responding as a *responding to* seems more fundamental than all its other dimensions, it is because the relation to the call unbalances the phenomenon of the response. It produces this disequilibrium not solely because the call is temporally and logically anterior to the response but also because no response could ever satisfy a demand that comes to us from the other. "The *answering* always supposes the other in a relation to itself, it keeps the sense of this dissymmetrical 'anteriority' down to the apparently most interior and most solitary autonomy of the 'as regards self,' of interior consciousness and moral consciousness jealous of its independence (another word for freedom)."[31] Finally, if the other *to* whom we respond is a singular other, the response as response *before* presupposes the presence of a universal authority. There is no response to the other without a third party who bears witness to the law.[32] The experience of the response that is at the center of the European concept of responsibility itself inscribes the place of the universal within responsibility. It inscribes the place of an authority that is no longer singular—that is, one which is not reducible to any particular language, nor even to the whole of European languages taken together—and before which the self is called to answer for all of its actions and thoughts. Derrida writes, "The expression 'before' marks in general, right on the idiom, the passage to an institutional agency of alterity. It is no longer singular but universal in its principle. One responds *to* the other, who can always be singular, and must in respect remain so, but one answers *before the law*, a court, a jury, an agency authorized to represent the other legitimately."[33] In short, the summons to respond before the other in order to answer for oneself (and for the other) turns the experience of responding into an experience of the universal, an experience of a respect for laws, obligations, and injunctions that arise from a universal order. This obligation that arises from a universal law contributes to the phenomenon's dissymmetry regarding itself. If there is an enigma of the response, it is because the relations that constitute it preclude any definitive saturation. But nothing is less certain than the idea that we only respond to, for (*de*), and before. One also responds for (*pour*), one responds equally in the name of the other, answering on behalf of the alterity of the other, that is to say, for his infinitude. Analyzing these modalities of the response are sure to further complicate its already very complex structure.

Let us come back, then, to the way in which responding to, responding for, and responding before are illuminated and intermingled in the "brief grammar of the response." Responding to refers to the other as any other, to the singular other whose call seems to pave the way for a relation of responsibility. Responding before defines responsibility as a relation of a universal authority before which the singular subject must appear, while responding for designates the obligation to justify oneself, one's actions and thoughts. These three structures of the response comprise the responsibility that European memory transmits to us, and which is presupposed by the justice and the justness of all of our theoretical, practical, and ethical-political decisions and comportments. These three modalities are not only intermingled in what Derrida calls *Europe-responsibility*, they are also implied by one another. Now, if I may be permitted to say so, in each of the three main discourses of European ethical thought—that is, the discourse where ethical duty is conceived as a contemplation of the supreme Good, or the discourse according to which ethical duty is a duty toward the singular other, and finally, the discourse that understands ethical duty as the duty to give account—one of the modalities of responding is generally privileged, while the responsibility that is tied to European memory, *Europe-responsibility*, would be the matrix in which the different ethical reflections are carved out in our culture. But it is also the case that this matrix would likewise be that which, from the very interior of this culture, would limit the scope of each of these individual ethics to the extent that the constitutive structure of an ethics coimplicates and communicates with the other structures of the phenomenon of the response. Responsibility would be assigned to us, then, thanks to our heritage. In the first place, responsibility would correspond to a responsibility toward the concept of responsibility to the extent that it is entailed in every responsible action or relation. Now, how should one respond to this concept? How should one respond for this concept (before it, in one's name, and in the name of the other)? Responding to the concept of responsibility subtends the obligation of staying in tune with the concepts of responsibility that have taken shape in the history of European thought.

A text like *The Gift of Death* should be able to clarify these things for us. Indeed, this text, which proceeds according to a deconstruction of the idea of a genealogy of the different concepts of responsibility—the genealogy proposed by Patočka in *Heretical Essays in the Philosophy of History*—brings a number of discourses on responsibility together to examine their differences and similarities, and makes them appear one before the other such that they answer for themselves before each other. Aside from Platonic dialogue, *The Gift of Death* puts a number of questions into play: Patočka's concept of a properly European responsibility, that is, Christian responsibility or, at least, a responsibility that corresponds to a Christianity that is still to come; the Heideggerian theory of indebtedness and of an originary responsibility that has been deliberately de-Christianized; the responsibility that, according to Levinas, results from our relation to the other as absolutely other; as well as the concept of responsibility proposed by Kierkegaard who, proceeding from a Christian reading of Abraham's decision, presupposes the suspension of the ethical order. I will be unable to do justice here to the complex treatment of all of the concepts of responsibility in *The Gift of Death*. We will have to content ourselves with a few rather schematic remarks on what Derrida calls "the secret nucleus of responsibility."[34] As we know, for Patočka it is a matter of linking responsibility to the secret, to the experience of the *mysterium tremendum*, or, to the secret of the Christian event, and of thereby demarcating it from the Platonic conception where responsibility must be exerted in broad daylight and, if possible, in public. According to Patočka, there is no place for the secret, and, thus, for true responsibility, in the Greco-Platonic tradition. Even if it is true that, for Patočka, the first awakening of responsibility in Greece corresponds to a conversion in the experience of death, that is, in the moment where "the soul is . . . gathering itself in preparation for death,"[35] it is only with the other way of apprehending death, that "comes from a gift received from the other, from he who, in his absolute transcendence, sees me without me seeing him" that responsibility, as such, comes about. Without a doubt, Derrida warns against the totalitarian danger that an alliance between the secret and responsibility threatens to imply.[36] However, in *Gift of Death*, Derrida also recognizes the necessity of linking responsibility (as well as the related concept of decision) to a certain secret.[37] We will only take up the following aspect of this problematic: according to the Greco-Platonic tradition, responsibility is linked in an essential way to an objective knowledge of the Good. Nevertheless, in subscribing to this necessity, Derrida shares Patočka's opinion, for whom any subordination of responsibility to knowledge comes back to its own nullification. Responsibility must also exceed the order of theoretical determination, without which it is nonetheless impossible. Derrida observes:

> Saying that a responsible decision must be taken on the basis of the knowledge seems to define the condition of possibility of responsibility (one can't make a responsible decision without science or conscience, without knowing what one is doing, for what reasons in view of what and under what conditions), at the same time as it defines the condition of impossibility of this same responsibility (if decision-making is relegated to a knowledge that it is content to follow or to develop, then it is no more a responsible decision, it is the technical development of a cognitive apparatus, the simple mechanistic deployment of a theorem).[38]

In order for a decision to be responsible it has to conform with both the phenomenal and the secret. It must be of the order of knowledge and nonknowledge, that is, simultaneously conscious and unconscious. If, for Patočka, these two aspects correspond to two moments in the genealogy of European responsibility, that is, to the Platonic and the Christian paradigms, then *The Gift of Death* shows that they are constitutive of the concept itself. In other words, all responsibility is aporetic. It is made up of the demand for public demonstration and the necessity to justify oneself, but, at the same time and as essentially, it involves singularity and what Heidegger calls *Verschwiegenheit*, discretion and secrecy in Dasein's response to the call of conscience. *Politics of Friendship* formulates this aporia in the following way:

> One *must* certainly *know, one must know it,* knowledge is necessary if one is to assume responsibility, but the decisive or deciding moment of responsibility supposes a leap by which an act takes off, ceasing in that instant to follow the consequence of what is—that is, of that which can be determined by science or consciousness—and thereby frees itself (this is what is called freedom), by the act of its act, of what is therefore heterogeneous to it, that is, knowledge. *In sum, a decision is unconscious*—insane as that may seem, it involves the unconscious and nevertheless remains responsible.[39]

If a thing like responsibility exists, it is thus necessarily aporetic. This amounts to saying that, to a certain extent, there is thus no rigorous concept of responsibility. With regard to the Kierkegaardian conception of responsibility, according to which the subject does not have to respond before others but solely before the absolute, Derrida writes: "Such is the aporia of responsibility: one always risks not managing to accede to the concept of responsibility in the process of *forming* it. For responsibility (we would dare not speak of 'the universal concept of responsibility') demands on the one hand an accounting, a general answering-for-oneself with respect to the general and before the generality, hence the idea of substitution, and, on the other hand, uniqueness, absolute singularity, hence nonsubstitution, nonrepetition, silence and secrecy."[40] Being attentive to the different concepts of responsibility in Europe, the task that Derrida proposes for himself in *The Gift of Death* is to show that each of these concepts presupposes the reduction of the aporetic structure of this thing called responsibility. The dissimulation of the aporetic essence of responsibility, and thus also of the absence of "coherence or consequence and, even lacking identity with respect to itself [of the concept of responsibility]," would be precisely that which gives the concepts of responsibility the ability to function; they are there "to obscure the abyss or fill in its absence of foundation."[41] Now, responding to European memory as the memory of the concept of responsibility consists in opening each of these concepts to other concepts; it is a matter of thinking of each of these concepts on the basis of the other concepts that Europe has formed. To respond to the concept of responsibility is, as we have said, to do justice to a thinking that came about between European languages. But, as Derrida observes in *The Other Heading*, the duty of responding to European memory also includes the duty of "opening Europe . . . onto that which is not, never was, and will never be Europe."[42] This duty "demands respecting and tolerating all that is not placed under the authority of reason" and even calls "for respecting whatever refuses a certain responsibility."[43] We respond to this duty in demonstrating that each of the concepts of responsibility that have been transmitted to us is devoted to the aporia. In exposing conceptual thought to its limit, such a response is faithful to the European heritage precisely insofar as it is a break with the tradition, opening itself to the other of Europe, and thus reopening the heritage otherwise with respect to the concept of responsibility.

Let us recall that it was phenomenology that elevated the concept of responsibility to its philosophical dignity. Given all that we have seen, it now seems obvious that if responsibility has been able to become a thematic priority in phenomenological reflection, then it is because the character of its response to a prior demand—one that emanates from the other—corresponds to a structure of phenomenal being insofar as the latter offers itself to an intuitive look and issues the demand to understanding as such that which then manifests itself. I have also been consistently speaking of responsibility as a phenomenon, that is, as showing itself to an immediate intuition in the structural totality of its essential moments. But have we not seen that the aporetic structure of responsibility prohibits the formation of a consistent and logical concept in the apprehension of its phenomenal essence? In the pages of *The Gift of Death* that Derrida consecrates to Patočka's attempt to offer a sufficient and adequate thematization of what responsibility must be, Derrida underscores the problematic nature of linking responsibility—which, according to the tradition, consists in responding to the other and before one's other and, if possible, publicly, indeed, in broad daylight—to the secret. Not only does such a link not conform to the phenomenological exigency for adequate thematization but it also does not fit in with the demand for thematization at all. But if there is only responsibility under the condition that one be unable to respond fully to the demand to answer for oneself, on the condition that there is a compromise with a certain irresponsibility, then this impossibility of satisfying thematic knowledge, rather than preventing responsibility, is precisely what makes it possible in the first place. Derrida remarks "that not only is the thematization of the concept of responsibility inadequate but that it is always so because it must be so."[44] When he adds that "on the other hand, the theme of thematization, the sometimes phenomenological motif of thematic conscience, is the thing that is, if not denied, at least strictly limited in its pertinence by that other more radical form of responsibility that exposes me dissymmetrically to the gaze of the other; where my gaze, precisely as regards me [*ce qui me regarde*], is no longer the measure of all things," it turns out that with the nonphenomenon of responsibility, what is in question is nothing less than phenomenological philosophy itself. As constitutive of responsibility, the secret that must inhabit it stops all acts of giving and self-presentation in its phenomenal essence. It subtracts them from any intuition that could be gathered together in a self-identity. Not without some resemblance to the aesthetic ideas evoked by Kant, "the concept of responsibility is," as Derrida writes, "one of those strange concepts that give food for thought without giving themselves over to thematization. It presents itself neither as a theme nor as a thesis, it gives itself without being seen [*sans se donner à voir*], without presenting itself in person by means of a 'fact of being seen' that can be phenomenologically intuited."[45] More precisely, what the impossibility of thematizing responsibility reveals is that phenomenology, which from its beginnings declared itself responsible for the concept of responsibility, reaches its limits just when it is a matter of thinking this thing that responsibility is. It reveals itself as incapable of sufficiently and adequately thematizing what responsibility is and must be. It thus lacks responsibility itself, if always "in order to be responsible it is necessary to respond to or answer to what being responsible means."[46] But it is precisely so that this dilemma becomes tangible in phenomenology, rather than in other discourses on ethics. This is the very reason why this philosophy, more than any other one, has the necessary resources to think responsibility otherwise. Paradoxically, it is the motifs of giving and appearing that are so dominant in phenomenology that permit us to bring our attention to what it is in responsibility that necessarily escapes thematization and phenomenology itself. The paradox is not any lesser for this realization. Indeed, although it is a philosophy that (as is the case with Husserl's philosophy) is made the heir of the Greco-Platonic idea of responsibility as *logon didonai,* in its subsequent developments it opened itself to a responsibility that comes to me from the transcendent other, who looks at me without me being able to keep him in my field of vision. To conclude, I will make use of a supplementary paradox, that of the relation between responsibility and Europe. It will allow for a certain kind of reflection—one that is still in the wake of phenomenology—to carry itself in advance of a concept of responsibility that (without covering up its European origin) opens itself to what differs from Europe and to alterity that is other than the one that still falls under the category of Europe's other. Rethinking the concept of responsibility otherwise is not only to betray phenomenology from within phenomenology but also to betray philosophy by complicating the relation that it has to Europe. But this comes back to thinking the philosophical otherwise. It consists in opening the philosophical to the heritage of the other and to what until now could only inappropriately be qualified as philosophical.

Notes

1. Cf. Karlheinz Stierle, "Interpretations of Responsibility and Responsibilities of Interpretation," *New Literary History* 25, no. 4 (1994): 853–854.

2. Hans Jonas, *Das Prinzip Verantwortung. Versuch einer Ethik für die technologische Zivilisation* (Frankfurt/Main: Suhrkamp, 1984), 22.

3. Jacques Derrida, "Force of Law. The 'Mystical Foundation of Authority,'" trans. Mary Quaintance, in *Cardozo Law Review* 11, nos. 5–6 (July/Aug. 1990): 953, 955.

4. Edmund Husserl, *The Crisis of the European Sciences in Transcendental Phenomenology*, trans. D. Carr (Evanston, IL: Northwestern University Press, 1970), 17.

5. Jacques Derrida and Elizabeth Roudinesco, *For What Tomorrow: A Dialogue*, trans. Jeff Fort (Stanford, CA: University of Stanford Press, 2004), 3, 5.

6. Derrida, "Force of Law," 955.

7. Derrida and Roudinesco, *Tomorrow*, 5 (translation modified).
8. Derrida, "Force of Law," 955.
9. Derrida, "Force of Law," 955.
10. Jacques Derrida and Pierre-Jean Labarrière, *Alterités* (Paris: Osiris), 76–77.
11. Jacques Derrida, *The Gift of Death*, trans. David Willis (Chicago: University of Chicago Press, 1995), 27.
12. Derrida and Roudinesco, *Tomorrow*, 5.
13. Jacques Derrida, *The Other Heading: Reflections on Today's Europe*, trans. Pascale-Anne Brault and Michael B. Naas (Bloomington: Indiana University Press, 1992), 41.
14. Derrida, *Other Heading*, 72.
15. Derrida, *Other Heading*, 41.
16. Derrida, *Other Heading*, 44.
17. Derrida, *Other Heading*, 41.
18. Derrida, *Gift of Death*, 48.
19. Derrida, *Other Heading*, 16.
20. Derrida, *Other Heading*, 17.
21. Derrida, *Other Heading*, 18 (translation modified).
22. Derrida, *Other Heading*, 17 (translation modified).
23. Derrida, *Other Heading*, 28–29.
24. Derrida, *Other Heading*, 76.
25. Jacques Derrida, *Politics of Friendship*, trans. George Collins (New York: Verso), 231.
26. Martin Heidegger, *Being and Time*, trans. J. Macquarrie and E. Robinson (London: SCM, 1962), 284.
27. Heidegger, *Being and Time*, 282.
28. Derrida, *Other Heading*, 52–53.
29. Derrida, *Politics*, 250.
30. Derrida, *Politics*, 250.
31. Derrida, *Politics*, 251–252.
32. See Derrida, *Politics*, 275–278.
33. Derrida, *Politics*, 252.
34. Derrida, *Gift of Death*, 114.
35. Derrida, *Gift of Death*, 40.
36. Derrida, *Gift of Death*, 34.
37. Furthermore, the analysis of the Kierkegaardian interpretation of the story of Abraham from the Gospel of Matthew finally shows that, like Platonism, Christianity causes a certain elimination of the secret. I quote: "But once the light is within us, within the interiority of the spirit, then secrecy is no longer possible." Derrida, *Gift of Death*, 100.
38. Derrida, *Gift of Death*, 24.
39. Derrida, *Politics*, 69.
40. Derrida, *Gift of Death*, 61.
41. Derrida, *Gift of Death*, 84.
42. Derrida, *Other Heading*, 77.
43. Derrida, *Other Heading*, 78–79.
44. Derrida, *Gift of Death*, 26.
45. Derrida, *Gift of Death*, 27.
46. Derrida, *Gift of Death*, 25.

10

AN IMMEMORIAL REMAINDER
The Legacy of Europe

THE QUESTION HAS BEEN ASKED OF WHAT REMAINS of Derrida's thought.[1] This question has not only been posed without any consideration of what Derrida himself has advanced as to the nature of memory and heritage—particularly in the context of his reflections on "Europe"— but also without any acknowledgment of his elaborations on "remaining" (*restance*) as opposed to "remainder" (*reste*), which is constituted by a part of a whole left over once the latter has vanished.[2] It is safe to say that the underlying insinuation of this question is that now that the chaff has been separated from the wheat, what remains of Derrida amounts to very little or nothing. Yet even when, on a more positive note, his work is judged to have been a contribution to topical issues, one that remains decisive, can such a remainder be called in any way a legacy? Undoubtedly, a remainder can be of importance to capitalizing memory, but does it therefore come with the injunction to be taken over and responded to in a responsible fashion? This, however, is what constitutes a legacy. Now, if the question of remaining has been an issue in Derrida, it is because it concerns nothing less than a condition of possibility of memory, heritage, or legacy. Remaining designates a structural feature of what, in a strict sense, has been bequeathed upon an addressee, and that continues to address itself to him or her in order to be responded to and appropriated (however selectively). More precisely, remaining names the condition for there to be something like a legacy in a strict sense, namely, that something in what is bequeathed must paradoxically withhold itself, maintain itself in reserve, and defy full appropriation. As the noun "remaining" (restance), based on a substantivation of the present participal of the verb "rester" indicates, remaining is not an identifiable remainder. It concerns a structure of withdrawal that is presupposed by any imparting of a legacy that at once opens the possibility of assuming a responsibility for what is bequeathed, and, at the same time, causes all appropriations of the legacy to remain partial and limited, that is, selective, in short.

It is this thought of remaining, without which there would not be anything like a heritage, that, among other things, Derrida has transmitted to us. It is a legacy that concerns the formal possibility of legacy itself, or, more precisely, since without such remaining no such thing as a heritage would exist, it concerns the very ("performative") imparting of legacy itself. But, however momentous, the Derridean legacy is not exhausted by this formal and ontological condition of possibility of what constitutes a legacy. What he has bequeathed on us is, furthermore, intimately tied to a reflection on "our" memory, "our" legacy, that is, the "double memory"—Greek and Judeo-Christian—of Europe (and, more generally, of the West). The point that I will make hereafter is that in all his work, Derrida has consistently reminded us of the fact that within our own heritage and memory something infinitely resists, and does so in the shape of an "infinitely impassible remainder [restance]" to all appropriations and reappropriations, as he writes in "Faith and Knowledge: The Two Sources of 'Religion' at the Limits of Reason Alone."[3] Derrida's legacy, I hold, is above all to have pointed out a certain immemorial remainder in Europe's double commitment to its Greek *and* Judeo-Christian heritage, a remainder that escapes and counteracts all attempts to conform that heritage to any fixed or dogmatic interpretation and destination. In what follows, I will also link this concern with an inassimilable remainder in our European legacy to the equally persistent issue in Derrida's thought of what he has termed "a new, very new Aufklärung,"[4] in other words, with an unrelenting critical vigilance concerning what in the name of Europe's heritage is made of this heritage. If something, then, "remains" of Derrida, it is insofar as he has drawn our attention to what remains inappropriable in our double memory, and which, by critically resisting all reappropriations, continues to challenge us without end. His work as a whole has been devoted to this remaining, or "immemorial remainder"; he has resolutely and unrelentingly sought to watch over, preserve, and maintain ("garder") this remainder throughout the entirety of his work. To think this immemorial remainder—a remaining that Schelling might have termed *unvordenklich*—and to watch over it, this is the task he has bequeathed on us. This is the legacy of his thought.

But before elaborating in more detail, not on what remains of Derrida for sure, but rather on what is the legacy of this thinker, let me linger for a moment on this notion of "remaining" itself, which, strangely enough, has drawn little or no attention from his commentators, in contrast to the many other neologisms that he has coined.[5] In "Signature Event Context," where, to my knowledge, the term remaining, more precisely, "the nonpresent remaining," is first introduced, the term designates something that constitutes every mark in its generality, that is, in its ideality of a grapheme, namely, the fact of being repeatable (hence identifiable), readable, and intelligible not only in the absence of its referent but also in the absence "of a determined signified or current intention of signification, as of every present intention of communication," in short, even then when a "differential mark is cut off from its alleged 'production.'"[6] Later—for example, in *Spurs. Questions of Style*—remaining is expanded to naming the structure of every text insofar as a text is defined by the possibility of lacking a definite meaning, remaining undecidable, and, therefore, escaping every hermeneutical horizon—although inviting such a horizon while simultaneously undoing it—and yet remaining fully readable. Finally, in *Limited Inc.*, after having emphasized that remaining does not mean "permanence" or "substance," Derrida expatiates on the modality of being of the structure in question and argues that, indeed, it escapes "the logic of presence or the (simple or dialectical) opposition of presence and absence."[7] He writes, "The rest of the trace, its remains [*restance*] are neither present nor absent. They escape the jurisdiction of all ontotheological discourse even if they render the latter at times possible."[8] Whether remaining concerns the constitutive structure of any mark, any text, or, in the context of that in which we are interested here, namely, anything that is bequeathed, transmitted, or handed over as a legacy, it designates a remainder (*reste*), as it were, in any mark, text, memory, or legacy, that defies all possible appropriation, even though this remainder, by virtue of undecidability, is the persistent and inevitable invitation to respond to it by seeking to make it one's own, but which, therefore, also limits all determining appropriations and thus remains a constitutive challenge. In fact, since there is no heritage (worth its name) without something that resists from within its transmission, it follows, furthermore, that the inheritor is as much, if not even more, indebted to what remains recalcitrant in that heritage to appropriation, than to what is considered to have effectively been handed over, for, indeed, without this abstraction of the heritage no bequeathing could have taken place to begin with. As a result, the "duty" of the thinker consists in watching over, and preserving, what of the legacy resists all appropriation, whatever its nature may be.

The debt and responsibility toward what thus withholds itself in any heritage will become clearer once we focus on the irreducible remainder in the double memory of Europe, in particular, within its Greek memory. But before exemplifying through a close reading of several pages of "Faith and Knowledge" such remainders within what the Greeks bestowed on Europe, I take this also as an opportunity to point out that Greek thought has been a persistent concern of Derridean thought, largely neglected by his commentators and critics who (myself included) have paid much more attention to his debates with thinkers such as Hegel, Husserl, or Heidegger. Undoubtedly, since we are addressing here the question of the memory of Europe—one aspect of which, is philosophy—the Greeks will obviously enjoy a privileged status in our discussion. But considering the amount of work that Derrida has persistently devoted to Greek thought from early on, it would be tempting to argue that rather than concerning modern thought, the legacy of Derrida is primarily determined by his rethinking of the Greeks.[9] In the interview following his presentation of "Double Mémoire," a letter addressed to "Old Europe" and presented on the occasion of the Festival d'Avignon in 2004, after having reminded his addressee that "philosophy is European," and that "the place of birth of the form of thought that is called *philosophia* ... is undeniably Greece," Derrida explains that, as a deconstruction of Eurocentrism, his work has borrowed its resources from, precisely, what has been deconstructed.[10] Such deconstruction is said "to have consisted in putting into question [the] philosophical representation of Europe by Europe, or this representation of philosophy by philosophy itself by way of its fundamental concepts."[11] In short, if what has been at issue in deconstruction is nothing less than the Platonizing interpretation of Europe's, or philosophy's, own origin in Greece, it is also clear that deconstruction is an attempt to oppose European philosophy's Platonizing interpretation of itself with something other—within Greek thought—that withstands Platonism and, in the same breath, philosophy's representation of its Greek origin.[12]

Indeed, it is qua Platonism, in short, in the shape of philosophy, or Western metaphysics, that Greek thought is a part of European memory. At least from "Plato's Pharmacy" on, Derrida has taken on the Platonizing appropriation of Greek thought, in particular of the Platonic texts themselves, by seeking to read, as he submits in "We Other Greeks," certain Greek words "that had already been marked by the irruption of the other" in Greek thought, and that are at work "in sentences, in scenes of discourse and writing, in works that, for this very reason, could not be closed upon themselves."[13] Platonism, insofar as it commands all of Western metaphysical—that is, ontological—thought, has from the start abstracted from these words, which stand for an other Greece within the Greece as we know it. More exactly, Platonism, the philosophy of Plato (as opposed to certain threads in Plato's texts), is, Derrida claims, the result of "a thetic abstraction at work [already] in the heterogenous text of Plato," that is, an abstraction by which certain theses and themes could be extracted from his writings. This abstraction, once "it has been supercharged and deployed, ... will be extended over all the folds of the [Platonic] text, of its ruses, overdeterminations, and reserves, which [it] will come to cover up and dissimulate."[14] By inquiring in "Plato's Pharmacy," into one such word that has already been marked by the infraction of the other, namely, *pharmakon*, Derrida confronts the abstraction of Platonism, that is, of the Greek memory at the heart of the European memory, with another kind of abstraction, namely, that which in Greek thought resists a unifying interpretation and recedes into oblivion at the moment the Platonic texts become appropriated by Platonism.

If I bring the question of abstraction to bear here on Derrida's reflections on double memory as the heritage of Europe, it is primarily because of "Faith and Knowledge," whose first part will be crucial for what I will construe as Derrida's legacy, and which is uniquely involved in this question to such a degree that it could even be read as a text in praise of abstraction. Indeed, against the all too often expressed claim that all concern for universality is abstract, and as such overrides all particularity, the issue of the so-called return of religion, and the divisions that accompany it, causes Derrida, in "Faith and Knowledge," to come out in a powerful defense of abstraction as the sole way not only of finding access to something universal but also as the condition for allowing the other to be other, singularly other, that is. After a terse evocation of the difficulties of speaking about religion today as if it was something readily identifiable, Derrida introduces the question of abstraction already in the first paragraph of the essay, when he holds that in order to muster the necessary courage to begin addressing the issue of religion, one must "pretend [*feindre*] for an instant *to abstract*, to abstract from everything or almost everything, in a certain way. Perhaps one must take one's chance in resorting to the most concrete and most accessible, but also the most barren and desert-like, of all abstractions"

(FK, 1). This acknowledgment of the need for abstraction at the very beginning of the first part of "Faith and Knowledge"—the part titled "Italics," a part that itself is exemplary in putting a politics of bracketing to work—amounts to a revaluation of abstraction that is seemingly unique in Derrida's work. Ultimately, the stakes of this evaluation consist in conceiving a form of abstraction, which, in distinction from what *Margins of Philosophy* called "an empirical abstraction without extraction from its own native soil," is, as we will see, a more than radical, that is, extreme kind of abstraction.[15] In any event, rather than entailing a loss of the object under investigation, the illusive subject matter that is religion today, itself calls, as Derrida points out, for abstraction in order to be able to be thought at all. In fact, the reference to Hegel's short essay "Who Thinks Abstractly?" not only serves to underline that abstraction is not what one commonly holds it to be but also that wishing to save oneself at all costs from abstraction amounts to wishing to save oneself from thinking as such, in short, to relinquish thought altogether.

By pretending to abstract, and, moreover, not only for an instant but also to abstract only "in a certain way," Derrida, undoubtedly, evokes the phenomenological form of abstraction (*epoche*). However, the claim that in order to be able to speak about religion today one must perhaps take one's chance "in resorting to the most concrete and most accessible, but also [to] the most barren and desert-like, of all abstractions," that is, I believe, to two markedly distinct, but also interlinked forms of abstractions, the Husserlian conception of abstraction is, from the start, confronted with several other forms of abstraction. There is thus, from the beginning, more than one kind of abstraction. Indeed, although I said that in a way "Faith and Knowledge" could be understood as in praise of abstraction, the latter has also an "evil" side, and this side, furthermore, is intimately linked to the subject matter here in question, namely, religion today. When, in paragraph 2, Derrida submits that he wishes "to link the question of religion to that of the evil of abstraction . . . to radical abstraction," that is, to "the deracination of abstraction," the resurgence of religion today is explicitly construed as a reaction against what is considered the evil of our time, namely, the radical uprooting, delocalization, and disincarnation of peoples and their culture by the worldwide spreading of Western technology, forms of living, and models of community. But Derrida also writes, "In order to think religion today abstractly, we will take these powers of abstraction as our point of departure, in order to risk, eventually, the following hypothesis: with respect to all these forces of abstraction and of dissociation . . . 'religion' is at the same time involved in reacting antagonistically and reaffirmatively outbidding itself" (FK, 2). At this point, the reason why precisely the subject matter "religion today," or the return of religion, calls itself for a certain abstraction in order to be able to be addressed by thought, becomes manifest. Without it, the fact that religion today is not only a reaction against the powers of abstraction but also one that, at the same time, capitalizes on such abstraction, and even exacerbates it, could not come into view. Now my prime concern here is not religion, and thus I will not, in what follows, expand on this guiding thesis of "Faith and Knowledge," which, if I am correct, corresponds to what has been referred to as "the most concrete and most accessible" abstraction, and which is taken up in greater detail in the second part of Derrida's essay.[16] By contrast, I intend to focus on what, in "Italics," is established with respect to "the most barren and desert-like" abstraction, which I consider to represent not only the core of Derrida's overall argument in "Faith and Knowledge" but also which, by touching on the question of the inappropriable remainders in the double memory of Europe, bears on what I hold to be Derrida's legacy. Yet, before we pursue this line of thought, let us remind ourselves that "Faith and Knowledge" is an inquiry into religion today and an attempt to rewrite Kant's *Religion within the Limits of Reason Alone* for the current situation. This context, in which not only the question of abstraction is posed but also, and intimately related to it, that of the possibility of "world" today, requires drawing on certain resources of *religio* itself if religion is to be rethought for our times in an enlightened manner. Indeed, among the three forms of detachment, and withdrawing abstraction from the world as we know it in order to conceive of another world—the island, the promised land, and the desert of revelation—Derrida centers in on the figure of the desert of revelation to open up within it another extreme desert—the epitome of abstraction—as a place that in spite of the threat of complete desolation that comes with it, perhaps, also harbors a promise of a world worthy of its name.

But first a brief note on those Greek words of which it is said that they are marked by the infraction of the other and to which Derrida has paid attention in his writings devoted to Greek themes.[17] Among them I single out *pharmakon* and *khora*. By centering his reading of Plato's *Phaedrus* on the word pharmakon, whose manifold meanings can neither be derived from one proper meaning nor dialectically sublated into one all-embracing signification, Derrida uses the resources of this word to construct the milieu of both the emergence *and* inversion of all the elemental concepts of Platonism. Indeed, one of the overarching agendas of "Plato's Pharmacy" is to question Platonism, which, with all its grand structural oppositions, "sets up the whole of Western metaphysics in its conceptuality."[18] With all its ambiguities and the reversions to which it lends itself, the pharmakon is shown to constitute "the original medium of decision, the element that precedes" Platonism as the dominant structure of the history of metaphysics, but that also "comprehends it, goes beyond it," and that can never be reduced to it.[19] The system, or chain of the meanings of the pharmakon that are distributed throughout the dialogue, and Plato's writings as a whole—a system in which Plato himself is caught, but which he also seeks to master by stopping the word's ambiguity and inserting the definition of pharmakon into a simple, clear-cut opposition, thus eventually encouraging the Platonist interpretation of his work—is within Plato's own text the matrix from which Platonism emerges, and, at the same time, "that which resists any philosopheme, indefinitely exceeding its bounds as nonidentity, nonessence, nonsubstance; granting philosophy by that very fact the inexhaustible adversity of what funds it and the infinite absence of what founds it."[20] If, while interpreting the *Timaeus*, Derrida has focused on the word khora, it is for similar reasons. In fact, he had already broached the problematic in question well before the publication of the essay "Khora," namely, toward the end of "Plato's Pharmacy" itself, where the issue of a third genre on this side of the Platonic oppositions is associated with "the passage beyond all 'Platonic' oppositions, toward the aporia of the originary inscription."[21] But in view of what we will encounter in "Faith and Knowledge," it is also of particular interest that with Plato the third genre is determined as "place" (*lieu*), and that itself, in order to conceive this place of extreme abstraction, requires a highly abstract move.[22]

As is well known, the problematic of a third genre, or khora, arises in the *Timaeus* at the very moment at which Plato, after having argued that the world has been created by the divine Demiurge as a perfect copy of the essences of the intelligible order, faces the necessity to account for the distinction between the original, or paradigm, and the copy, the intelligible and the sensible, the invisible and the visible, and so forth. As a pre-originary origin that does not let itself be framed by any genre of being, or discourse, that is, an origin that escapes both the polarities of the sensible/intelligible, visible/invisible, form/without form, and so forth, as well as the logos/mythos distinction, Plato shows his embarrassment in the *Timaeus* of being unable to name and identify khora and, after a brief elaboration, does not explicitly return to it again.[23] Indeed, although khora can accommodate all kinds of determinations, translations, and identifications, it does not properly possess any one of them to the extent that as a "general place," it receives them only in order to give place to them.[24] As a result, khora as a "general place," must, in Heidegger's words, "be bare of all the modes of appearance, any modes that it may receive from anywhere." From this the question arises whether the meaning of khora may not signify "that which separates itself from every particular, that which withdraws, and in this way admits and 'makes room' precisely for something else."[25] In any case, as we will see, such withdrawal will also be for Derrida a prime characteristic of khora. As he argues, even though Plato interrupts the narrative of the dialogue only for a relatively brief moment to develop his thought about khora, the whole of the *Timaeus* manifests the constraint of responding to this impossibility of properly identifying it by producing on all of this dialogue's textual levels formal analogies to it, or stories that themselves are contained in other stories. Based on a magisterial reading of the textual complexities of the dialogue, Derrida concludes that the whole of the *Timaeus* is a "mise en abyme of the discourse on khora."[26] It must be noted that Plato's embarrassment at his inability to give form to khora is not simply the result of a failure of philosophical discourse. The "structural law" that prohibits naming khora, and thus saying what khora is, as well as the constraints that bear on the *Timaeus* insofar as on its conceptual and especially narrative level the text reduplicates what has been said about khora, is also testimony to an essential indeterminacy and abstraction of khora: "a secret without secret [that] remains for ever impenetrable on the subject of it/her," and which "khora must, if you like, *keep*; it is just what *must be kept for it*, what *we* must keep for it."[27] In other words, then, the word's indeterminacy, as well as the irreducibility of what it designates, must be respected and preserved "as such," in all its abstraction. Khora, which "is neither generative nor engendered but which carries philosophy," is a word that names an immemorial remainder in Greek philosophy, something that reserves itself, and the task of thought consists in attending to what of it withdraws itself, and thus abstracts itself, from the abstraction that Platonism represents insofar as the latter reductively isolates various themes and theses in this "theatre of irony" that is the *Timaeus*, "where the scenes interlock in a series of receptacles without end and without bottom."[28]

By drawing attention to these Greek words in Plato's texts that are the foundation of the conceptuality of Western metaphysics, something other within these founding texts of our heritage comes into view that this heritage is unable to appropriate, or rather, whose very lack of appropriation is the condition for the installation of philosophy in all its conceptuality. This remainder not only resists metaphysical appropriation, but it is also of the order of a critical power that, in principle, causes all forms of appropriation of the founding texts to be limited, and even to be deconstructable. This thought of an immemorial remainder in our Greek heritage, one that itself is not only undeconstructable but also the source of the deconstructability of all interpretative appropriations of our heritage, makes up the core of the kind of uncompromising vigilance of what Derrida has referred to as "a new, very new *Aufklärung*," and that continues to instruct the essay on "Faith and Knowledge."[29] The thought of this immemorial remainder undoes in all interpretations of the Greek heritage, and claims that are made in its name, the possibility of any absolutist stance, not to speak of the interested adaptations of the tradition in dogmatic or ideological perspectives. But since, as we have seen, our heritage is not only Greek but also includes a Judeo-Christian memory, the same obtains for this part of our memory that is intimately cojoined to the first.

Indeed, in the context of his elucidation in "Faith and Knowledge" of the notion of the "most barren and desert-like" abstraction, two names are invoked, the Greek name khora and the Jewish name of the "'messianic.'" But before clarifying how both names are linked not only to the thought of an immemorial remainder in our double memory but also to the question of abstraction, it is necessary to reconstruct, in at least a very succinct manner, the arguments that impel the invocation of these two names. While wondering how to think religion today, in an enlightened and tolerant way, and, in a way similar to Kant, within the limits of reason alone—that is, in the sense of a religion "which, without again becoming 'natural [that is, pagan] religion' would today be effectively universal" (FK, 14), and be constitutive of "world," hence, beyond its Christian or even Abrahamic paradigm—Derrida evokes two temptations, one Hegelian, the other Heideggerian. The Hegelian temptation is that of onto-theology, according to which absolute knowledge is the truth of religion. Yet, as Derrida remarks, even though this temptation is distinct from faith, onto-theology, which undoubtedly destroys religion, is, "also perhaps what informs . . . the theological and ecclesiatical, even religious, development of faith" (FK, 15). The Heideggerian temptation consists in grounding all revelation (*Offenbarung*) in the more originary light of "revealability" (*Offenbarkeit*). And yet, the possibility of the more fundamental structure of revealability is, perhaps, also something that becomes only conceivable as a result of revelation, that is, in the wake of positive religion.[30] In the face of the aporias that these two temptations represent, and, especially, in the case of the Heideggerian temptation, the increasing obscurity of the light that is said to be more originary than that of revelation compels Derrida to make the decisive step toward, and in view of, "a *third place* that could well have been *more than* archi-originary, the most anarchic and anarchivable place possible, not the island nor the promised land, but a certain desert—not the desert of revelation, but a desert *within* the desert, the one which makes possible, opens, hollows out, or infinitizes the other. Ecstasy or existence of the most extreme abstraction" (FK, 16; trans. mod.). The third place, that Derrida cuts open within the problematic of religion with the help of the resources of religion itself, a place of still an*other* light—"*Light* [always] *takes place*" (FK, 6)—is distinct from all the other abstract spaces that are the island, the promised land, and the desert we know (i.e., the one of the revelations of historical religions). This third place is more originary, or rather it is "*more than* archi-originary," in other words, it is not a place (and a light) that would come before another, and that would be the truth, or the ground, for what "depends" on it or is "made possible" by it. Rather than an *archae* that gives the law, this place is anarchic and, furthermore, does not let itself be archived or memorized but remains absolutely immemorial. This abstract place toward which Derrida steps up his pace is not abstract as is the Platonic space of the Isles of the Blessed (and more generally of all forms of utopian worlds), the Jewish concept of a promised land, or all the Graeco-Christian deserts of historical religions, which as "aporetical places ... shape our horizon, here and now" (FK, 7). In distinction from the desert we know, including the desert of negative theology, Derrida refers to this place as "a certain desert," more precisely a "desert within the desert," which both makes the desert of revelation possible and, at the same time, hollows it out, or infinitizes it, thus preventing it from ever coming fully into its own. The third place in question, one that puts the desert into the desert, as it were, is a space considerably more abstract than the abstractness and emptiness of the desert we know, one which notwithstanding its extreme abstraction, or precisely because of it, is perhaps the promise of a world to begin with. But this place is not only a place of spacing but also of temporizing. As "ecstasy or existence of the most extreme abstraction," it is a place whose abstraction is so extreme that it is never allowed to come to a rest in (an) itself. Always ahead of itself, always withdrawing from itself, this place never becomes present. It is a nonpresent place, outrageously abstract. Its temporality is such that it resists ever becoming even an abstract place, thereupon remaining a place of "the most extreme abstraction."

Needless to say, with this third utmost abstract and anarchic place, without any interiority whatsoever in which roads in any sense (sensible or intelligible, properly or figuratively) could be traced, hence more aporetic than ever—a place whose consideration arose from the question of whether today a new *Religion within the Limits of Reason Alone* could provide a template for a universal world while keeping both the Hegelian and Heideggerian temptations in check—the question of how to orient oneself in this desert becomes an issue. In the same way as with the other three places for which religion in particular offers guidelines for orientation, "religion" provides the resources for how to proceed within this place abstract beyond measure. However, what religion means in this case must be rethought beyond the historical religions and all their secular variations, as we know them, because what is at stake with the third place is the possibility of a world to begin with, one that would be truly universal. With the two etymological sources of religio in mind, religio deriving either from *religare*, to link or re-link, or from *re-legere*, to gather together, to collect, Derrida submits: "That which would orient here 'in' this desert, without pathway and without interior, would still be the possibility of a *religio* and of a *relegere*, to be sure, but before the 'link' of *religare* . . . , before the link between men as such or between men and the divinity of the god it would also be like the condition of the 'link' reduced to its minimal semantic determination" (FK, 16). What permits orientation in the "desert *within* the desert" is, first, the possibility of linking, of a religio and a relegere in advance (yet not, therefore, more originary) of the link accomplished in religare, that is, in linking men to men, and men to God; and second, the possibility prior to all identity of a minimal self-linkage (or reference to oneself) as the condition of a link to others. For, indeed, no link to others is possible without a certain reserve, such as "the holding-back of scruple (religio), the restraint of shame, a certain *Verhaltenheit* as well . . . , the respect, the responsibility of repetition in the wager of decision or of affirmation (re-legere) which links up with itself in order to link up with the other" (FK, 16).[31] In essence, the orientation that a certain return of religion permits in the hyper-abstract place that represents a template for world in a strict sense is one that consists in cutting roads for a possible linkage of oneself to oneself and to others, one that "would precede all determinate community, all positive religion, every onto-anthropo-theological horizon. It would link pure singularities prior to any social or political determination, prior to all intersubjectivity" (FK, 16–17).³² In other words, the social bond that the linkage in question would establish is no longer one between already hardened identities or determined subjects, but one between others in general, others in the very purity of their singularity, without any horizon of any sort giving as yet a concrete form and substance to the links between these singularities. Undoubtedly, such a conception of world can "resemble a desertification, the risk of which remains undeniable, but [this desertification] can—on the contrary—also *render possible* precisely what it appears to threaten. The abstraction of the desert can thereby open the way to everything from which it withdraws" (FK, 17).³³ Abstract to the extreme, such a social bond is, indeed, the condition for there to be World in the first place, a world worthy of its name, and consequently, the abstraction in question is one that needs to be cultivated. Without abstracting, without putting for an instant, at least, all determinations between brackets, without risking a desertification, there is no hope whatsoever for a universal world.

Derrida proposes two names for this ambiguous, duplicitous source, or origin that provides orientation in the extreme abstract space of the desert within the desert, which, although it also runs the risk of desertification, provides the conditions for "a universalizable culture of singularities," that is, for a world (FK, 18). He writes, "Here origin is duplicity itself, the one and the other. Let us name these two sources, these two fountains or these two tracks that are still invisible in the desert. Let us lend them two names that are still 'historical,' there where a certain concept of history itself becomes inappropriate. To do this, let us refer—*provisionally*, I emphasize this, and for pedagogical and rhetorical reasons—first to the 'messianic,' and second to the chora" (FK, 17).

Several remarks are warranted here. First, the names given to the two tracks to be cleared in the desert are names that are only "lent" to them, one Greek, the other Jewish (and Christian), and thus refer to the double memory and heritage of the West alone. These names are given only provisionally to the tracks to be cleared, and merely for pedagogical and rhetorical reasons, in other words, also for historical reasons. However, the stakes of a reflection today on religion within the limits of reason alone are, as we have seen, those of a universal world. To name the tracks that are still invisible in the desert of extreme abstraction and that are still in want of being cleared, but that need to be drawn for a universal world to become a possibility, can therefore only be a provisional act if these names are intelligible only within the European and Western traditions. But, at the same time, these names are not just any names within that tradition. Indeed, each one of them designates an immemorial remainder in that tradition that resists all particular appropriations of that tradition, and that concerns, as will become clear hereafter, the spatial and temporal forms of the experience of a world that would be genuinely universal and refers to something anterior to the world as understood by philosophical Platonism and Jewish-Christian religion.

Before I turn to these two names themselves, let me point out that even though Derrida's inquiries into what in Plato resists Platonism seems to overshadow his concern with the analogous structure in the Jewish heritage of Europe, the two tracks that these names designate have been present in Derrida's work from early on, at least since "Violence and Metaphysics." But in "Faith and Knowledge" they come together in explicit fashion. If this is so, it is not only because of the twofold nature of the European heritage, but also because of the concern with world, with a world that would be genuinely universal, and that would be experienced as a "place" for all. Indeed, the reflections on the messianic and khora concern nothing less than the possibility of such an experience of world, that is, they concern the spatial and temporal "forms" of an "alter-mondialiste" world, a world clear of all ethnocentricity, European and non-European alike.

The name for a first track to be cleared in the abstract place of the extreme desert is "the *messianic*, or messianicity without messianism. This would be the opening to the future or to the coming of the other as the advent of justice, but without horizon of expectation and without prophetic prefiguration" (FK, 17).[34] The messianic, as one of the two sources for orientation in the abstract space distinct from the island, the promised land, and the desert of Greco-Christian religion, names the unconditional openness to the to-come, an openness that is radical in that it does not limit in advance what possibly can come, or happen, by way of a horizon of expectation or anticipation. Such openness to the future implies exposure to "absolute surprise and, even if it always takes the phenomenal form of peace or of justice, it ought, exposing itself so abstractly, be prepared (waiting without awaiting *itself*) for the best as for the worst, the one never coming without opening the possibility of the other" (FK, 17–18). In other words, the messianic is a form of temporality whose ecstatic nature is never fulfilled, or saturated, by any messianism, or Messiah, and names, provisionally, "a general structure of experience" (FK, 18). This "form" of time, which despite its name does not belong to any Abrahamic religion from which it has been abstractly lifted, is the first form of intuition, as it were; more precisely, the first condition for an experience (and the occurrence) of a world that would be unconditionally open to the future and to all others. Because of its radical ecstatic nature, the form of temporality constitutive of such experience is, then, also the first form of what can only be called a very new transcendental aesthetics in which the conditions of experience are also, as the issue of "performativity" in the essay suggests, the conditions for the occurrence of world.[35]

Intimately connected to "this abstract messianicity" as the temporal form of experience is an equally abstract faith as "a believing, . . . a credit that is irreducible to knowledge and [a] trust that 'founds' all relation to the other in testimony" (FK, 18). Indeed, a desire for, and an awaiting of, justice, or rather, a faith defying "the risks of absolute night," that is, the risk that the advent of justice in the face of the to-come might turn out to be a disaster, is inscribed into this unconditional openness toward the future named "messianic."[36] This desire for justice, in other words, for each singularity to have a chance to occur, is one for "a universalizable culture of singularities," a culture that would permit a relation to the other as another singular other (and that would allow one to be recognized in turn as such) in advance of (and thus in abstraction from) any determined dogmas that could saturate, or to use Husserlian language, fulfill this faith. In the same way as the ecstatic temporization constitutive of experience that is a general, or universal, structure of experience, this faith is a general condition of experience tied to its temporal structure, which, rather than simply a given, needs to be cultivated or, say, performed, in order to have constitutive force. It is the abstract condition for the social bond and has to be cultivated in this very abstraction from all determined social relations, to provide the ground for a culture of singularities, that is, of others, and to provide such a culture with a chance of becoming universal. Derrida adds, "The universalizable culture of this faith, and not of another or before all others, alone permits a 'rational' and universal discourse on the subject of 'religion'" (FK, 18).

The specifically temporal dimension of "messianicity without messianism," as well as the faith in justice that is its correlate, make up the core of that part of the double memory of Europe, or the West, that is, of Jewish extraction. Yet when Derrida holds that the messianicity in question, "stripped of everything, as it should, this faith without dogma ... cannot be contained in any traditional oppositions, for example that between reason and mysticism" (FK, 18), a question imposes itself. Indeed, does Derrida, in spite of his invocation of the double memory of Europe, not confer a special privilege to our Greek memory in determining "our" European heritage? Is this search into general structures of experience that are to confront both Platonism as the dominant structure of the history of Western metaphysics, and the historical religions of the West, with truly universal conditions of a world not profoundly indebted to the Greek side of our heritage? In particular, is the operation by which the temporal condition is abstracted from the historical religions, not the philosophical, hence, Greek operation (or performance?) par excellence? Undoubtedly, even though they are the result of an, indeed, "purely rational analysis," and a reflection that does not flinch (*réfléchissant sans fléchir*)—that is, one that not only does not sway or give ground but also one that, by not bending upon itself in self-closure, remains relentlessly open to what it reflects upon—messianicity and faith, as Derrida understands these notions, cannot be accounted for by the elementary oppositions of Greek, that is, Platonist, thought, such as, for example, knowledge versus ignorance, opinion versus dogmatic faith, or reason versus mysticism. But, in the very gesture of inquiring into the temporality that orients a space such as the desert within the desert, and that is irreducible to reason and mysticism, knowledge and dogma, is this not a specifically Greek gesture, one that, it seems, is at stake precisely in Plato's notion of a third genre, in the thought of khora?

However, before trying to answer this question, let me first take up the name for the second source, or track, that cuts open a way within the abstraction of the desert. After the "messianic" as a name for a certain temporal experiential track, the name *khora* serves to designate the spatial configuration of the experience in question. Within the general structures of experience drawn out by this unheard of kind of transcendental aesthetics, khora designates spacing—"the place of absolute exteriority"(FK, 19) that all places as we know them presuppose—as a form, or condition, of the experience of world. Indeed, for a culture of singularities to be possible, not only ecstatic temporality is required but also a spacing that secures the irreducible distance between the singularities, without which they would not be able to maintain their otherness with respect to one another.

As a notion that Plato introduces in the *Timaeus* "without being able to reappropriate it in a consistent self-interpretation," and which thus points within what is Greek beyond the Greek toward something other, this Greek name enjoys manifestly a certain privilege for Derrida, for, indeed, he writes that "from the open interior of any corpus, of any system, of any language or any culture, *khora* situates the abstract spacing, *place itself*, the place of absolute exteriority, but also the place of a bifurcation between two approaches to the desert" (FK, 19; trans. mod.). And yet as will become clear hereafter, this privilege is only a function of the very resources contained in this Greek name for opening Greek thought to its other. Indeed, this Greek word overflows the Greek paradigm by which it cannot be appropriated, and khora thus possesses a generality that names the place itself exterior to any interiority, and in which all linguistic, cultural, or ethnic self-relatedness is inscribed. In addition, this Greek word situates the place of a bifurcation of two ways of approaching the desert, the first of which is the *via negativa*, itself a Graeco-Abrahamic hybridization, and for that very reason *not* universalizable: "it speaks solely at the borders or in view of the Middle-Eastern desert, at the source of monotheistic revelations and of Greece" (FK, 19).[37] By contrast, the second way of approaching the desert rests on an experience of a resistance within the Graeco-Abrahamic complex itself to the cross-like linkage of both. In a way similar to the abstract faith as a necessary correlate of the temporal track through the extreme desert, this experience of resistance is intimately linked to the spatial way that cuts across its abstract expanse and represents a formative condition for securing the universalizibility of a culture of singularities. Derrida writes that "in addition to investigating the onto-theologico-political tradition that links Greek philosophy to the Abrahamic revelations, perhaps we must also submit to the experience [*épreuve*] of that which within this linkage resists it, which will always have resisted it, from within or as though from an exteriority that works and resists inside" (FK, 20; trans. mod.). This experience of a resistance within the Graeco-Abrahamic, that is, within the Christian synthesis of the Greek *and* the Abrahamic, whose universalizability is compromised by its onto-theologico-political agenda, is, however, the experience of something that, by contrast, is, perhaps, universalizable. According to Derrida, the Greek word khora offers itself as a name for this very resistance. He explains:

> *Chora*, the "experience of chora," would be . . . the name for place, a place name, and a rather singular one at that, for that spacing which, not allowing itself to be dominated by any theological, ontological or anthropological instance, without age, without history and more 'ancient' than all oppositions

(for example, that of sensible/intelligible), does not even announce itself as 'beyond being' in accordance with a path of negation, a *via negativa*. As a result, *chora* remains absolutely impassible and heterogeneous to all the processes of historical revelation or of anthropo-theological experience, which at the very least suppose its abstraction. (FK, 20–21; trans. mod.)

The thoroughly abstract place in question is a place that as such, and precisely because it lacks an "as such," resists, in Greek thought, as well as in the Graeco-Abrahamic hybrid complex, that is, also within the nonuniversalizable idiom of Europe, or the West, all determining domination. It infinitely abstracts itself from, and resists, all places, as the sole place in which the other can unconditionally come and in which justice can take place. Khora "will never have entered religion and will never permit itself to be sacralized, sanctified, humanized, theologized, cultivated, historicized. Radically heterogeneous to the safe and sound, to the holy and the sacred, it never admits of any *indemnification*. This cannot even be formulated in the present, for chora never presents itself as such. It is neither Being, nor the Good, nor God, nor Man, nor History. It will always have been . . . the very place of an infinite resistance, of an infinitely impassible persistence [*restance*] an utterly faceless other" (FK, 21).

In short, then, khora is a name for something so utterly impassible within Graeco-Abrahamic hybridization (and the universalization that it claims), which, because it does not let itself be reappropriated by the hybrid complex in question, is of the order of a remainder that infinitely resists all appropriation within any finite philosophical, theological, or anthropological configuration even though they presuppose its abstract place. Like "the messianic without messianicity" in one part of the double memory of Europe, khora in its Greek part is an immemorial remainder that withdraws from what it renders possible. According to "Faith and Knowledge," "this Greek noun [khora] says in our memory that which is not reappropriable, even by our memory, even by our 'Greek' memory: it says the immemoriality of a desert in the desert of which it is neither a threshold nor a mourning" (FK, 21). As the reference to immemoriality suggests, that which remains in infinite resistance to all appropriation in the "cultural" memory of Europe, including our Greek memory, is something "older" than thought and the live memory that it presupposes, that resists all appropriation by cultural memory and all particular formations of thought, and that, therefore, has the potential of referring to a beyond of the idiomatic and is, perhaps, universalizable. To have reminded us of this double immemorial remainder, or the duplicity of the origin of Europe, or the West, which subtracts and abstracts itself from what it makes possible, and never enters religion or philosophy, and which, therefore, remains the source of the essential instability of all such formations, this is, I hold, the legacy that Derrida has bequeathed on us. It is an injunction to watch over this immemorial remainder by never letting down one's guard in the face of claims that seek, in the name of particular idioms, absoluteness and universality.

I return to the question left in abeyance concerning a certain Greek bias in Derrida's exploration of the remainder in question. If there is a bias here it would certainly have to do with the importance conferred upon the notion of khora. Undoubtedly a Greek conception, it would thus seem that, although this word names in Greek the other of Greece within Greece, the Greek idiom is given the privileged position of being able to point to an other that within its own, but also within every other idiom, or hybridization of idioms, provides the basis for a universal, trans-idiomatic place. But does Derrida simply accord an unwarranted preeminence to the Greek paradigm? In response, let us remind ourselves that the word khora was chosen provisionally and for pedagogical and rhetorical reasons. Indeed, among "the names that are given us as our heritage" (FK, 20), khora is *the* "Greek name" (FK, 21), and thus a name we have at our disposal for something that is not Greek anymore but universalizable. Consequently, if there is any privilege associated with the Greek idiom is it not for the fact that Greek language has a reserve of names for what resists all nonuniversalizable idioms, and which articulates something that, in principle, is shareable by all traditions? A word such as khora signals within the Greek idiom a resistance against its own idiomaticy. But could not also something similar be said of the word, "the *messianic*, or messianicity without messianism," which articulates the abstract relation to the to-come by subtracting from messianicity all hints of fulfillment?

In any case, as I have shown, the two names messianicity and khora are names in our tradition that offer orientation—one temporal, the other spatial—in the absolutely abstract place of the desert within the desert. They are the conditions necessary for a possible universalizable culture of singularities based on a minimal social bond, that is, of a world. In conclusion, I wish to point out that in the context of recasting Kant's *Religion within the Limits of Reason Alone* in light of "religion today," Derrida follows up on the new transcendental aesthetics that provides the performative conditions for a world by an inquiry into an analytic of pure practical reason, as it were. To show this, I return one more time to this faith in a world that I have linked to the immemorial remainder at the core of the double memory of Europe. If in "Faith and Knowledge," where the question about religion today is posed within the limits of reason alone, the culture of singularities that would make up such a world is further determined in terms of a culture of tolerance, that is, in terms of a concept whose meaning stems unmistakably from the sphere of religion, this is, of course, in conformity with the demands that devolve from the central question of religion. Yet, because of its origins in early Christianity, and the still essentially Christian nature of this notion during the Enlightenment, Derrida "immediately places quotation-marks around this word in order to abstract and extract it from its origins. And thereby ... announce, through it, through the density of its history, a possibility that would not solely be Christian" (FK, 21–22). Now, let us bear in mind that tolerance has been "a secret of Christian community" (FK, 22), in other words, of the historical actualization of a possibility for being-together, for being in community, and of which the early Christian community (and later Christianity) was the first, according to the French Enlightenment thinker Voltaire cited by Derrida, to give the example. It offered the world a purely moral and universal ideal of being in communion with one another, to emulate. But by putting this concept of tolerance in quotation marks, thereby abstracting it from its origins, Derrida gestures toward another kind of tolerance, free, indeed, of all particular creeds, while, at the same time, also mustering all the resources of religio. He writes, "Another 'tolerance' would be in accord with the experience of the 'desert in the desert,' it would respect the distance of infinite alterity as singularity. And this respect would still be *religio, religio* as scruple or reticence, distance, dissociation, disjunction, coming from the threshold of all religion in the *link of repetition to itself*, the threshold of every social or communitarian link" (FK, 22).

By understanding tolerance from the experience of the extreme desert, and the possibilities that religio offers for orienting oneself within it, "tolerance," as a condition for being together in the sense of a world and a culture of singularities, becomes respect. Free from all ties to historical creeds, as it must be for there to be the possibility of world, tolerance must be an active respect for that which makes the other other, differently worded, for what by linking him-or herself to him- or herself (relegere)—thus abstracting, reserving, holding back oneself from others, dissociates him or her from others—so that they become capable of relating to them (religare) in the first place. Tolerance as a condition for a place called world names a way of relating to the other in its alterity, one that respects the singularity of the distance that he or she must uphold to be a singularity to begin with. The world that such abstract tolerance would make possible, is a world in a strict sense. Based on the dissociation, disjunction, discretion, and respectful reservation (*retenue*) that the other demands so as to be able to remain singular, and that he or she must never surrender for the sake of a common substrate, essence, or identity, but must hold on to as a remainder that cannot be reappropriated, the world in question would be a just world, a place where each discrete singularity would be able to have a place, or rather, to take place.

Notes

1. See, for example, "Was bleibt von Derrida?" in *Information Philosophie* 3 (2010): 28–35, where the editors of the journal invited Alexander G. Düttmann, Dieter Mersch, Andreas Niederberger, and Bernard Waldenfels to respond to this question.

2. *Restance* has been translated either as "remaining" or "remainder." In what follows I will also indiscriminately use both possible translations. For a discussion by Derrida of the translation of the term "remainder," see Jacques Derrida, *Limited Inc.* (Evanston, IL: Northwestern University Press, 1988), 52. Let me also point out that it would be interesting to explore whether restance itself is not also a translation of corresponding Heideggerian notions such as *Bleibe* and *Wahrniss*. Not unrelated to the notion of restance is certainly also the notion of *demeurance* in Maurice Blanchot and Jacques Derrida, *The Instant of My Death/Demeure: Fiction and Testimony*, trans. E. Rottenberg (Stanford, CA: Stanford University Press, 2000), 91.

3. Jacques Derrida, "Faith and Knowledge: The Two Sources of 'Religion' at the Limits of Reason Alone," trans. S. Weber, in *Religion*, eds. J. Derrida and G. Vattimo (Stanford, CA: Stanford University Press, 1998), 31 (translation modified). Hereafter cited in text as FK.

4. Jacques Derrida, afterword to *Limited Inc.*, 141.

5. One notable exception is Matthias Flatscher's fine discussion of this neologism in an excursus on Derrida in *Logos and Lethe: Zur Phänomenologischen Sprachauffassung im Spätwerk von Heidegger und Wittgenstein* (Freiburg: Karl Alber, 2011), 207–210. Arguing that the notion of restance is intimately interconnected with that of *iterability* (hence, with all repetition with a difference), Flatscher suggests that the term is a nonmetaphysical variation on what traditionally has been conceived as the hyletic, materiality, or sensibility, which can no longer be comprehended within the framework of the dichotomy between the noetic and the aesthetic.

6. Jacques Derrida, *Margins of Philosophy*, trans. A. Bass, (Chicago: University of Chicago Press, 1982), 318.

7. Jacques Derrida, *Limited Inc*, trans. S. Weber, (Evanston, IL: Northwestern University Press, 1988), 53.

8. Derrida, *Limited Inc*, 83.
9. See also Paul Allen Miller, who has pointed out that Derrida's engagement with the Platonic corpus, in particular, is long-standing and that he "has always returned to the founding gestures of occidental philosophy and their simultaneous encoding and resistance in the Platonic corpus." Paul Allen Miller, "The Platonic Remainder. Derrida's *Khora* and the *Corpus Platonicum*," in *Derrida and Antiquity*, ed. M. Leonard (Oxford, UK: Oxford University Press, 2010), 331.
10. Jacques Derrida, "La 'vielle Europe' et la nôtre," in *Le Théâtre des idées. 50 penseurs pour comprendre le XXie siècle*, ed. N. Truong (Paris: Flammarion, 2008), 21–22.
11. Derrida, "La 'vielle Europe' et la nôtre," 21–22.
12. As Vincent Descombes has pointed out, the question raised by various French thinkers in the sixties about the end of philosophy implies that "philosophy is *the ideology of the western ethnos.*" Derrida, he argues, subscribes, or rather "has no objection" to this "reductive formula . . . except for the fact that to say it is impossible." Vincent Descombes, *Modern French Philosophy*, trans. L. Scott-Fox and J. M. Harding (Cambridge, UK: Cambridge University Press, 1980), 137. However, if Derridean thought is, indeed, involved in a deconstruction of Western ethnocentrism, it is, I add, first of all insofar as Western ethnocentrism is based on a Platonist interpretation of *philosophia*.
13. Jacques Derrida, "We Other Greeks," trans. P.-A. Brault and M. Naas, in *Derrida and Antiquity*, ed. M. Leonard (Oxford, UK: Oxford University Press, 2010), 33. Inquiring into the place of Greek thought within Derrida's writings, particularly into Derrida's interpretation of Sophocles's *Oedipus at Colonus*, Andrew Benjamin points to "the founding relation to strangeness" that, according to Derrida, is from the start inscribed in Greek philosophy. As an "affirmation of 'hybridity' (or 'bastardry,' etc.)," Greek philosophy is thus "*ab initio* more-than-one." Andrew Benjamin, "Possible Returns. Deconstruction and the Placing of Greek Philosophy," in *Derrida and Antiquity*, ed. M. Leonard (Oxford, UK: Oxford University Press, 2010), 209–210.
14. Jacques Derrida, "Khora," in *On the Name*, trans. D. Wood et al. (Stanford, CA: Stanford University Press, 1995), 119–120.
15. Jacques Derrida, *Margins of Philosophy*, trans. A. Bass (Chicago: University of Chicago Press, 1982), 215.
16. For a superb discussion of religion as a reaction against, and a simultaneous capitalization on, the forces of abstraction, see Michael Naas, *Miracle and Machine: Jacques Derrida and the Two Sources of Religion, Science, and the Media* (Bronx, NY: Fordham University Press, 2012).
17. In the wake of Derrida, Nicole Loraux has shown that *oikein*, which designates the Greek conception of autochthonous inhabitation, or dwelling in the civic space, is another such word without an *as such* in Plato's text. See Nicole Loraux, *Né de la terre. Mythe et politique à Athènes* (Paris, Seuil, 2009), 181–186. See also Nicole Loraux, "La métaphore sans métaphore: A propos de l'"Orestie,'" *Revue philosophique* 2 (1990): 247–268, where the "matric words," *phren* and *haima*, in Aeschylus's *Oresteia* are shown to be words that resist the sensible/intelligible distinction.
18. Jacques Derrida, *Dissemination*, trans. B. Johnson (Chicago: University of Chicago Press, 1981), 76. Let us also point out that footnote 43 in "Plato's Pharmacy," where Derrida, while referring to the chapter "Questions of Method" from *Of Grammatology*, writes that "one could say that the *pharmakon* plays a role *analogous*, in this reading of Plato, to that

of *supplément* in the reading of Rousseau," shows that though not a Greek word, the word "supplément" in the French idiom is already understood from those words in the Greek idiom that are indicative of an other of the Greek in Greek language and thought. Jacques Derrida, *Of Grammatology*, corrected ed., trans. G. C. Spivak, Baltimore: Johns Hopkins University Press, 1997, 96.

19. Derrida, *Dissemination*, 99.

20. Derrida, *Dissemination*, 70. When Plato, in "Letter VII," states that he does not have a systematic doctrine and has not composed in writing a work in that respect, as some pretend to have acquired it from his own instruction, he seems at first to distance himself from any Platonizing interpretation of his thinking. But this disclaimer that "there is no way of putting [the subjects to which he devotes himself] in words like other studies," is made "only" in the name of life-philosophizing where acquaintance with the subject is generated in the soul "like a blaze kindled by a leaping spark . . . and at once becomes self-sustaining" without ever congealing in any systematic form. Plato, *The Collected Dialogues*, eds. E. Hamilton and Huntington Cairns (Princeton: University of Princeton Press 1980), 1588–1589. For a more detailed discussion of "Plato's Pharmacy," see my "Giving to Read" in *The Wild Card of Reading: On Paul de Man* (Cambridge: Harvard University Press, 1998), 149–180.

21. Derrida, *Dissemination*, 160.

22. Derrida, *Dissemination*, 159–161. The reference to abstraction here is to the introduction by Albert Rivaud to the *Timaeus* in Platon, *Oeuvres Complètes* Paris: Societé d'édition "Les Belles Lettres," 1925, Vo. X, 66–67. Derrida, after having submitted that "the more radically you break with a certain dogmatism of the place or the bond (communal, national, religious, of the state), the more you will be faithful to the hyperbolic, excessive . . . demand, to the *hubris*, perhaps of a universal and disproportionate responsibility toward the singularity of every other," speaks of *khora* as precisely a place and place giving well beyond not only all such dogmatisms but also any negative theology. Jacques Derrida, "Abraham, the Other," in *Judeities. Questions for Jacques Derrida*, ed. B. Bergo et al. (Bronx, NY: Fordham Press, 2007), 13, 33. As regards the translation of khora as place (*topos*), see John Sallis, *Chorology. On Beginning in Plato's Timaeus* (Bloomington: Indiana University Press, 1999), 116, 153–154. For the prephilosophical meanings of the word khora, see Sallis, *Chorology*, 24, 116–117.

23. Jacques Derrida, "Khora," 89. This is a point that, as Sallis has pointed out, was made already by Aristotle in *On Generation and Corruption*. But as Sallis argues, on the contrary, the khora remains in force throughout the Timaeus "by the way in which this discourse traces the errancy, that is, marks the traces of its operation in the very midst of the god's productions." Sallis, *Chorology*, 132. Derrida, for his part, will show that the whole of Plato's dialogue is regulated by a mise en abyme of what itself does not let itself be properly said, that is, khora.

24. Derrida, "Khora," 99–100.

25. Martin Heidegger, *Introduction to Metaphysics*, trans. G. Fried and R. Polt (New Haven, CT: Yale University Press, 2000), 69–70.

26. Derrida, "Khora," 104.

27. Derrida, "Khora," 94, 117, 97.

28. Derrida, "Khora," 126, 119–120, 119.

29. The thought of something undeconstructable, such as justice, for example, is necessarily co-implied by everything deconstructable. The idea of the undeconstructable

therefore does in no way suggest that there is a beyond of deconstruction or even something like postdeconstruction. For a fine discussion of the status of the nondeconstructable, see Alexander Garcia Düttmann, *Derrida und Ich. Das Problem der Dekonstruction* (Bielefeld: Transcript, 2008).

30. Whether or not "revealability" (as opposed to "revelation") is understood as a transcendental condition of possibility for revelation, or, rather, as the factum of being revealed, or being in the open, it is the very possibility of drawing such a difference in a rigorous manner, namely, without any contamination, that is at issue here. Generally speaking, although Derrida does in no way put the necessity of making this distinction into question, the Heideggerian temptation consists in assuming that the difference between revelation and revealability is unproblematic. Yet the very possibility that revealability, however it is understood, may originate in the positive religions of revelation, shows it to be aporetic and to require a step toward a third place. The same logic applies in the case of the distinction between religion and its speculative truth.

31. See also: "a certain rupture, a certain departure, a certain separation, an interruption of the bond, a radical unbinding remains also, I believe, the condition of the social bond as such." Derrida, "Abraham, the Other," 5.

32. Any horizon of interpretation predicated on an understanding of Being (ontology), an understanding of God (theological), or the human being (anthropological) misses out on the abstractness of the desert within the desert. As Kant already noted, creation without the human being is nothing but "a mere desert." Immanuel Kant, *Critique of the Power of Judgment*, trans. P. Guyer and E. Matthews (Cambridge: Cambridge University Press, 2000), 308. To think the desert in all its abstraction requires also removing the human from it.

33. Since, indeed, this whole problematic concerns the spatial and temporal conditions for there to be a world in extreme abstraction, it is important to linger just for a moment on how "rendering possible" is to be understood here. As we have seen, khora (in spite of the imaginary of matrix, womb, and mother that Plato evokes) does not engender, rather it "gives place [*lieu*]," which "does not come to the same thing as to make a present of a place," but, as Samuel Weber translates, "to give way to" something, in short, to make possible, to make something happen. Derrida, "Khora," 100. Khora, consequently, is not of the order of a formal transcendental condition of possibility. Rather, as a giving way to something, khora "carries" what it makes possible in that it permits the repetition of what has been given way and to repeat it with a difference, thus, allowing for a relation of freedom to what is repeated. Derrida, "Khora," 126.

34. In our heritage the Greeks provide only the spatial conditions for a world. There is nothing like an open future for the Greeks and the unpredicatability that it implies.

35. Derrida evokes the need for "a new transcendental aesthetic" for the first time in *Of Grammatology*, 290. The conditions of the experience of the world defined by such an aesthetic are, at the same time, the conditions for the performative inception of such a world, in a way similar to Kant's contention that "the conditions of *possibility of experience* in general are at the same time conditions of the *possibility of the objects of experience.*" Immanuel Kant, *Critique of Pure Reason*, trans. P. Guyer and A. W. Wood (Cambridge: University of Cambridge Press, 1999), 283.

36. This is also one reason why the name "messianic," however charged, and even though it abstracts from all eventual fulfillment by messianism, or a messias determined in advance, offers itself to naming the condition of possibility for the experience of a universal

world. Such an experience presupposes the faith that in spite of the fact that the worst can happen just as well as justice, a world is possible, and will prevail, and which, by way of its "performative" nature, actively contributes to its formation.

37. For a discussion of the *via negativa* characteristic of negative theology, see, in particular, Jacques Derrida, "How to Avoid Speaking: Denials," in *Languages of the Unsayable: The Play of Negativity in Literature and Literary Theory*, ed. S. Budich and W. Iser (New York: Columbia University Press, 1989), 3–70; for a discussion of the connection of via negativa and the desert, see Jacques Derrida, "Passions: 'An Oblique Offering,'" in *On The Name*, trans. D. Wood et al. (Stanford, CA: Stanford University Press, 1995), 3–31.

11

BEYOND THE IDEA OF EUROPE

The essays collected in this volume are testimony of my lasting concern with how to think philosophically of Europe. If, indeed, this is an issue it is because Europe cannot, as philosophers from Nietzsche to Husserl and beyond have observed, be identified as merely a geographical entity. Considering the multiplicity of languages, ethnicities, and cultures that it comprehends, it can neither simply be identified in empirical terms as representing a common and homogeneous culture. Unlike other parts of the world whose place can be identified by the site they occupy on a map and by the culturally distinct features that characterize the group of people that live together on this territory, Europe, in Husserl's words, is "a spiritual shape."[1] He writes: "The title 'Europe' clearly refers to the unity of a spiritual life, activity, creation, with all its ends, interests, cares, and endeavors, with its products of purposeful activity, institutions, organizations."[2] And if this is so, it is, as he asserts in *The Crises of European Sciences and Transcendental Phenomenology*, because Europe is driven by "the genuine idea of universal philosophy," and thus by the *telos* of a "responsibility for the true being of mankind."[3] What follows from this spiritual shape of Europe and the "infinite task" that it represents is not only that Europe is never allowed to come to a rest in self-identity but also that this task affects Europe in its spiritual nature and demands of itself relentless self-criticism and development.[4] As a result of such self-understanding, Europe's identity is never settled. Europe is always on the threshold toward the accomplishment of itself as a spiritual project, task, dream, or utopia: one that itself is not defined once and for all, but that, on the contrary, undergoes inevitable modifications at its own hands. As a spiritual shape Europe is thus not only an entity not yet present in itself and still to come but also a "place" on the limit that divides it from itself and opens it to the other.

In Massimo Cacciari's words:

> Europe is "suspended" in its own geographic configuration. It is a place that from era to era seems necessary to redefine. This trait already resounds in the Greek term *topos*. In fact, *topos* does not indicate a "container" where to accumulate different elements however distinct, but the extreme limit, the *eschaton*, where these same elements arrive in their movement. Therefore, one recognizes the place only when one reaches the "threshold," its limit, that is, there where it is made *cum-finis*, near, close, contiguous to the other from itself, where it reveals something *communis* with the other. Europe is there where it "touches" the extraneous, the stranger. Europe can try to know itself only there where it encounters, in every sense, the wonderful-frightening [Greek: *thauma*] of the stranger.[5]

In several of the essays included in this book Europe's outreach and exposure to the other, or the stranger, has been addressed, not only in terms of an openness that presupposes as a condition an essential distancing of itself from itself but also an endowment of the other, the foreigner, so as to put itself into question.

In these concluding pages, I wish to linger on the manifold of modes of self-reflection, self-representation, and self-conception to which this precarious nature of what is European has given rise. Indeed, *Europe* has been repeatedly described as a project, a task, a promise, a dream, or a utopia. It has been conceptualized as an image, a shape, a figure, and above all as a concept and an idea. The essays collected in this volume have thus inquired into a variety of these notions in terms of which Europe has been thought, but also into a number of topics with which Europe has been closely associated to such a degree that they concern the very nature of Europe's essence, such as the horizon, the world, transparency, light, the concept, the relation to otherness, responsibility, and so forth.

Among these ways of thinking about Europe, the notions of Europe as a figure, a concept, or an idea are philosophically highly charged. Broadly speaking, as a figure Europe is the schema, or image, of an intelligible entity; as a concept it is a cognitively fully determined representation of the entity in question, whereas as an idea it is, particularly from a Kantian perspective, this entity in the shape of a task that does not cognitively exhaust the entity in question. As a concept, Europe, philosophically speaking, is one of its most significant representations, given that as a concept Europe can claim philosophical dignity.[6] But apart from the fact that Europe, beginning with Greece, is the place where the notion of *concept* originates and can thus, by contiguity, be associated with it, and that as a concept Europe serves as the standard against which it can be critically measured in all its historical deficiencies and shortcomings, such a representation also has its intrinsic limits. Indeed, as a concept this representation aims at a full determination of what Europe is, at identifying and fixing it according to its essence. But what about the characterization of Europe as an idea? An *idea* is, undoubtedly, also a philosophical notion, and in fact one which from Plato to Kant enjoys an even greater prestige than the concept. Significantly enough, the reference to Europe as an idea is not only one of the ways in which today we have come to think and to speak about Europe, in fact it has for some time become more common to refer to Europe as an idea than as a concept. Is this reference to Europe as an idea an index of a new way by which Europe meets its constitutive task of redefining itself? Does this philosophical designation fit Europe, therefore, more properly than say a concept of Europe? What are the stakes of calling it an idea rather than something else? Does this representation of Europe as an idea best convey what we think today when we reflect on Europe? Or does this term *idea*, while articulating perhaps something about Europe that makes it a more adequate denomination, at the same time also limit the meaning of *Europe*?

However, to refer to Europe as an idea does not necessarily mean that *idea* has a philosophical meaning. More often than not one can safely assume that *idea* just refers to some vague representation of Europe as a unity of meaning, or project, and of being more than just an empirical conglomerate of distinct nations. However nebulously, the term conveys a sense of unity and identity of its object. But the use of *idea* to speak of Europe also leaves one with the impression that the term is employed in the absence of a better word, especially since no reflection on the precise meaning of the term accompanies its manifold usages. Indeed, most of the time no precise content is associated with it at all. Yet, what happens when a determined content held to be the unifying substrate of Europe becomes associated with its idea? It certainly does not mean that the idea has already become a more philosophical concept. When, as with white supremacy in the United States, the idea of Europe heralds the superiority of the Caucasian race, the notion is an expression of ideological idiocy. But if on the contrary the idea designates freedom, the right to have rights, democracy, and the political as the privileged sphere of existence of man, on the one hand; and on the other, the sciences, rationality, and universality, then the prephilosophical connotations of the idea are left behind. Such content associated with the idea of Europe renders the unifying and identifying thrust that is only vaguely present in the ordinary understanding of the notion of the idea so much more salient. Comprehending all the above mentioned attributes of Europe as the idea of Europe thus also highlights the idea's unity: its uniqueness, no doubt, but also its single nature, the oneness of the one idea of Europe.

To speak of the idea of Europe is not only to speak of what unifies Europe, of what gives it its identity, but also of the one idea that can accomplish such unification and identification. Recently it has been argued that the time has come to reject the claim that there is one unitary idea that would provide Europe with its identity and that Europe "must begin by rejecting the idea that we need an idea of Europe."[7] In lieu of a singular unifying idea of Europe, which Anya Topolski holds to be a thing of the past, Europe should abandon the idea in which it considers itself grounded and replace it with an identity based on the idea that Europe "is a space for plurality;" for a plurality of ideas, in short, "a Europe of Ideas." Topolski concludes: "Let us reject the idea of Europe and embrace a Europe of ideas," a Europe that is "a space for the clash of ideas."[8] Obviously, the assumption is that Europe as a unified idea is a navel-gazing Europe impervious to all that is different from it. But this program of replacing the one idea of Europe by a Europe of competing ideas involves different concepts of the idea. The clashing ideas for which Europe should be the space are not of the same order as the one idea of Europe. On the contrary, with the abandonment of the one unifying idea, the philosophical sense of the idea as a unifying and identifying representation is relinquished, and its meaning reverts back to its vague common use. The clashing ideas Topolski calls for merely amount to opinions, views, representations, or beliefs. Without the idea's oneness and unifying thrust, they turn into the object of a struggle that divides, rather than unifies.

But precisely because the idea, understood in its ordinary sense, is a vague, if not empty representation, a mental form only, the call for a clash of ideas could also encourage projections to provide the empty form of the idea with some content. Seen in this way, the agon of ideas would paradoxically be a struggle for the one idea that could unify Europe with itself. Traditionally, Europe has been associated with such things as democracy, the Enlightenment, rationality, the sciences, universality, and so forth. These are interrelated aspects of the content of the idea of Europe itself and not in a clash with one another. On the contrary, they are indistinguishable from the conception of Europe as an idea to begin with. Philosophically speaking this is evidence of the fact that rather than an empty abstract representation that can be filled arbitrarily by a variety of contents, as an idea of Europe, the idea has a very specific content. Although further implicit aspects of that content can be added to it in an explicit manner, thus making the idea more concrete, this cannot be done simply at one's will. For, indeed, if it should prove to be the case that an idea qua idea is not just any mental representation, but that such a notion comes from the start with certain determinations, not just any content will do. These determinations are, first of all, a function of the content of an idea as an idea, which is anything but a homogenous, undifferentiated whole; on the contrary, it is an internally multiple though intimately interrelated set of ideas, such as those of reason, universality, the sciences, democracy, human rights, progress toward freedom, and so forth. If the idea of Europe is an idea in the singular, it is by virtue of the fact that in itself it is a unified complex of numerous ideas. Any idea intent on competing with the one idea of Europe would thus also have to meet the challenge of the richness of the idea of Europe's internal complexity of concurring ideas.

Let me linger a bit more on the conception of Europe as a place of competing ideas; more precisely, on the underlying understanding that Europe as an idea is characterized by an intrinsic plurality and, thus, creative potential of ideas. At the very moment Europe is not understood in merely geographical terms but, as Husserl holds in the "Vienna Lecture," as "a spiritual shape" according to which "the English Dominions, the United States, etc., clearly belong to Europe, whereas the Eskimos or Indians presented as curiosities at fairs, or the gypsies, who constantly wander about Europe, do not"—or to follow Nietzsche, as a "cultural concept" shared by "only those nations and ethnic minorities who possess a common past in Greece, Rome, Judaism and Christianity"—Europe appears despite all the exclusions as an entity characterized by extraordinary plurality and diversity of languages, cultures, traditions, and ethnicities.[9] As the essay "The Form of the Concept" in this book demonstrated, this diversity is a significant feature of Europe that has repeatedly been highlighted (by Hans-Georg Gadamer, for one) and that has been made possible by the absence in Europe of a dominating central state apparatus (such was the case in China, for example, which was largely responsible for blocking its expansion in the fifteenth century when in many respects it was more highly developed than the West).[10] The idea of Europe is not an aggregate of such differences, be they cultural, ethnic, linguistic, and so forth, but made up by a unified complex of traits that make such plurality possible. Indeed, from the start the idea of Europe inscribes within itself an essential dimension of otherness—a structural exposure to what Cacciari described as "the extraneous, the stranger."

But what does it mean that Europe, rather than a geographical entity, is a spiritual topology, and that as an idea Europe, rather than the expression of a common culture, is a spiritual figure? It means, first and foremost, that the idea of Europe is not merely rooted in actual languages, traditions, religions, customs, nor in what in North America is nowadays called "cultures." It follows from this that to hold that Europe as an idea is just one *particular* idea restricted to a particular world and its humanity, presupposes the assumption that there are not simply non-European cultures, traditions, worlds, and so on, but also other nongeographical configurations whose unity is of the order of an idea. If the idea of Europe is a particular idea, it is one among many other ideas that other cultures can claim as their own, the sheer existence of which then relativizes the very claim to universality that it makes. Here, too, the question arises of what concept of idea subtends this argument. If there are a manifold of ideas claiming universality, are these ideas even ideas to begin with? A clash of ideas, all of which pretend to universality, is a contradiction in terms. If there is a universal idea, then there can only be one if its thrust is to be universal. Or if there are several ideas that can make this claim, they are the same and, thus, no competition is possible between them.

In any event, since the unitary thrust of the notion of idea presupposes an essential affirmation of difference and otherness, it is difficult to see what other nongeographical ideas there are that would be in competition with the idea of Europe and that, as a result, would reduce it to being just a parochial idea. Without speculating on where alternative nongeographical configurations could be found—in fact I agree with Jean-Luc Nancy that "up until now, one cannot say that any other configuration of the world or any other philosophy of the universal and of reason have challenged" the West's shaping of the course of the world—let me for the time being only point out that the notion of an idea that names such a configuration—the idea of Europe, for example—is itself not only "something genuinely European," as Josef Simon points out, it is, first of all, a Greek term, a Greek notion.[11]

Does it not follow from this that even before posing the question of what the idea of Europe positively consists of, and especially before taking issue with the idea of Europe—either in order to propose a Europe of ideas, or in order to accuse Europe's arrogance of conceiving of itself as an idea in the first place—should one not first have to clarify how one understands the notion of idea in all these cases? And is such explication feasible without taking the originary meaning of "idea"—*idea* or *eidos*—that is, its Greek meaning, and the history of the expression in the history of Western thought into account? Indeed, to refer to Europe as a project, a projection, a concept, a figure, an idea, are not just innocent designations. This is above all the case when we speak of Europe as an idea by way of a Greek philosophical word. Something more precise than the ordinary and prephilosophical sense of the idea as a fleeting subjective content, a vague representation, or a hazy inkling of something by consciousness is meant when one speaks of Europe as an idea. If, furthermore, one takes into account that the term *idea* in the Western tradition is a prominently philosophical term, then something more "philosophical" is involved when the idea is evoked in conjunction with Europe as a spiritual figure rather than a geographical expanse. In order to gauge what is philosophical about the idea when associated with Europe, it may be good to remind ourselves that an idea is always an idea of something, and that in an idea one must thus distinguish its object, or content, from itself as a structure, or a form (of representation). Since in the case of an idea, this distinction between form and content is of a very specific nature, we are already anticipating the philosophically technical sense in which the term has to be taken. But let us not move too quickly ahead, and remind ourselves again that to speak of an idea, in the context of the problematic of Europe, is not just any word but a Greek word and a Greek thing. In its passage from the prephilosophical Greek language to its philosophical use, the notion of idea, which first designated the outward appearance or visible outline of a thing or person—but also already what kind or sort of thing it is, or to which it belongs—undergoes a fundamental transmutation in that it now designates a thing's or person's *invisible* and incorporeal form. This revolutionary metamorphosis is unique in that the idea, which until then permitted the recognition of something by way of its sensible contours, now refers to an invisible form beyond appearances that can be beheld intellectually and that when applied to sensible appearances allows for their intelligibility.[12] With this distinction of the intelligible status of the idea, Greece paved the way not only for the sciences but also for a universal ethics. Although it is in Greece that the passage from the extraphilosophical understanding of the idea to its philosophical sense occurs, the notion in question, when applied to Europe, is not therefore simply to be retraced to its Platonic sense as the proper nature or true intellectual ground of things, or in a more Aristotelian fashion, as the originary forms in which all things participate. Only by reflecting on when and where Europe becomes wedded to the notion of an idea is it possible to see in what sense 'idea' has to be taken in this context.

But when and where was Europe elevated explicitly, and for the first time, to the rank of an idea? Today, the reference to Europe as an idea is so common that the expression is taken for granted. George Steiner's essay *The Idea of Europe*, for example, at no point pauses to reflect on the appellation in question.[13] Unless I have missed something (which, of course, is not excluded) there is not yet any conceptual history of the expression "the idea of Europe." Undoubtedly, it was Georg Simmel, who as early as 1915 published an essay titled "Die Idee Europas," but as far as I can see, to speak of Europe as an idea is a relatively recent development.[14] If the expression gained its momentum only after the publication of Husserl's 1935 Vienna Lecture in the early 1960s, it must also be noted that even in this lecture, or in *The Crisis of European Sciences*, the expression "the idea of Europe" is not to be found. Husserl still speaks of "the concept of Europe," in conformity with a tradition that has been canonized with the publication of an entry on Europe in the *Historisches Wörterbuch der Philosophie*.[15] But when in the Vienna Lecture Husserl speaks of philosophy as the discovery by the Greeks of infinity, and thus "as [an] idea, as the idea of an infinite task" and "as the primal phenomenon of spiritual Europe," this "philosophical-historical idea (or the teleological sense) of European humanity" can be construed as being the idea that drives Europe, and that therefore Europe is an idea in the sense of an infinite spiritual task.[16] The same holds true of Husserl's contention in *The Crisis of European Sciences* that "European humanity bears within itself an absolute idea."[17] This idea refers to universal reason as it emerged in the European sciences and philosophy but not, per se, the "idea of Europe." Notwithstanding the fact that Husserl does not explicitly coin the expression "the idea of Europe," its use by Steiner and other phenomenologically oriented thinkers, such as Jan Patočka or Jacques Derrida, can probably be traced to the Vienna Lecture.[18]

Without yet inquiring in what specific sense *idea* is understood when Europe is invoked as an idea, its association with philosophy, the sciences, or rational thought in general links the reference to Europe as an idea to the Enlightenment. To speak of Europe as an idea is to invoke the Greek heritage of Europe, as opposed to Europe's Christian past in the Middle Ages, which dominated the Romantics' nostalgic reflections on Europe by

Novalis and Friedrich Schlegel. As Christoph Jamme has pointed out, for Schlegel the cultures of Asia—Indian culture, in particular—are a prefiguration of the future of Europe because as highly unified cultures they offer a model for what a future Europe would look like: one that, like the Europe of the Middle Ages, would have overcome its plurality and all its divisions through the religious and political unification by Christianity.[19] Reunited with itself according to an oriental model, Europe would then also be on par with these non-European cultures, not as competing ideas but as integrated cultures under a dominant religious principle. However, to refer to Europe as an idea is to evoke the other origin of Europe in Greek and Roman antiquity, distinct from the Christian heritage of Europe, that is, a Europe whose identity is oriented in accordance to the demands of reason. In distinction from Novalis' dream of "*Eine* Christenheit," of a theologico-political identity that erases all plurality and makes Europe alike other cultures equally entrenched in self-enclosed identities, Europe understood in terms of the idea of reason is not a Europe that has eliminated all difference; on the contrary, it is characterized not simply by the unity of Europe as a plurality of cultures, languages, histories, and so forth, but by its structural openness to the other.[20] Characterized as an idea, Europe signifies another relation to the other and speaks to a different type of identity than one based on empirical unification and self-enclosure.

As an idea Europe is thus intimately associated with the Enlightenment. Let us remind ourselves again that for Husserl, the idea immanent to Europe as a spiritual rather than geographic shape or figure is an idea that originates in Greece and that teleologically drives the history of European humanity. Husserl calls this idea in the Vienna Lecture "the historical teleology of the infinite tasks of reason."[21] With this the idea of Europe is, as far as its content is concerned, not only defined as the realization of something essentially Greek under the name or in the form of the object of Europe. But this also means that the sense in which *idea* is taken here—as a telos, as an infinite task—is also testimony to an entirely different understanding than that which one finds in Plato or Aristotle. Idea in the context of the expression "idea of Europe" is to be understood in a modern sense, as a representation of reason that can only be approximated in an infinite process: as an idea in the Kantian sense.

However much it is intertwined with the destiny of its object, the idea of Europe, understood according to Kant's reinterpretation of the Platonic concept, is not something that, like a concept, represents or reflects the essence of a completed thing. Indeed, in distinction from a concept that legislates about what Europe has been and is as such, Europe, as an idea in the Kantian sense, is something that will never be realized in full. As an idea in a Kantian sense Europe remains an undetermined, not yet definite presence. As something that can only be tangentially approximated but never completely accomplished in reality, such an idea remains in a way exterior, something outside Europe in all its cultural and historical reality; something intimate, however, that is also foreign to itself and to be striven for as an infinite task. If this is so, it follows that the idea is not something invented by Europe with the purpose to be imposed on others in order to gain hegemony over them. It is, on the contrary, something that concerns Europe itself, its own identity, first and foremost: namely, the demand to Europeanize itself so as to be itself.[22]

I reemphasize that in the expression "the idea of Europe," *idea* is not only to be taken in a specific philosophical sense but, as is also clear from the Vienna Lecture, it encapsulates the exigencies of Greek and European philosophy. Europe here is one with philosophy. When we speak of the idea of Europe we suggest that *Europe* is another name for philosophy. But is this not a preposterous or outrageous claim? Is Europe's raising itself to the status of an idea not an act of supreme arrogance? This is a question that in this or other forms has been raised repeatedly in postcolonial and cultural studies. For economic reasons I refer here only briefly to an essay by Hans Schelkshorn, "Der Hochmut Europas und die Philosophie."[23] According to the author, philosophy has from its inception in Greece, and regardless of all epochal breaks, "been carried by a deep current of imperial thinking" until today.[24] Furthermore, if its possession is accompanied by "a consciousness of superiority that is itself anchored in philosophy," philosophy as such is inherently an articulation of a Greek and European claim to superiority and exclusivity, which provided "over millenaries the European world domination with ideological support."[25] This claim to superiority is wedded to philosophy to such a degree that even when it puts itself self-critically into question and demands the dismantling of its inherent imperialism, these gestures are still "accompanied by a certain arrogance in that European philosophy desperately clings to its claim of exclusivity."[26] As Schelkshorn avers: "Under the spell of the idea of the uniqueness of European philosophy even the discourse about the crisis of the Occident remains a monolog of European philosophy with itself, in which the imperial logic of exclusion reproduces itself one more time."[27] I have no intention to deny that Greek and European philosophy is not free of arrogance; I only wish to point out that it is a sign of a misconception of what philosophy is all about, to hold that this arrogance is intrinsic to philosophy itself. Nor will I take issue with Schelkshorn's claim that there are philosophies other than the Greek-European ones, such as the syntheses between non-European spiritual or religious traditions and European philosophy; in short, that there are "several origins of the birth of philosophy."[28] I limit myself to pointing out that this claim is based, as well, on an understanding of philosophy as an ideological construct, or a view of the world (*Weltanschauung*), a misunderstanding that, in fact, denies other cultures the singularity of their own modes of thinking. There are certainly, as Heidegger puts it, several great origins, and philosophy has to open itself to them, but these are origins of other modes of thought than Greco-European philosophical thought. By contrast, what I wish to take issue with in the present context is the implicit claim in the characterization of philosophy as being built on a deep current of imperial thinking, that "the idea of the uniqueness of European philosophy" is the foundation of "the idea of Europe"—that it is Europe's self-proclaimed uniqueness that has motivated it to arrogantly raise itself to the status of an idea, inflating its particularity and imperial designs into universalism. Such a conclusion only reveals a lack of knowledge of what an idea is in the first place, and thus also misses out on the internal potential of an idea such as Europe to critically confront the misuses to which it has historically lent itself. It is a misunderstanding of the notion of the idea itself, one that also fails to grasp the resources that the notion of idea harbors, and that might have the potential for going beyond the idea of Europe in an attempt to conceptualize limits in which the notion of the idea envelops its object, that is, "Europe."

Now with the crisis of Europe that results from the decline of its position in the world, and the horrific catastrophes that it has experienced within itself—and that, at the same time, have opened its eyes and forced it to acknowledge the atrocities that, as a colonizing power, it has committed in the name of its values, thus also compromising them—the idea of Europe has evidently become problematic. Rather than a worldwide force and model, Europe is said to have become provincialized, barely an acting factor anymore in the shaping of the world. To refer to Europe in this sense is to refer to it as a hegemonic power and not as an idea. But such provincialization of Europe is also an occasion for critically turning to itself—the occasion of introspection. With the definite end of Europe as a hegemonic power, the possibility arises of bringing the idea of Europe itself into sharper focus, not only where its content is concerned but also the form that this content takes when it is conceived as an idea. This is what I now wish to explore.

I take my starting point in the "Annexes" published to Jan Patočka's *L'Europe après l'Europe* (in the translation from the Czech into French by Erika Abrams).[29] From the title of the book—*L'Europe après l'Europe*—it is clear that after Europe has come to an end, we are not simply done with Europe. In fact, the end of Europe in the sense of the loss of its economic and political supremacy in the world presents Europe with an opportunity; with a chance, as the Czech philosopher puts it, to reconceive of itself. In order to gauge the context for such a chance, it is important to realize that, as Patočka points out at the beginning of *Plato and Europe*, the end of Europe by way of Europe's self-destruction "has drawn the entire world into this, just as she had appropriated before the whole world in a material fashion."[30] By forcing the rest of the world to engage in those horrendous enterprises of self-destruction by "projecting the division of Europe upon a division of the world," inheritors of Europe have emerged who "will never allow Europe to be [again] what it once was."[31] It is important to see that this result is in fact the outcome of Europe's success; more precisely, of its successful Europeanization of the world. In *L'Europe après l'Europe*, Patočka notes that "the collectivities that are in the process of awakening, as well as those who affirm themselves for the first time as political giants are . . . formally Europeanized in the sense that indisputably they adopt technology, production and the forms of European organization," even though "they remain intimately foreign to the spiritual substance of Europe."[32] The new emerging humanities not only remain foreign to it, "their relation to this substance is even strained if not antagonistic," in that the rational foundations of what has been taken over from Europe are amalgamated with traditions and motifs that are not only hostile to Europe but whose origins are often very archaic, some of which are retraceable to the stone age.[33] If this situation is a chance for Europe to reflect on itself and to have a future after its end, it is precisely because of the formal universality that it itself has taken on throughout the world, or to put into more contemporary language, in the thus globalized world. Indeed, this state of affairs confronts Europe with the fact that, paradoxically, it itself has remained foreign to its own substance. Not only that: if Patočka can characterize the successful Europeanization of the world as "a generalization of the shipwreck of Europe," it is because the unforeseeable alloy that European rationality has undergone through its globalization rests on and perpetuates the very reasons that have caused, to begin with, the European catastrophe from within.[34] For this reason, the dismal situation of a successfully Europeanized world that takes over from Europe harbors the possibility of another Europe—I would say, of the *other* Europe (if not the Europe of the other), if that expression (the *other* Europe) had not already been reserved for Eastern Europe (for example, by Patočka himself).

In order to understand Patočka's argument, let me first recall that in distinction from Edmund Husserl, who, in the wake of a long tradition, retraces the idea of Europe to that of philosophy—that is, to the Greek idea of a rational science and a universal truth that not only meets the demand of being able to account for itself but also imposes itself without distinction on everybody—Patočka, by contrast, locates the origin of Europe in the Greek, Platonic conception of the "care of the soul [*epimeleia tes psyches*]." Among everything that Europe has inherited, this conception is what, after Europe's shipwreck, could still "affect us in a way so that we could again find hope in a specific perspective, in a specific future, without giving in to illusory dreams and without undervaluing the toughness and gravity of our current situation."[35] For Patočka this conception of the care of the soul is not an altogether different motif from the Husserlian notion of reason and rationality. On the contrary, the motif of tending to the soul consists only in a recasting and deepening of the foundations of European rationality in order to be able to overcome the crises of Europe. Indeed, in the notion of the care of the soul whose aim, as Patočka does not cease to remind us, is to endow it with full transparency and clarity, all the defining features of rationality find their first philosophical and historical articulation.[36] It is a clarity that the soul achieves as a result of looking into what is, into the most perfect being—the *eide*, the forms, or looks of what is—and which, as the most perfect beings, are also those that are entirely knowable. Their being is of such a nature as to have the potential (*dunamis*) of being fully cognizable because it is of the order of the intelligible itself. Ultimately, the gaze into what is, is a gaze into the idea beyond all ideas: the idea of the Good (*agathon*), which must not be understood in a narrow moral sense but that has "ethical" implications in a way that concerns the intelligibility of all that is.[37] It is, therefore, crucial to understand that the notion of the care of the soul is not simply an approach that concerns the life of the individual but is, from the start, intrinsically tied to the life in community—a point that though present from the beginning in Patočka's reflections on the care of the soul, is perhaps more forcefully emphasized in his later writings.[38] Furthermore, in these later writings, the cared for soul is characterized as an "open soul." Patočka writes: "The open soul is in its essence, a soul that has been put in contact; it is not a being that is closed upon itself . . . it is possible to say that in a way its essence is to be outside itself," outside itself in the world whose horizon it actively opens up.[39]

So for Patočka, it is not the idea of a rational science and its implicit universality but the inherent rational nature of the care of the soul that is the embryonic form of Europe.[40] Yet, as he argues, especially in *Heretical Essays in the Philosophy of History*, this conception has undergone a number of transformations of which only the last, its Christian appropriation, is at the foundation of Europe. For what interests us here, namely, the reasons that have led to the end of Europe and its concomitant generalization in a globalized world, the turn that the notion of the care of the soul undergoes in the sixteenth century, is what must concern us first and foremost. In a most succinct form this turn occurs when in the life of Western Europe "another motif comes to the fore, opposing the motif of the care of the soul"—though not simply from the outside but by a motif that, as Patočka notes, is "originally held in captivity" by the Christianized conception of the care of the soul—namely the motif to dominate; the will to rule.[41] He writes that this new motif that, beginning with the sixteenth century, comes "to dominate one area after another, politics, economics, faith, and science, transforming them in a new style [is] not a care *for the soul*, the care to *be*, but rather the care to *have*, care for the external world and its conquest."[42] Since this motif of "*having* over *being* excludes unity and universality . . . the expanding western Europe lacks any universal bond, any universal idea which could be embodied in a concrete and effective bonding institution and authority."[43] Let us remind ourselves at this point that Patočka's concern with the care of the soul is an attempt at deepening the foundations of European rationality. More generally, the essays and fragments collected in *L'Europe après l'Europe* stand under the sign of the "idea of an ultimate foundation," or an "idea of the well-founded."[44] This theme of "the wellfounded," which deserves a careful analysis of its own, guides Patočka's attempt to deepen the foundations of European rationality. Husserl is credited for having begun this urgent task in *The Crisis of European Sciences and Transcendental Phenomenology*, and Patočka sets out to follow the direction that Husserl outlined even though he failed to solve the problem. While hereafter I will repeatedly evoke some of the main aspects of Patočka's novel approach to the task in question, it may be appropriate to try, in spite of the dense and, at times, elliptic elaborations in *L'Europe après l'Europe* (229ff), to pinpoint as succinctly as possible in what Husserl's failure consists. It seems to me that when asking why, besides the inertia of the tradition, ancient mathematics and the metaphysics of the ideas related to it maintained themselves for such a long time, Patočka's response—that the force of this metaphysics and the secular theology that it implies—is rooted "in the deepest layers of human existence . . . layers from which the drive emerges to call and exhort the souls to live a life in truth which constitutes what is most proper to them."[45] As we will see, for Patočka, Husserl's answer to the task of recasting the foundations of European rationality by way of an objectification of subjectivity in the form of the transcendental ego falls short of accomplishing this. On the contrary, a deepening of the foundation of rationality can only be achieved through "the Socratic-Platonic idea of a total reflection" (235), by which the first reflection originating in the deepest layers of human existence, and the second reflection that concerns our appropriation and domination of the content of the world, are dialectically overcome in the conception of an "open soul."[46]

At this juncture it may be appropriate to recall that, according to Patočka, the idea of rationality that emerged as such only in Europe emerges simultaneously with the idea of its opposite, namely, "the anonymous tradition of non-reason," or irrationalism, which is constantly displaced by reason.[47] This latter conception of irrationalism is one, he writes, "that also could only emerge on the European soil, and thanks to the means that Europe provides."[48] For this very reason the idea of irrationality is twofold. First, Patočka refers with it to the myths or traditions of other civilizations. Indeed, in view of Europe's culture of reason and rationality, the foreign traditions and archaic motifs that have become amalgamated with European rationality in the process of the Europeanization of the world are inevitably of the order of the irrational. But this motif of irrationality is of particular significance in *L'Europe après l'Europe* in that European civilization is shown here to harbor its own peculiar irrationalisms as well. It is important to note that these irrationalisms, which include archaisms, certain traditions, and nativisms, are not simply particularities or idiomaticies of singular cultures. They are defined negatively with respect to the rational, whereas particularities and idiomaticies concern the way the universal is articulated in a culturally different way in each case, given that all testimony bearing to the universal can only take place through the particular, and in an inevitably particular form. Whereas the particular is an inescapable mode for articulating the universal, archaisms, nativisms, and irrationalities have a debilitating effect on it. Certain motifs that are specifically European, and that are not simply of the order of inevitable particularity, are mixed into Europe's self-defining concern with reason and universality—with the idea of Europe itself. In the same way, as is the case with all the other, non-European traditions, there is also "a native irrationalism peculiar to Europe."[49] In his characterization of the assimilation by other cultures of the European heritage, Patočka qualifies the native content and form with which European rationality undergoes unexpected alloys, as archaisms.[50] Let me linger for a moment on this notion of "archaisms" which, in distinction from the native irrationalism that both Europe and other traditions share, Patočka reserves for certain substrata that non-Western cultures mix into their appropriation of European rationality.

Greek philosophy, as it begins to take shape in the sixth century, is not the result of what has come to be known as the "Greek miracle." As Jean Pierre Vernant remarks, "there is no immaculate conception of Reason."[51] Johannes Lohmann, though without employing the term *archaisms*, has described "the prodigious transformation that human thought underwent during the classical-Greek epoch" as historically the first liberation of human thought from the primitive experience of the world in "original language," that is, in language as rooted in the magical and conjuring function of the name. The radical change consisted in Greek language becoming "*logos*, that is, the consciously experienced form of thought itself," a *concept* of language, whose correlate is the *concept* of world, *physis*. But this emergence of something wholly other in Greece—Greek philosophy—did not take place at one go.[52] In the case of the Presocratics, it has been shown that, on the contrary, it is the result of a methodic translation through a manifold of stratifications of what Clémence Ramnoux has called "the archaic," a cultural stratum of representations with its own vocabulary, structures, and modes of concatenations, and that is reinterpreted by philosophy so as to give rise to an entirely new kind of style and structure of thought; that is, rational thought with its language freed of all such archaisms and reduced to abstractions and essentials.[53] The question raised by this accomplishment of Greek philosophy in which a recourse to archaisms takes place, but in order to completely recast them in view of a universal discourse free of archaisms, is whether non-Western cultures have been at all involved in a similar process; in other words, whether the archaic has undergone a similar "laicization" in other cultures, in particular when they became Europeanized through the assimilation of certain aspects of European rationality that they permeated with native archaisms. Patočka does not seem optimistic in this respect. In any event, the native irrationalisms that are present in Europe's actual conception of reason and universality, and to which Patočka draws our attention, are not to be understood as of the order of archaisms to begin with. Rather than belonging to archaisms, to what Ramnoux calls "le lointain"—the far off, the distant, the remote—they are of the order of what is close, in fact, rather close, namely the relatively recent phenomenon of Christianity, historically, in the context of which a rediscovery and renewal of the Platonic notion of the care of the soul finds its latest articulation. What has caused Europe to self-destruct in a process that, through the Europeanization of the rest of the world has drawn the non-Western world into the same movement, derives from the pernicious amalgamation of the idea of rationality and universality with irrational motifs native to Christianity.

Undoubtedly, the idea of reason, and hence of universality, originates with Plato and is thus Greek in origin. But, as Patočka argues, the original meaning of Plato's discovery of universality undergoes a significant change when it is taken up by Christian theology. For Plato, the signification of this discovery of reason and universality concerns, first and foremost, the soul as the place of knowledge, and consists in the conviction that the new consciousness to which it gives rise leads to a complete transformation of the human being—in a process which Patočka refers to as "a reflective renewal of life"—with the effect of thoroughly reforming not merely the individual but the collective form of his existence; the political nature of his existence, in particular.[54] Yet, when this attempt at "a reflective renewal of life" is taken up by Christian theology and its conception of history, and Europe is thus born, the possibility of organizing European humanity in an unprecedented and unheard of fashion on the basis of the spiritual principle of the care of the soul is quickly aborted by the tenets of theology itself. More specifically, this process in which the relinquishment of the political dimension of the motif in question takes place is historically grounded in Europe's expansion to the West, and the simultaneous essential transformation by the Reformation "of the orientation of Christian praxis, turning from the sacred to the secular, acquir[ing] that political significance that will manifest itself in the organization of the North American continent by

Protestant radicalism."⁵⁵ As regard the specific forms that the irrationalisms native to Europe take and that become amalgamated with the ideas of reason and universality involved in the care of the soul Christian style, I can limit myself here to evoking only the two most important ones.

First, at the moment God becomes the one who alone detains true knowledge, what is proper to the human being, namely, the soul's ability to look into the essence of what is—"the being which agelessly, eternally is" and to which it thus becomes bonded—loses the weight that it enjoyed in Greek thought.⁵⁶ As a consequence, the authentic nature of what is human, rather than being understood in terms of a knowledge of the Good through which human beings could, in a way, become immortal and equal to the Greek gods, is in Christianity held to reside in man's practical attitude, in the operative actions in which he is involved—labor, in short—at the service of God in this world, in the down here.⁵⁷ Transposed to a world entirely disenchanted and dedivinized by Protestant theology, the Greek idea of reason and universality generates, as Patočka remarks, a new attitude "that until then was unknown to the spirit, an attitude that one could qualify as purely objective [*sachlich*], consisting in understanding things from the things themselves and their thingly structures without mixing anything heterogeneous into them."⁵⁸ Needless to say, this new attitude made possible by Christianity's practical attitude regarding work and service to God in a thoroughly secular world changes the nature of knowledge in its entirety, which from now on becomes a knowledge of domination of a thoroughly objectified world. The "unique accomplishment" of Christianity's appropriation of the Platonic motifs of reason and universality, which had been developed in the context of a concern with the soul and in view of a reorganization of community on universal grounds, thus amounts to an abortion of its initial goal.⁵⁹ Oriented exclusively toward the things in the world in an objectivist, physicalist way, to the exclusion of the human beings within the world, the new attitude that emerges with Christianity "necessarily skirts the content of the world" and thus also "finds itself incapable of constructing a mundane science."⁶⁰ Indeed, as Patočka emphasizes, mathematics, now aiming at "universalist tasks of a new style," as opposed to the role it enjoyed in Greek thought, play a significant role in the new attitude toward the world that reigns in the sciences. Freed from the metaphysical realism of the ideal objectities, mathematics as a purely formal discipline and as "the model for the new reflection that aims at the world, and the down here," no longer seeks to map out the realm of the Ideas. Aiming at the universe of realities, it understands its formal structures primarily as the correlate of practical operations in and on the world.⁶¹ Such a mode of reflection, however, as Patočka submits, is unable to respond to the structures and real needs of European society in that it entirely abstracts from the opportunity that the renewal in Europe—or as Europe—of the idea of the care of the soul offers for "reforming as a whole the tenor and collective form of [European humanity's] existence, particularly, of political life."⁶²

The second motif that severely curtails the renewal of the principle of rationality and universality in Christian Europe concerns its very conception of the soul, or subject. According to Patočka, the correlate of the European sciences' concern with an entirely objectified, or physicalist world, is a conception of the subject as an imperialist entity from which the world in its entirety can be drawn: a subject that is absolute and which, when speaking of European consciousness, he characterizes as "a consciousness that one could say to be closed upon itself by way of its infinity."⁶³ He concludes: "The *proton pseudos* of Europe is thus wed to its closure upon itself for having been rendered absolute."⁶⁴

Patočka writes, "Rooted in the deepest layers of our human existence, ... the impulsion to call upon the souls, and exhort them to a life in truth is what is most proper to these layers."⁶⁵ Yet, even though "the secular empire of theology" has its source in these deepest layers of human existence (as is demonstrated by its ability to urge the discipline upon human beings to excel in worldly activity in a disenchanted and dedivinized world, and so to find a way to themselves by virtue of this trial), the disenchantment and dedivinization in question and the exclusive theoretical and practical concern with the world stifled the community of self and other to which the reflection on the souls' impulsion to a life in truth should have led. As a result of the secular empire of theology, the thrust of rationality is thus thoroughly reduced to the sphere of objectivity of a here below suspended from a beyond. At the hands of the sciences' mundane, or rather secular orientation, "the Platonic-Socratic idea of a total reflection" that concerned the world *and* the human being becomes replaced by "a partial reflection only, which, pretending to be total, in fact, condemned total reflection to oblivion."⁶⁶ At the root of the catastrophe of Europe is this theologically motivated reduction of rationality to the objectified world and expansion of the soul to an absolute subject. Further implications of the limitation of rationality and universality to the objective world of things, and the conception of the subject as absolute, will be spelled out hereafter. At this point let me only emphasize that the two motifs show Europe to be tied in the same way as all other traditions to a native irrationalism of its own, an irrationalism profoundly linked to Christianity in its Protestant form on whose soil the Greek idea of reason and universality enjoyed its renewal in Europe.[67]

This irrationalism, or hyperbolism of Europe's nativeness that emerged in the shape of a new rationality in Europe some four hundred years ago, is what caused the end of Europe from within. But for Patočka, as we have seen, the end of Europe has, perhaps, a positive signification. Indeed, for him "the post-European epoch stands under the sign of chance," on condition that in rethinking Europe, one avoids falling back on past errors.[68] However, for this to take place, Europe will have to face the enormous task of "deepening the foundations of rationality in relation to that at which one had arrived in Europe during the historical period dominated by it."[69] In *L'Europe après l'Europe* we read: "It must suffice here to call to attention some of the fundamental conditions without which one cannot hope to succeed. One cannot generalize Europe as has been done hitherto contenting oneself with transplanting and taking up again results, but only by reflecting on the presuppositions that are responsible for the limits of rationality hitherto."[70] Indeed, what is required is "the urgent task of deepening the foundation of European rationality which alone could make a true debate with all the living traditions of the concrete world possible."[71] The deepening of Europe's foundation in an effort to yield a foundation that is "well-founded," rather than an exercise of bending in on itself, is thus also predicated on an opening to other traditions within the concrete world. As we have seen, the post-European world is one in which the whole world has been Europeanized. A well-founded foundation would thus be one that would have inquired into the limits that native traditions, be they European or non-European, have imposed on the idea of reason and rationality itself. But only through a radical inquiry, first and foremost, into its own nativisms can Europe hope to develop a well-founded foundation and thus reach out to others.

Let us remind ourselves again that for Patočka the idea of Europe is, in the same way as for Husserl, that of reason and universality. Let us also not lose sight of the fact that it has only been in Europe that this idea has arisen in explicit fashion, and that it is only in Europe that this idea has been involved in a, however failed, "reflexive renewal of life."[72] In spite of the "successful Europeanization" of the world, no other culture has taken the place of Europe's demanding of itself such a renewal. They have limited themselves to mixing their own historical patrimony into what they have taken over from Europe, namely a certain conception of world-oriented rationalism, or become entrenched in nostalgic and at times violent fundamentalisms, resisting what Max Weber characterized as the intellectualization, and, hence, disenchantment (*Entzauberung*) of the world. If the non-Western world has become Europeanized as a whole, a reflection on the idea of Europe is certainly no longer the privilege of Europe alone. Yet if the non-Western world has become Europeanized without the spirit of Europe, it follows that it cannot draw on the resources of the European tradition to take critical issue with the form of rationality that they have assimilated. If Europe after Europe still has a crucial role to play, it is because the idea of reason and universality that are, in Husserlian terms, its telos, or destiny, provide it with the task and the means to deepen its own understanding of what such a legacy demands of it. It alone would, therefore, seem to have the potential for bringing about a world capable of what Patočka calls a "reflexive renewal of life" by freeing rationality and universality from native irrationalisms and archaisms. But if in order to do this, Europe must find ways of relating to other cultures in a way that is free of its past arrogance, the first step in this direction consists in coming to grips with its own native irrationalisms.

As Patočka avers, even though the conception of reason (and thus also of universality) that has dominated European thinking and its self-conception is "insufficient, and has provoked crises," such as the crisis of Europe itself, "it remains that it will always be impossible to respond otherwise than through reason to the questions posed and the crises caused by reason."[73] This demand, although based on the very exigencies of reason, will immediately raise the objection, as Patočka himself acknowledges, that Europe's inquiry into its own limits, and the means to overcome them, amounts to nothing less than a perpetuation of the "spiritual supremacy of Europe."[74] Yet, such self-inquiry in no way precludes an "extra-European reflection, on the contrary, it sets it into movement and enriches it."[75] For Patočka, Europe's inquiry into the limits of reason, especially in the scientific and technical sense of reason, can avoid the suspicion that such a reflection only serves Europe's desire for supremacy by being accompanied by actions at other levels, such as those of economy and politics. But even though Patočka's inquiry into the nativism and irrationalities of European reason already goes some way toward accomplishing a reflection on "the extra-European spiritual 'substances,'" the notion of universality implicit in reason demands, in my view, an even deeper exploration of the contingent native irrationalisms of Europe that prevent the reflection in question from becoming limited from within.[76] It could perhaps be said that the task of scrutinizing the idea of reason and universality for the inevitable limits owed to its emergence in Europe is an infinite task bestowed on Europe by its very tradition.

In light of this pressing inquiry into the nativisms and irrationalities intertwined with the idea of Europe as the idea of reason and universality, I raise the question whether by thinking of Europe as the idea of reason and universality, the very notion of the *idea* does not belong to a stratum—perhaps not of nativism and irrationality but of a particularity, or idiomaticity—that even though it is indispensable to articulating reason and universality at all, nonetheless restricts its universal thrust. Undoubtedly, such a question seems farfetched, even counterintuitive, because the notion of the idea as a philosophical notion that refers to something purely intelligible—to an essence (*ousia*) that per se denotes something universal, something *katholou*, free from everything sensible, hence from everything particular—is already intrinsically universal.[77] So how could the idea of Europe condition reason and the claim to universality that Europe, the idea of Europe, designates?

As a representation of an essence, a *noeton*, or mere object of thought, an idea grasps this essence in its very unification, uniqueness, and singularity. It establishes the essence that it represents as beyond all becoming, change, hence as self-subsistent. It thus refers to what strictly is—being itself—to what is eternal, atemporal, and ahistorical. If this is so, then the question can certainly be asked whether, when said of Europe, for example, this notion suggests that Europe, with its demands of reason and universality as transcultural demands in essence, are essentially European and belong to it as a privileged possession of something eternal. But at the same time a more important question arises, whether the notion of an idea of Europe resumes, or absorbs in advance what Europe could be all about, blocking in advance any possible development of reason and universality? Undoubtedly, to ask what Europe is, is to ask a question of identity, and the notion of the idea is an inevitable answer to this question, especially if Europe is not yet something that is, but a task: an infinite task at the limit. But if the nature of Europe is such that it still needs to be produced, or that it is something to come, then the notion of an idea of Europe that states in advance what it is, freezes it into a form that does not allow for further development.⁷⁸ Differently put, does the elevation of reason and universality to the status of an idea called Europe not permanently fix their nature, taking, as it were, the possibility of further reasoning about reason out of reason, thus preventing any attempt at deepening it in order to increase its universal range?

But there is more. To conceive of the rationalism and universality with which Europe identifies as an idea is not merely to suggest that contentwise it understands itself as originating in Greece but also that it formally conceives of itself according to an exclusively Greek philosopheme, namely, the idea. Even though in the archeology of this notion from its archaic origins, and to some extent common understanding (in which it primarily refers to sensible looks, or forms, such as the visible exterior form of an individual or a thing), to its philosophical status (in which it concerns invisible, that is, purely intelligible objects of thought), the Greekness of this Greek notion is not simply Greek anymore in an idiomatic sense, the question arises, nonetheless, whether in order to secure the universal thrust of the idea of reason and universality associated with Europe, it might be necessary to uncouple this idea from the extraordinary charge that it carries as a remnant of Greek metaphysics.⁷⁹ Following Patočka we have seen that certain native irrationalisms inherent to Christian Europe have obliterated the "total reflection" that the Greek idea of the care of the soul comprehends. But must we not go one step further, and ask whether the conception of reason and universality is also limited from within by this intrinsically Greek concept of the idea, and hence by Greek metaphysics? Is it perhaps necessary to question the references to "looks," forms, appearances, and shapes that inform this Greek concept, even there where their objects are solely intelligible, and to inquire into the implications that these significations have for understanding reason and universality itself? In order to secure the thrust of the demands that come with reason and universality as European ideas, might it therefore be necessary to liberate them of Europe's "incorrigible Platonism" of which Derrida speaks in a section of *The Gift of Death* that is largely devoted to Patočka?⁸⁰

In short, if Europe has come to an end, is it also, perhaps, because it has come to an end as an *idea*, and that if this end is a chance for a Europe after Europe, in a Europeanized world, the idea (of Europe) will have to make room for another "representation"? Unless, of course, the notion of the idea still harbors an untapped potential of going beyond itself, beyond the idea itself; beyond the idea in a Greek sense. Considering the fact that in

Greece itself the philosophical notion of the idea must have been received as something exceedingly strange, if not foreign, to go beyond the idea—apart from restoring and reviving to this notion the strangeness that in the fourth century Greece must have been peculiar to it—then involves an even greater strangeness and otherness: the double foreignness as it were, of the idea beyond the idea.

If the idea of Europe is merely confined to the rational organization of its economy and its societies with their plural languages and cultures, as is mostly, although not exclusively, the case in the current union since it is no less a project of a community of values, then the idea of Europe in an emphatic sense—as the project and promise of universal openness to, and responsibility for the other—has today, perhaps, more critical power than ever. Indeed, the European Union must not be conflated with Europe as an idea. One can also say, therefore, that Europe has certainly not lived up to its own idea in the traditional sense. But the question that needs pondering is whether conceiving of this idea of Europe as an *idea*—as a representation in which Europe bends back on itself in a loop of self-identification and gives itself to itself—is of the order of a last native irrationalism, perhaps, and thus a reservation that holds up its exposure and responsibility to the other. But if Europe, or rather its idea, is, as Husserl pointed out *Crisis*, the idea of philosophy, then Europe cannot claim, as the sages did in early Greece or in other non-European cultures, that it possesses truth. It cannot on the basis of the fact that the idea of a universal and rational humanity has grown on European, and, in particular, Christian soil, claim and reserve rationality and universality as its own exclusive property, and in the same breath, pride itself to be the very incarnation of humanity itself, and to be the sole carrier of the torch of humanity.[81] As the idea of reason and universality, this idea demands of Europe the courage to critically put its own traditions and beliefs into question. Yet if this is the heritage that constitutes it, Europe must also proceed in renouncing any claim to a fixed identity and, hence, of giving itself to itself. In other words, it must muster the courage to critically interrogate its status as an idea, through which it gives itself to itself and by the same stroke arrests itself. Only so will it be able to secure the universal appeal and thrust of its idea to begin with. This questioning would then also amount to a deepening of the concept of the idea, conceiving of a concept of the idea "beyond the idea" in which the idea of Europe, rather than giving itself to itself in a movement of self-identification, would come to be an idea that comes from the other rather than from itself.[82] Indeed, in the globally

Europeanized world a novel idea of Europe as the idea of reason and universality could, in principle at least, also come from the non-Western world.

The end of Europe and the beginning of a post-European world makes it incumbent on Europe, which has understood itself so far from the idea of reason and universality, to revisit the concept of the idea with which it represented itself. Given its history in which it hegemonically ruled the world on the basis of its self-proclaimed superiority as the incarnation of humanity itself, its responsibility today consists in giving the idea of reason and universality a deeper foundation by going beyond the idea. If this is to be accomplished by uncoupling its idea not only from all native European irrationalisms but also, and perhaps more fundamentally, from a Greek nativism however subtle concerning the idea itself, this cannot take place exclusively by Europe's opening itself to other native traditions, simply replacing its own traditions by other, exotic ones. The chance given to Europe as a result of the catastrophe of Europe in a post-European context is, to paraphrase what Patočka advanced about reason, to rethink, first of all, the idea of Europe as that of reason and universality, beyond the idea—not by abandoning this notion but by way of the means that the very notion of idea possibly provides. This is the chance of conceiving an idea of reason and universality that rather than restricted to the idea of European humanity, would be one that, from the start, comes from the others as a task incumbent on humankind as a whole—without, if I may say so, the sole ballast of Greek and Christian metaphysics and theology. To put it differently: If the idea of Europe has come to an end, Europe needs another renaissance. One this time that is not based on the rediscovery of its own foreign origins in Greece, that is, not of the idea of rationality and universality in the form of a worldly science that it took in the West but on the discovery of another kind of foreignness, the foreignness of the non-European others. Yet, and this is crucial, one that is *apart, and beyond* the latters' own archaic and native irrationalisms in contrast to which the *idea* of an idea of Europe would still reveal itself as something merely native, thus not sufficiently meeting the philosophical demand of what Patočka calls "the idea of what is well-founded."[83]

A moment ago I held that in the aftermath of Europe, an idea of Europe that rather than being closed on itself, but which from the outset is an idea of openness, must accomplish such a rethinking of Europe not by abandoning itself to some exotic otherness but by exploring its own strangeness with respect to Europe itself. The first step in such a direction consists in the exploration of its own untapped resources. Instead of limiting oneself to rehearsing what the ideas of Europe have been so far—such as reason, freedom, democracy, and so forth—and establishing the deficit of their realization, I thus propose that European reflection bend back on itself, on its idea as an idea, not, however, with the intent of closing itself on itself, but of capturing the potential for an openness to others within the idea as an idea. For the resources inherent to the notion of the idea to accomplish this, I turn to Martin Heidegger's elaborations in *Zur Bestimmung der Philosophie* on the relation between an idea and its object. With, unmistakably, Kant's elaboration on the regulative nature of ideas in the First Critique in mind, Heidegger points out that an idea is marked by a certain negativity, since unlike a concept, an idea "does *not* give its object in complete adequation, in the completed, and full determinateness of its essential elements."[84] "Definite moments" of its object, but also singular characteristic ones must, of course, be given in its idea. Yet even though an idea illuminates its object only in an aphoristic, limited illumination, what is significant is that new characteristic moments of the idea's object—"new essential elements [*Wesenselemente*]"—can always become salient and attach themselves onto (the term Heidegger uses is *Ansetzung*, that is, adding on, appending, or affixing) the already established features of the object and modify them. The object, however, is allowed to keep its final indeterminateness. The idea, by contrast, as regards its own sense, leaves nothing open. It consists of "an unambiguously delimited interconnection of the motivations regulated according to essential laws that concern the determinability of the never completely determined object of the idea, and that come into view as a unity of sense."[85] It follows from this that the object's final indeterminateness is not just any indeterminateness, as in the case of a fuzzy representation or guesswork, but a determined indeterminateness. The idea lets the object be undetermined, to remain autonomous, capable of exhibiting new essential features, and this possibility is what the idea gives to the object, whose indeterminateness, or incomplete determination, is, therefore, in Heidegger's terms, a determined one. This gift by the idea to the object is the idea's specific sense and accomplishment. Let us, therefore, look at this gift in greater detail. What it offers to the object is not a merely formal, empty, or arbitrary possibility, but a possibility that, as Heidegger avers, is "determined, and always renewed according to essential laws," that are the object's own laws.[86] These laws must be laws that originate with the object itself because as heteronomous laws they would annihilate its autonomy, and especially the freedom of its openness to modifications by the outside, the foreign, or other. But if it is through its idea that the object receives this possibility of self-modification by way of the affixture of new and other features of itself, the implications are that the object has laws of its own only insofar as it is open to the outside, the foreign, or other. More precisely, the object receives laws of its own not by itself but as a gift from what is not itself. It is its idea that makes it possible to bequeath an autonomy on it as a gift received in its exposure to what it is not, and on the basis of this gift alone is it capable of self-modification. If the idea makes such self-modification of the object possible—and only if it is the object that modifies itself according to laws of its own that are a gift to it by what it is not, is there such a thing as a self-modification—this is not a transformation through which the object would close itself on itself in self-sufficiency. On the contrary, it allows the object to undergo modifications of itself by itself and by its outside, the foreign, or other.

To summarize: The relation between an idea as a determined unity of sense and its object is thus a relation in which the object is characterized by the structurally always-open possibility of bringing to light new implications of its already established features, but also totally novel characteristics that are allowed to become attached to them, thus enriching and modifying them. This process is one according to essential laws of the object itself, but that, at the same time, it possesses only through its openness to otherness. It also follows from this that the idea allows its object to determine itself according to laws in a process that, in principle, never comes to a closure in full determination, and that structurally leave it open to further features, without ever freezing into a final identity. Such is the case, in particular, if the regulation or orientation that the objects' idea provides, allows for the *Ansetzung* of new features to the object that also come to it from its outside, the foreign, and the other, allowing for a modification of it by what is other than it, according to essential rules, of course—not only the rules of the unity of sense that constitutes the idea but that are also "proper" to the object in the complex way we have seen.

How do these reflections on the relation of an idea to its object bear on an idea beyond the idea called for where the idea of Europe is concerned? On an idea that given the Europeanized, or globalized, world, is no longer one of Europe alone? By definition, an idea is an idea of reason: of universal intelligibility, in other words. It follows that an idea must allow its object to modify its determinations in such a way that it, by itself, meets this standard without which it would not even be what it is in all its distinctness. From what we have seen, an idea beyond the idea would be one in which its object is let to modify *itself by itself*, and at the same time *by what it is not*, through the *Ansetzung* to itself of new features that come both from itself and the other. However, such a self-modification is truly one only if it takes place freely, without irrationalisms; without retrenchment in nativisms, or archaisms. Rather than enabling Europe to give itself to itself by representing itself as an idea, the idea beyond the idea would thus allow Europe to expose itself to the gift by the other. Such an idea beyond the idea would also no longer be of the order of a representation of Europe.

In chapter 8 of this book I have shown that the idea of Europe cannot be an idea in the Kantian sense, that of the infinite approximation of a telos. But if the aim of rethinking the idea of Europe in post-Europe is to secure a "well-founded" idea, an idea beyond the idea, then this structural potential of an openness to additions in its object, be that object Europe or humanity in its entirety—additions that rather than arbitrary are, to quote Heidegger one more time, "regulated according to essential laws regarding the determinability of the object as a unity of sense"—must be given a *regulative* function in thinking or rethinking the idea of Europe: regulative, not in the sense of an infinite approximation, but in the sense that this rule must be met in full at any moment.[87]

Notes

1. Edmund Husserl, "The Vienna Lecture," in *The Crisis of European Sciences and Transcendental Phenomenology*, trans. D. Carr (Evanston, IL: Northwestern University Press, 1970), 273.
2. Husserl, "The Vienna Lecture," 273.
3. Husserl, *Crisis of European Sciences*, 12, 17.
4. Husserl, "The Vienna Lecture," 289.
5. Massimo Cacciari, "Europe or Philosophy," *Phenomenology and Mind*, no. 8 (2015): 139.
6. The monumental *Historisches Wörterbuch der Philosophie* is, to my best knowledge, the first dictionary featuring an entry on Europe from the perspective of the history of concepts (*Begriffsgeschichte*). See J. Ritter, ed., *Historisches Wörterbuch der Philosophie* (Darmstadt: Wissenschaftliche Buchgesellschaft, 1972), 2:824–828.
7. Anya Topolski, "From the Idea of Europe to a Europe of Ideas," openDemocracy, May 24, 2014, opendemocracy.net/can-europe-make-it/anya-topolski/from-idea-of-europe-to-europe-of-ideas.
8. Topolski, "From the Idea of Europe."

9. Husserl, "The Vienna Lecture," 273; Friedrich Nietzsche, *Human, All Too Human: A Book for Free Spirits*, trans. R. J. Hollingdale (Cambridge, UK: Cambridge University Press, 1996), 365. For a discussion of Husserl's remarks regarding Eskimos and Gypsies, see Rodolphe Gasché, *Europe, or the Infinite Task. A Study of a Philosophical Concept* (Stanford, CA: Stanford University Press, 2009), 352–353.

10. See Dan Diner, *Aufklärungen. Wege in die Moderne* (Stuttgart: Reclam, 2017), 25ff.

11. Jean-Luc Nancy, *The Creation of the World or Globalization*, trans. F. Raffoul and D. Pettigrew (Albany, NY: SUNY Press, 2007), 34; Josef Simon, "Europa als philosophische Idee," in *Europa Philosophie*, ed. W. Stegmaier (Berlin: de Gruyter, 2003), 15.

12. Jean-François Mattéi, *Le Procès de l'Europe. Grandeur et misère de la culture européenne* (Paris: PUF, 2011), 58.

13. George Steiner, *The Idea of Europe: An Essay* (New York: Overlook Duckworth, 2015).

14. Georg Simmel, "Die Idee Europa," *Gesamtausgabe* (Frankfurt: Suhrkamp, 2000) 13:112–116.

15. Husserl, "The Vienna Lecture," 299.

16. Husserl, "The Vienna Lecture," 291, 276, 269.

17. Husserl, *Crisis of European Sciences*, 16.

18. Jan Patočka, *Plato and Europe*, trans. P. Lom (Stanford, CA: Stanford University Press, 2002); Jacques Derrida, *The Other Heading: Reflections on Today's Europe*, trans. P.A. Brault and M. B. Naas (Bloomington: Indiana University Press, 1992).

19. Christoph Jamme, "Die 'geistige Geographie' Europas," in *Europa—Stier und Sternenkranz. Von der Union mit Zeus zum Staatenbund*, eds. A. B. Renger & R. A. Issler (Bonn: V&Runipress, 2009), 574. In this context of the Romantics' turn to the orient as a model for recovering a form of medieval Europe in the present, one may also mention Maria Zambrano's contention that "the forgotten wetnurse of Europe" is Africa "which Europe, because of its arrogance, has forgotten." See Maria Zambrano, *Der Verfall Europas*, trans. C. Frei (Vienna: Verlag Turia and Kant, 2004), 84.

20. Quoted after Jamme, "Die 'geistige Geographie' Europas," 573.

21. Husserl, "The Vienna Lecture," 299.

22. See Tadashi Ogawa, "Eurozentrismus, Eurozentrik und Ent-Europäisierung," in *Grund und Grenze des Bewustseins: Interkulturelle Phänomenologie aus japanischer Sicht* (Würzburg: Königshausen & Neumann, 2001), 121–131.

23. Hans Schelkshorn, "Der Hochmut Europas und die Philosophie," in *Die Philosophie und Europa. Zur Kategoriengeschichte der, europäischen Einigung*, ed. W. Griesser (Würzburg: Königshausen & Neumann, 2015), 135–160. I can limit myself to evoking this essay because the argument that it makes is a most succinct condensation of the postcolonial criticism of European philosophical thought.

24. Schelkshorn, "Der Hochmut Europas und die Philosophie," 135. And if one agrees that philosophy originates in Greece, and is thus essentially Greek in nature, it is difficult to see how it could possibly free itself from its imperial features.

25. Schelkshorn, "Der Hochmut Europas und die Philosophie," 136.

26. Schelkshorn, "Der Hochmut Europas und die Philosophie," 159.

27. Schelkshorn, "Der Hochmut Europas und die Philosophie," 159.

28. Schelkshorn, "Der Hochmut Europas und die Philosophie," 160.

29. The additions I will be concerned with, "Ce qu'est l'Europe—Sept fragments," and "L'époque posteuropéenne et ses problèmes spirituels," date from 1988 and 1974, respectively.

All page numbers in the text refer to Jan Patočka, *L'Europe après l'Europe*, trans, E. Abrams (Paris: Verdier, 2007).

30. Jan Patočka, *Plato and Europe*, trans. P. Lom (Stanford, CA: Stanford University Press, 2002), 9. Translation modified.

31. Jan Patočka, *Heretical Essays in the Philosophy of History*, trans. E. Kohak (Chicago: Open Court, 1996), 92; Patočka, *Plato and Europe*, 9.

32. Patočka, *L'Europe après l'Europe*, 208.

33. Patočka, *L'Europe après l'Europe*, 208, 211.

34. Patočka, *L'Europe après l'Europe*, 211.

35. Patočka, *Plato and Europe*, 12.

36. The metaphors of light, radical clarity, and the sun are intimately interwoven with the notion of the care of the soul and with that of reason. See chapter 3 in this book.

37. For how "goodness is fundamental in any explanation," see Julia Annas, *An Introduction to Plato's Republic* (Oxford: Clarendon Press, 1981), 244–247.

38. Marc Crépon remarks in this "Postface" to *L'Europe après l'Europe* that besides being an ontological project in that the "soul becomes aware of the place that it occupies in the whole of what is . . . it is a critical and political project because the care of the soul cannot be reduced to the care of *one's* own soul. It is always at the same time and in constitutive fashion, a care for the *soul* of the community." And thus it is also "a project of life." Marc Crépon, "Histoire, Ethique et Politique: La Question de l'Europe," in *L'Europe après l'Europe*, 293–294.

39. Patočka, *L'Europe après l'Europe*, 239. For an extensive discussion of this notion of an "open soul," which Patočka most likely borrows from Henri Bergson, see Francesco Tava, "The Brave Struggle: Jan Patočka on Europe's Past and Future," *The Journal of the British Society for Phenomenology* 47, no. 3 (2016), especially 252–253.

40. See, for example, Patočka, *Plato and Europe*, 149. As Patočka emphasizes in *L'Europe après l'Europe*, it is already in Greece that the notion of the care of the soul divides in two different pursuits, one that consists in the philosophical exploration of the essence of the world in view of a universal science (Democritus, and the materialists), and another that enquires into the possibility of a transformation of human life made possible by this universal science, that is, the Socratic-Platonic one. It is the ancient materialist pursuit that, starting with the sixteenth century, begins to dominate in Europe. See, for example, Patočka, *L'Europe après l'Europe*, 135, 287.

41. Patočka, *Heretical Essays*, 83.

42. Patočka, *Heretical Essays*, 83.

43. Patočka, *Heretical Essays*, 84.

44. Patočka, *L'Europe après l'Europe*, 79, 81.

45. Patočka, *L'Europe après l'Europe*, 232.

46. In addition to these reasons for Husserl's failure to accomplish the task he has set for himself in the *Crisis* book, there is, I think, another, deeper reason for Patočka's criticism, which concerns the status of the formal and ideality. Tentatively only the following: regarding the relation in ancient mathematics between mathematical idealities and the realm of the ideas, as opposed to modern mathematics' concern with universal formal structures that are the correlate of operations on the universe of reality, Patočka objects to Husserl for not having sufficiently seen that modern mathematics' concern with a universe of purely formal structures for gaining access to the universe of realities implies a forgetting of what

The Heretical Essays had qualified as ancient mathematics' concern with the "content, and the donation of the form," as opposed to modern mathematics' "emphasis on product over content, on mastery rather than understanding;" in short, a forgetting of the intrinsic connection between the Platonic reign of the Ideas and the motif of the care of the soul. Patočka, *Heretical Essays*, 86.

47. Patočka, *Heretical Essays*, 83.
48. Patočka, *L'Europe après l'Europe*, 187.
49. Patočka, *L'Europe après l'Europe*, 210.
50. Patočka, *L'Europe après l'Europe*, 210. See, in particular, 211.
51. Jean Pierre Vernant, "La formation de la pensée positive dans la Grèce archaïque," in *Mythe et pensée chez les Grecs* (Paris: Maspéro, 1965), 2:123.
52. Johannes Lohmann, "Über den paradigmatischen Character der griechischen Kultur," in *Die Gegenwart der Griechen im neueren Denken*. Festschrift für Hans-Georg Gadamer, eds. D. Henrich et al. (Tübingen: J. C. B. Mohr, 1960), 179, 172, 174.
53. Clémence Ramnoux, "L'Archaïsme en philosophie," in *Etudes Présocratiques* (Paris: Editions Klincksieck, 1970), 27–35. For how this same principle applies to Plato's thought, see Henri Joly, *Le Renversement Platonicien: Logos, Episteme, Polis* (Paris: Vrin, 1974).
54. Patočka, *L'Europe après l'Europe*, 236.
55. Patočka, *Heretical Essays*, 84.
56. Patočka, *Heretical Essays*, 108.
57. Patočka, *L'Europe après l'Europe*, 227. Patočka is referring here to the origin of the conception of labor as a devotion to God in the culture and life of the medieval cloisters, and which finds its culmination in what Max Weber qualifies as "protestant ethics." By this reference it is also made clear that the seed of Protestantism is already planted in medieval Catholicism.
58. Patočka, *L'Europe après l'Europe*, 227–228.
59. Patočka, *L'Europe après l'Europe*, 236.
60. Patočka, *L'Europe après l'Europe*, 236.
61. Patočka, *L'Europe après l'Europe*, 231.
62. Patočka, *L'Europe après l'Europe*, 236.
63. Patočka, *L'Europe après l'Europe*, 216.
64. Patočka, *L'Europe après l'Europe*, 216.
65. Patočka, *L'Europe après l'Europe*, 232.
66. Patočka, *L'Europe après l'Europe*, 235.
67. It is also here that Patočka's reference to a heretical Christianity should be mentioned to overcome the continued indebtedness of historical Christianity and its conception of the care of soul to its Platonic solution through knowledge of what is. Only a heretical Christianity could truly accomplish the Christian conception of the care of the soul by way of a radical break with Platonism, and a fortiori, the thoroughly new beginning of Europe that it promised to be. See Rodolphe Gasché, *Europe, or the Infinite Task. A Study of a Philosophical Concept* (Stanford, CA: Stanford University Press, 2009), 241–47, 261–62.
68. Patočka, *L'Europe après l'Europe*, 53.
69. Patočka, *L'Europe après l'Europe*, 212–213.
70. Patočka, *L'Europe après l'Europe*, 213.
71. Patočka, *L'Europe après l'Europe*, 213.
72. Patočka, *L'Europe après l'Europe*, 236.

73. Patočka, *L'Europe après l'Europe*, 190.
74. Patočka, *L'Europe après l'Europe*, 241.
75. Patočka, *L'Europe après l'Europe*, 241.
76. Patočka, *L'Europe après l'Europe*, 241.
77. The kind of question I am seeking to pose here is already prefigured in a sense by Patočka's recourse to a heretical Christianity to radically break with Platonism in historical Christianity in order to achieve a novel, truly Christian conception of the care of the soul that would make good on Christian Europe's initial promise.
78. This question is all the more important as Europe is not only an economical but, above all, political project.
79. See chapter 7 in this book. The point that Greek philosophical language is no longer idiomatic, hence, no longer a native language, has been forcefully argued by Martin Heidegger, for example. But can one hold, as does Heidegger in *What Is Philosophy?*, that Greek philosophical language is a language that transcends all idiomaticity without conceiving of such a liberation from the idiomatic as an infinite task? See Martin Heidegger, *What Is Philosopy?*, trans. W. Kluback and J. T. Wilde (Estover, Plymouth: Vision Press, 1989).
80. Jacques Derrida, *The Gift of Death*, trans. D. Wills (Chicago: University of Chicago Press, 1992), 28.
81. See Patočka, *L'Europe après l'Europe*, 212, 235.
82. I borrow the expression "beyond the idea" from Jean-Luc Nancy, who in "Finite History" speaks of the need of rethinking history "beyond the idea" of history. See Jean-Luc Nancy, *The Birth to Presence*, trans. B. Holmes et al. (Stanford, CA: Stanford University Press, 1993), 149.
83. Patočka, *L'Europe après l'Europe*, 81.
84. Martin Heidegger, *Zur Bestimmung der Philosophie, Gesamtausgabe* (Franskfurt/Main: Klostermann, 1987), 56/57:13–14. Emphasis mine.
85. Heidegger, *Zur Bestimmung der Philosophie*, 56/57:14.
86. Heidegger, *Zur Bestimmung der Philosophie*, 56/57:14. The idea lets the object have its own laws.
87. Heidegger, *Zur Bestimmung der Philosophie*, 56/57:14.

BIBLIOGRAPHY

Annas, Julia, *An Introduction to Plato's Republic*, Oxford, UK: Clarendon Press, 1981.
Arendt, Hannah. *Between Past and Future: Eight Exercises in Political Thought*. New York: Penguin, 2006.
———. *The Human Condition*. Chicago: University of Chicago Press, 1958.
———. *The Life of the Mind: One/Thinking*. New York: Harcourt Brace Jovanovich, 1978.
———. *Men in Dark Times*. New York: Harcourt Brace, 1983.
Arendt, Hannah, and Karl Jaspers. *Briefwechsel 1926–1969*. Munich: Piper, 2001.
Auerbach, Erich. "Figura." In *Scenes from the Drama of European Literature*, translated by R. Manheim, 11–76. Minneapolis: University of Minnesota Press, 1984.
Aylesworth, G. E., trans. *The Heidegger-Jaspers Correspondence (1920–1963)*. Humanities Books, 2003.
Benjamin, Andrew, "Possible Returns: Deconstruction and the Placing of Greek Philosophy." In *Derrida and Antiquity*, edited by M. Leonard, 207–234. Oxford, UK: Oxford University Press, 2010.
Blanchot, Maurice, and Jacques Derrida, *The Instant of My Death/Demeure: Fiction and Testimony*. Translated by E. Rottenberg, Stanford, CA: Stanford University Press, 2000.
Borradori, Giovanna. *Philosophy in a Time of Terror: Dialogues with Jürgen Habermas and Jacques Derrida*. Chicago: University of Chicago Press, 2003.
Bowra, C. M. *The Greek Experience*. New York: Praeger, 1969.
Brague, Rémi. *Europe: La voie romaine*. Paris: Criterion, 1993.
Cacciari, Massimo. *Der Archipel Europa*. Translated by G. Memmert. Köln: DuMont, 1998.
———. "Europe or Philosophy." In *Phenomenology and Mind*, no. 8 (2015), 139–145.
———. *Gewalt und Harmonie*. Translated by G. Memmert. Munich: Carl Hanser, 1995.
Crépon, Marc, "Histoire, Ethique et Politique: La Question de l'Europe." In Jan Patocka, *L'Europe après l'Europe*, translated by E. Abrams, 275–295. Paris: Verdier, 2007.
Davis, Bret W. "Dialogue and Appropriation: The Kyoto School as Cross-Cultural Philosophy." In *Japanese and Continental Philosophy: Conversations with the Kyoto School*, edited by Bret W. Davis, Brian Schroeder, and Jason M. Wirth, 33–51. Bloomington: Indiana University Press, 2010.
Derrida, Jacques, "Abraham, The Other." In *Judeities, Questions for Jacques Derrida*, edited by B. Bergo et al., 1–35. Bronx, NY: Fordham Press, 2007.
———. *Dissemination*. Translated by Barbara Johnson. Chicago: University of Chicago Press, 1981.
———. "Double Mémoire." In *Le Théâtre des idées: 50 penseurs pour comprendre le XXIe siècle*, edited by N. Truong, 15–27. Paris: Flammarion, 2008.
———. "Faith and Knowledge: The Two Sources of 'Religion' at the Limits of Reason Alone," translated by S. Weber. In Jacques Derrida and Gianni Vattimo, *Religion*, 1–78. Stanford CA: Stanford University Press, 1998.
———. "Force of Law: The 'Mystical Foundation of Authority.'" trans. M. Quaintance, in *Cardozo Law Review* 11, nos. 5–6 (July/Aug. 1990), 919–1045.

———. *The Gift of Death*. Translated by David Wills. Chicago: University of Chicago Press, 1995.
———. "How to Avoid Speaking: Denials." In *Languages of the Unsayable: The Play of Negativity in Literature and Literary Theory*, edited by S. Budich and W. Iser, 3–70. New York: Columbia University Press, 1989.
———. "Khora." In *On the Name*, translated by D. Wood et al., 89–130. Stanford, CA: Stanford University Press, 1995.
———. *Limited Inc.* Translated by S. Weber. Evanston, IL: Northwestern University Press, 1988.
———. *Margins of Philosophy*. Translated by A. Bass Chicago: University of Chicago Press, 1982.
———. *Of Grammatology*. Translated by G. C. Spivak. Baltimore: Johns Hopkins University Press, 1997.
———. "On a Newly Arisen Apocalyptic Tone in Philosophy." In *Raising the Tone of Philosophy: Late Essays by Immanuel Kant, Transformative Critique by Jacques Derrida*, edited by Peter Fenves, 117–171. Baltimore: Johns Hopkins University Press, 1993.
———. *The Other Heading: Reflections on Today's Europe*. Translated by P. A. Brault and M. Naas. Bloomington: Indiana University Press, 1992.
———. "Passions: An Oblique Offering." In Jacques Derrida, *On the Name*, translated by D. Wood et al., 3–31. Stanford, CA: Stanford University Press, 1995.
———. *Politics of Friendship*. Translated by George Collins. New York: Verso, 2006.
———. *The Problem of Genesis in Husserl's Philosophy*. Translated by M. Hobson. Chicago: University of Chicago Press, 2003.
———. *Rogues: Two Essays on Reason*. Translated by P. A. Brault and M. Naas. Stanford, CA: Stanford University Press, 2005.
———. *Speech and Phenomena*. Translated by D. Allison. Evanston, IL: Northwestern University Press, 1973.
———. "We Other Greeks," trans. P. A. Brault and M. Naas. In *Derrida and Antiquity*, edited by M. Leonard, 17–41. Oxford, UK: Oxford University Press, 2010.
———. *Writing and Difference*. Translated by A. Bass. Chicago: Chicago University Press, 1978.
Derrida, Jacques, and Anne Dufourmantelle. *Of Hospitality*. Translated by R. Bowlby. Stanford, CA: Stanford University Press, 2000.
Derrida, Jacques, and Jean-Pierre Labarrière. *Altérités*. Paris: Osiris, 1986.
Derrida, Jacques, and Elizabeth Roudinesco, *For What Tomorrow: A Dialogue*. Translated by Jeff Fort. Stanford: University of Stanford Press, 2004.
Descombes, Vincent. *Modern French Philosophy*. Translated by L. Scott-Fox and J. M. Harding. Cambridge, UK: Cambridge University Press, 1980.
Diner, Dan. *Aufklärungen. Wege in die Moderne*. Stuttgart: Reclam, 2017.
———. *Lost in the Sacred: Why the Muslim World Stood Still*. Translated by S. Rendall. Princeton, NJ: Princeton University Press, 2009.
Düttman, Alexander Garcia. *Derrida und Ich. Das Problem der Dekonstruktion*. Bielefeld: Transcript, 2008.
Düttman, Alexander Garcia et al. "Was bleibt von Derrrida?" In *Information Philosophy* 3 (2010), 25–28.
Fink, Eugen. *Metaphysik der Erziehung im Weltverständnis von Plato und Aristoteles*. Frankfurt/Main: Klostermann, 1970.

Flatscher, Matthias. *Logos und Lethe: Zur Phänomenologischen Sprachauffassung im Spätwerk von Heidegger und Wittgenstein*. Freiburg: Karl Alber, 2011.
Freeman, Kathleen. *Ancilla to the Pre-Socratic Philosophers*. Cambridge, MA: Harvard University Press, 1983.
Gadamer, Hans-Georg. *Das Erbe Europas: Beiträge*. Frankfurt/Main: Suhrkamp, 1989.
———. "Europa und die Oikumene." In *Europa und die Philosophie*, edited by H.-H. Gander, 67–86. Frankfurt/Main: Klostermann, 1993.
———. "Hermeneutics and Historicism." In *Truth and Method*, 2nd ed., translated by J. Weinsheimer and D. G. Marshall, 505–541. New York: Continuum, 1995.
———. "Karl Löwith zum 70. Geburstag." In *Natur und Geschichte. Karl Löwith zum 70. Geburtstag*, edited by H. Braun and M. Riedel, 455–457. Stuttgart: Kohlhammer 1967.
———. "Rhetorik, Hermeneutik und Ideologiekritik." In *Gesammelte Werke*, 2:232–250. Tübingen: Mohr, 1993.
———. *Vernunft im Zeitalter der Wissenschaft*. Frankfurt/Main: Suhrkamp, 1976.
Gasché, Rodolphe. *Europe, or the Infinite Task: A Study of a Philosophical Concept*. Stanford, CA: University of Stanford Press, 2009.
———. "Giving to Read." In Gasché, Rodolphe, *The Wild Card of Reading: On Paul de Man*, 149–180. Cambridge, MA: Harvard University Press, 1998.
———. "Remainders of Faith: On Karl Löwith's Conception of Secularization." *Divinatio. Studia Culturologica Series* 28 (2008): 27–50.
Gollwitzer, Heinz. "Europa." In *Historisches Wörterbuch der Philosophie*, edited by J. Ritter, 824–828. Darmstadt: Wissenschaftliche Buchgesellschaft, vol. 2, 1972.
Gordon, Peter Eli. "Rosenzweig Redux: The Reception of German-Jewish Thought." *Jewish Social Studies* 8, no. 1 (2001): 1–57.
Granel, Gérard. "L'Europe de Husserl." In *Écrits logiques et politiques*, 37–58. Paris: Galilée, 1990.
Habermas, Jürgen. *Philosophical-Political Profiles*. Translated by F. G. Lawrence. Cambridge, MA: MIT Press.
———. *The Postnational Constellation. Political Essays*. Translated by M. Pensky. Cambridge, MA: MIT Press, 2001.
Hegel, Georg Wilhelm Friedrich. *Early Theological Writings*. Translated by T. M. Knox. Chicago: University of Chicago Press, 1948.
———. Introduction to *The Philosophy of History*. Translated by L. Rauch. Indianapolis: Hackett, 1988.
———. *The Philosophy of History*. Translated by J. Sibree. New York: Dover, 1956.
Heidegger, Martin. *Being and Time*. Translated by J. Macquarrie and E. Robinson. London: Harper and Row, 1962.
———. *Zur Bestimmung der Philosophie, Gesamtausgabe*. Frankfurt/Main: Klostermann, vol. 56/57,1987.
———. "Die Herkunft der Kunst und die Bestimmung des Denkens." In *Denkerfahrungen*, 135–149. Frankfurt/Main: Klostermann, 1983.
———. *Introduction to Metaphysics*. Translated by G. Fried and R. Polt. New Haven, CT: Yale University Press, 2000.
———. *What Is Philosophy?* Translated by W. Kluback and J. T. Wilde. Estover: Vision, 1989.
Heidegger, Martin, and Erhart Kästner. *Briefwechsel 1953–1974*. Edied by H. W. Petzet. Frankfurt: Insel, 1986.

Held, Klaus. "The Origin of Europe with the Greek Discovery of the World." *Epoché* 7, no. 1 (Fall 2002): 81–95.
Hersch, Jeanne. *Das philosophische Staunen. Einblicke in die Geschichte des Denkens.* Munich: Piper, 1981.
Husserl, Edmund. *The Crisis of European Sciences and Transcendental Phenomenology.* Translated by D. Carr. Evanston, IL: Northwestern University Press, 1970.
———. *La Crise des sciences européennes et la phénoménologie transcendentale.* Translated by Gérard Granel. Paris: Gallimard, 1976.
———. "Grundlegende Untersuchungen zum phänomenoligschen Ursprung der Räumlichkeit der Natur." In *Philosophical Essays: In Memory of Edmund Husserl*, edited by M. Farber, 307–325. New York: Greenwood Press, 1968.
———. *Ideas: General Introduction to Pure Phenomenology.* Translated by W. R. Boyce Gibson. New York: MacMillan, 1931.
Jamme, Christoph. "Die 'Geistige Geographie' Europas." In *Europa—Stier und Sternenkranz: Von der Union mit Zeus zum Staatenbund*, edited by A. B. Renner and R. A. Isler 571–582. Bonn: V&R unipress, 2009.
Jaspers, Karl. "Die Achsenzeit der Weltgeschichte." *Der Monat* 1, no. 6 (1948): 3–9.
———. *The Origin and Goal of History.* Translated by M. Bullock. New Haven, CT: Yale University Press, 1953.
———. *Psychologie der Weltanschauungen.* Berlin: Springer, 1919.
———. "Vom Europäischen Geist." In *Rechenschaft und Ausblick. Reden und Aufsätze*, 233–264. Munich: Piper, 1951.
Johnson, Roberta. "The Context and Achievement of *Delirium and Destiny*." In *Maria Zambrano, Delirium and Destiny: A Spaniard in Her Twenties*, 213–325. Translated by C. Maier. Albany, NY: SUNY Press, 1999.
Joly, Henri. *Le Renversement Platonicien: Logos, Episteme, Polis.* Paris: Vrin, 1974.
Jonas, Hans. *Das Prinzip Verantwortung: Versuch einer Ethik für die technologische Zivilication.* Frankfurt/Main: Suhrkamp, 1984.
Jullien, François. *A Treatise of Efficacy: Between Western and Chinese Thinking.* Translated by J. Lloyd. Honolulu: University of Hawai'i Press, 2004.
———. *De l'Universel, de l'uniforme, du commun et du dialogue entre les cultures.* Paris: Fayard, 2008.
Kant, Immanuel. *Critique of the Power of Judgment.* Translated by P. Guyer and E. Matthews. Cambridge: Cambridge University Press, 2000.
———. *Critique of Pure Reason.* Translated by P. Guyer and A. W. Wood. Cambridge, UK: Cambridge University Press, 1999.
Der Kleine Pauly. *Lexikon der Antike.* Edited by K. Ziegler and W. Sontheimer. Munich: Deutscher Taschenbuch, 1979.
Kosellek, Reinhardt. Foreword to *My Life in Germany before and after 1933. A Report*, by Karl Löwith, ix-xv. Translated by E. King. Urbana: University of Illinois Press, 1994.
Landgrebe, Ludwig. *The Phenomenology of Edmund Husserl: Six Essays.* Ithaca, NY: Cornell University Press, 1981.
Latzel, Edwin. "The Concept of 'Ultimate Situation' in Jaspers' Philosophy." In *The Philosophy of Karl Jaspers*, edited by P. A. Schilpp, 177–208. New York: Tudor, 1957.
Lohmann, Johannes. "Hans-Georg Gadamer: Wahrheit und Methode. Grundzüge einer philosophischen Hermeneutik. Tübingen: Mohr 1960. XVII, 486 S." *Gnomon* 37 (1965): 709–718.

———. "Über den paradigmatischen Charakter der griechischen Kultur." In *Die Gegenwart der Griechen im neueren Denken: Feschrift für Hans-Georg Gadamer*, edited by D. Henrich et al., Tübingen: J. C. B. Mohr, 1969.
Loraux, Nicole. "La métaphore sans métaphore: A propos de l'Orestie." *Revue philosophique* 2 (1990), 247–268.
———. *Né de la terre. Mythe et politique à Athènes*, Paris: Seuil, 2009.
Löwith, Karl. *Gott, Mensch und Welt in der Metaphysik von Descartes bis zu Nietzsche*. Göttingen: Vandenhoeck & Ruprecht, 1967.
———. "Heidegger: Thinker in a Destitute Time." In *Karl Löwith, Martin Heidegger and European Nihilism*, edited by R. Wolin, 31–134. Translated by G. Steiner. New York: Columbia University Press, 1995.
———. "The Japanese Mind. A Picture of the Mentality That We Must Understand if We Are to Conquer." In *Sämtliche Schriften*, 2:556–570. Stuttgart: J. B. Metzlersche, 1983.
———. "Japan's Westernization and Moral Foundation." In *Sämtliche Schriften*, 2:541–555. Stuttgart: J. B. Metzlersche, 1983.
———. *My Life in Germany before and after 1933. A Report*. Translated by E. King. Urbana: University of Illinois Press, 1994.
———. *Nature, History, and Existentialism and Other Essays in the Philosophy of History*. Edited by A. Levison. Evanston, IL: Northwestern University Press, 1966.
———. "Unzulängliche Bemerkungen zum Unterschied von Orient und Okzident." In *Die Gegenwart der Griechen im neueren Denken. Festschrift fur Hans Georg Gadamer*, edited by D. Henrich, W. Schulz, and K.-H. Volkmann-Schluck, 141–170. Tübingen: J.C.B. Mohr, 1960.
———. "Das Verhältnis von Gott, Mensch und Welt in der Metaphysik von Descartes und Kant." In *Sitzungsberichte der Heidelberger Akademie der Wissenschaften*, 1–26. Heidelberg: Carl Winter, Universitatsverlag 1964.
———. *Von Rom nach Sendai, Von Japan nach Amerika: Reisetagebuch 1936 und 1941*. Edited by K. Stichweh and U. Von Bülow. Marbach: Deutsche Schillergesellschaft, 2001.
Lukacs, Georg. *The Theory of the Novel: A Historico-philosophical Essay on the Forms of Great Epic Literature*. Translated by A. Bostock. Cambridge, MA: MIT Press, 1971.
Mattéi, Jean-François. *Le Procès de l'Europe: Grandeur et misère de la culture européenne*. Paris: PUF, 2011.
Miller, Paul Allen. "The Platonic Remainder: Derrida's *Khora* and the *Corpus Platonicum*." In *Derrida and Antiquity*, edited by M. Leonard, 321–341. Oxford, UK: Oxford University Press, 2010.
Muschg, Adolf. "Meine Japanreise mit Löwith." In *Von Rom nach Sendai, Von Japan nach Amerika: Reisetagebuch 1936 und 1941*, by Karl Löwith, 111–155. Edited by K. Stichweh and U. Von Bülow. Marbach: Deutsche Schillergesellschaft, 2001.
Naas, Michael. *Miracle and Machine: Jacques Derrida and the Two Sources of Religion, and the Media*. Bronx, NY: Fordham University Press, 2012.
Nancy, Jean-Luc. *The Birth to Presence*. Stanford, CA: Stanford University Press, 1993.
———. *The Creation of the World or Globalization*. Translated by F. Raffoul and D. Pettigrew. Albany, NY: SUNY Press, 2007.
———. "Euryopa: Le regard au loin." In *Contributions*, 5–15. Leipzig: University of Leipzig, 1994.

———. *The Inoperative Community*. Translated by P. Connor et al. Minneapolis: University of Minnesota Press, 1991.
———. "Our History." *Diacritics* 20, no.3 (1990): 97–115.
———. *La Remarque Spéculative*. Paris: Galilée, 1973.
Natorp, Paul. "Philosophie und Psychology," *Logos* 2/4 (1913), 176–202.
Nietzsche, Friedrich. *Beyond Good and Evil: Prelude to a Philosophy of the Future*. Translated by W. Kaufman. New York: Vintage, 1989.
———. *Human, All Too Human: A Book for Free Spirits*. Translated by R. J. Hollingdale. Cambridge, UK: Cambridge University Press, 1996.
Ogawa, Tadashi. "Eurozentrismus, Eurozentrik und Ent-Europäisierung." In *Grund und Grenze des Bewusstseins: InterkulturellePhänomenologie aus japanischer Sicht*, 121–131. Würzburg: Königshausen & Neumann, 2001.
Otto, Walter, Vishnu-Narayana. Texte zur indischen Gottesmystik, Translated by R. Otto, Jena: Eugen Diederichs, 1917.
Patočka, Jan. *L'Europe après l'Europe*. Translated by E. Abrams. Paris: Verdier, 2007.
———. *Heretical Essays in the Philosophy of History*. Translated by E. Kohak. Chicago: Open Court, 1996.
———. *Plato and Europe*. Translated by P. Lom. Stanford, CA: Stanford University Press, 2002.
Plato. *The Collected Dialogues*. Edited by E. Hamilton and H. Cairns. Princeton, NJ: Princeton University Press, 1980.
Ramnoux, Clémence. "L'Archaisme en philosophie." In *Etudes Présocratiques*, 27–35. Paris: Editions Klincksiek, 1979.
Riedel, Manfred. "Karl Löwiths philosophischer Weg." *Heidelberger Jahrbucher* 14 (1970): 120–133.
Ries, Wiebrecht. *Karl Löwith*. Stuttgart: J. B. Metzlersche, 1992, 11–12.
Ritter, Joachim. "Europäisierung als europäisches Problem." In *Metaphysik und Politik. Studien zu Aristoteles und Hegel*, 321–340. Frankfurt/Main: Suhrkamp, 1977.
Sallis, John. *Chorology: On Beginning in Plato's Timaios*. Bloomington: Indiana University Press, 1999.
Savinio, Alberto. *Destin de l'Europe*.Translated by L. Chapuis. Paris: Christian Bourgois, 1990.
———. *Encyclopédie nouvelle*. Translated by N. Frank. Paris: Gallimard, 1980.
Scheler, Max. *The Nature of Sympathy*. Translated by P. Heath. London: Routledge & Keegan Paul, 1954.
Schelkshorn, Hans. "Der Hochmut Europas und die Philosophie." In *Die Philosophie und Europa: Zur Kategoriengeschichte der europäischen Einigung*, edited by W. Griesser, 135–160. Würzburg: Königshausen & Neumann, 2015.
Schmitt, Carl. *Land and Sea: A World-Historical Meditation*. Translated by S. G. Zeitlin. Candor, NY: Telos, 2015.
Simmel, Georg. "Die Idee Europa." In *Gesamtausgabe*, 13: 112–116. Frankfurt: Suhrkamp, 2000.
Simon, Josef. "Europa als philosophische Idee." In *Europa Philosophie*, edited by W. Stegmaier, 15–35, Berlin; De Gruyter, 2003.
Steiner, George. *The Idea of Europe: An Essay*. New York: Overlook Duckworth, 2015.
Stierle, Karlheinz. "Interpretations of Responsibility and Responsibilities of Interpretation." In *New Literary History*, 25, no. 4 (1994), 853–854.

Ströker, Elizabeth. *Husserl's Transcendental Philosophy*. Translated by L. Hardy. Stanford, CA: Stanford University Press, 1993.
Tassin, Etienne. "De l'Europe philosophique à l'Europe politique." In *Existe-t-il une Europe philosophique?*, edited by N. Weill, 129–145. Rennes: Presses Universitaires de Rennes, 2005.
Tava, Francesco. "The Brave Struggle: Jan Patočka on Europe's Past and Future." In *The Journal of the British Society for Phenomenology*, 47 no. 3 (2016), 242–259.
Topolski, Anya. "From the Idea of Europe to a Europe of Ideas." openDemocracy, May 24, 2014, opendemocracy.net/.
Van Peursen, Cornelius A. "The Horizon." In *Husserl: Expositions and Appraisals*, edited by F. Elliston and P. McCormick, 182–201. Notre Dame: University of Notre Dame Press, 1977.
Vernant, Jean-Pierre. "La formation de la pensée positive dans la Grèce archaique." In *Mythe et pensée chez les Grecs*, 2, 95–124. Paris: Maspero, 1965.
Weil, Simone. *The Iliad or The Poem of Force*. Translated by M. McCarthy. Wallingford, PA: Pendle Hill, 1973.
Zambrano, Maria. *Der Verfall Europas*. Translated by C. Frei. Vienna: Turia & Kant, 2004.

INDEX

Abraham, 162, 167n37, 184–85
Abrams, Erika, 204
Aeschylus, 83, 86n20, 189n17
Archimedes, 68
Arendt, Hannah, 57, 64n11, 66, 73, 86n20, 88
Aristotle, 40–42, 63n1, 64n15, 107n14, 119, 123, 125, 190n23, 200–1
Assmann, Jan, 84n9
Augustine, Saint, vii–viii

Benjamin, Andrew, 189n13
Bergson, Henri, 222n39
Blanchot, Maurice, 188n2
Blumenberg, Hans, 4
Borradori, Giovanna, 139
Bowra, C. M., 37–38
Brague, Rémi, xiii
Buddha, 67, 72, 79
Burckhardt, Jacob, 102

Cacciari, Massimo, xiv, 4–10, 111, 194, 198
Cohen, Hermann, 95
Confucius, 67, 79
Crépon, Marc, 222n38

Davis, Bret W., 100–1, 109n72
Democritus 222n40
Derrida, Jacques, 34, 40, 43–46, 110–19, 126–30, 131nn8–9, 133, 138–147, 151–65, 168–87, 188n2, 188n5, 189n9, 189nn12–13 189nn17–18, 190n22, 191n30, 191n35, 200, 215
Desanti, Jean-Toussaint, 30
Descombes, Vincent, 189n12
Descartes, René, 119
Diner, Dan, 64n5
Düttmann, Alexander Garcia, 191n29

Elijah, 68
Empedocles, 3

Ferris, David, 85n16
Fink, Eugen, 41–42, 44–45, 91
Flatscher, Matthias, 188n5
Freud, Sigmund, 34

Gadamer, Hans-Georg, xiii, 49–63, 87, 89, 93, 197
Gasché, Rodolphe, xvn7
Gasset, Ortega y, xivn2
Goethe, Johann Wolfgang, 81
Gordon, Peter Eli, 108n37
Granel, Gérard, 29–30, 33, 46
Grimm, Jacob, 61

Habermas, Jürgen, 61–62, 91–92, 106n11
Hearn, Lafcadio, 96
Hegel, Georg Wilhelm Friedrich, ix, xiii, 3, 9, 16, 39, 55, 73, 85n12, 90, 94–96, 101–2, 106, 109n66, 119, 171, 173, 177, 179
Heidegger, Martin, xiv, 24, 30, 33, 35, 39, 45–6, 47n3, 48n10, 65, 84n8, 87, 89–90, 95–96, 106n11, 107n14, 119–27, 132nn12–14, 151, 158, 160, 162–63, 171, 176–79, 188n2, 191n30, 203, 218, 220, 224n79
Held, Klaus, 131n10
Heraclitus, 3, 68, 88, 105, 122
Herodotus, 82
Hersch, Jeanne, 3
Hölderlin, Friedrich, 39
Homer, 68, 81–83
Husserl, Edmund, 1–2, 19–21, 29–31, 35–36, 39–40, 47n3, 65, 87–89, 106n10, 110, 115, 117, 120–21, 126, 132n14, 133, 135, 138, 150–51, 153, 155–56, 166, 171, 173, 182, 193, 197, 200–1, 205–7, 212–13, 216, 221n9, 222n46

Index

Isaiah, 68

Jamme, Christph, 201
Jaspers, Karl, xiii, 64n5, 65–83, 84nn1–2, 84nn6–10, 85n13, 85n15, 85nn17–20, 108n54
Jeremiah, 68
Jonas, Hans, 150
Jullien, François, 134, 149n28

Kant, Immanuel, xv, 3, 46, 84n11, 135–141, 143–47, 165, 174, 177, 186, 191n32, 191n35, 195, 201–2, 218
Kästner, Erhart, 39
Keyserling, Hermann, 77, 84n7
Kierkegaard, Soeren, 150, 162–63, 167n37
Kosellek, Reinhard, 91

Landgrebe, Ludwig, 20
Lasaulx, Ernst von, 67, 72, 84n7
Levinas, Emmanuel, 40, 162
Lohmann, Johannes, 56–57, 208
Loraux, Nicole, 189n17
Löwith, Karl, xiii, 87–106, 106n6, 106nn10–11, 107n18, 108n37, 108n54, 109n59, 109n66, 109n72
Lukacs, Georg, xiii, 84n1

Maisuradze, Giorgi, 85n13
Marx, Karl, 30, 33, 57, 91, 105
Miller, Paul Allen, 189n9
Mo-ti, 67

Naas, Michael, 189n16
Nancy, Jean-Luc, xiv, 12–26, 27n4, 33–34, 114, 198, 224n82
Natorp, Paul, 141
Niebuhr, Rheinhold, 93
Nietzsche, Friedrich, 4, 57, 87–88, 106n6, 107n18, 134, 150, 193, 197
Nishida, Kitaro, 100–1, 104, 109n72
Novalis, 201

Otto, Rudolf, 53
Otto, Walter, 85n13

Pan, 42, 44
Parmenides, 68

Patočka, Jan, xiv, 35–41, 46, 48n10, 48n16, 155, 162–65, 200, 204–215, 217, 220nn39–40, 222n46, 223n57, 223n67, 224n77
Peursen, Cornelius A. Van, 21
Plato, 14, 35, 38–39, 41–44, 63, 68, 119, 125, 135–36, 162, 172, 174–78, 181, 183, 189n18, 190n20, 191n33, 195, 201, 209, 223n53, 223n67

Ramnoux, Clémence, 208–9
Riedel, Manfred, 92
Ritter, Joachim, 61
Rivaud, Albert, 190n32
Rosenzweig, Franz, 95–96, 108n37
Rousseau, Jean-Jacques, 190n18

Sallis, John, 190nn22–23
Sartre, Jean-Paul, 19
Savinio, Alberto, xiv, 2–3
Scheler, Max, 54
Schelkshorn, Hans, 202–3
Schelling, Friedrich Wilhelm Joseph, 169
Schlegel, Friedrich, 201
Schmitt, Carl, 6
Schopenhauer, Arthur, 57, 88
Shuzo, Kuki, 92
Simmel, Georg, 89, 200
Simon, Josef, 198
Socrates, 79
Sophocles, 86n20, 189n13
Spinoza, Baruch, 107n18
Steiner, George, 200
Strauss, Viktor von, 67, 72, 84n7
Susuki, D. T., 104.

Thales, 3
Thucydides, 68
Tillich, Paul, 93
Topolski, Anya, 196
Tse, Chuang, 64n4
Tsu, Lieh, 67

Unamuno, Miguel de, xiv2n

Valéry, Paul, 129
Vernant, Jean Pierre, 208

Vico, Giovanni Battista, 91
Voltaire, François Marie Arouet, 187

Weber, Alfred, 67, 84n7
Weber, Max, 213, 223n57
Weber, Samuel, 191n33

Weil, Simone, 86n20
Wittgenstein, Ludwig, 30, 33

Zambrano, Maria, vii–x, xivn2, 221n19
Zarathustra, 67
Zeus, 12

RODOLPHE GASCHÉ is Distinguished Professor and Eugenio Donato Chair of Comparative Literature at the University of Buffalo. He is author of numerous books, including *Persuasion, Reflection, Judgment: Ancillae Vitae* (Indiana UP, 2017).

www.ingramcontent.com/pod-product-compliance
Lightning Source LLC
Chambersburg PA
CBHW030538230426
43665CB00010B/938